POST-COMMUNIST MALAISE

MEDIA MATTERS

Patrice Petro and Cristina Venegas, Series Editors

Media Matters focuses on film, television, and media within a transnational and interdisciplinary frame: environmental media, media industries, media and democracy, information media, and global media. It features the work of scholars who explore ever-expanding forms of media in art, everyday, and entertainment practices. Under the co-direction of Patrice Petro and Cristina Venegas, the series is sponsored by the Carsey-Wolf Center at the University of California, Santa Barbara. The Center seeks to foster innovative and collaborative research that probes the aesthetic, political, economic, artistic, and social processes of media in the past and in our own time.

Nataša Ďurovičová, Patrice Petro, and Lorena Terando, eds., *At Translation's Edge*
Elena Gorfinkel and Tami Williams, eds., *Global Cinema Networks*
Zoran Samardzija, *Post-Communist Malaise: Cinematic Responses to European Integration*

POST-COMMUNIST MALAISE

Cinematic Responses to European Integration

ZORAN SAMARDZIJA

RUTGERS UNIVERSITY PRESS
New Brunswick, Camden, and Newark, New Jersey, and London

Library of Congress Cataloging-in-Publication Data

Names: Samardzija, Zoran, author.
Title: Post-communist malaise : cinematic responses to European integration / Zoran Samardzija.
Description: New Brunswick : Rutgers University Press, [2020] | Series: Media matters | Includes bibliographical references and index.
Identifiers: LCCN 2019034571 | ISBN 9780813587141 (paperback) | ISBN 9780813587158 (cloth) | ISBN 9780813587165 (epub)
Subjects: LCSH: Motion pictures—Europe, Eastern. | Post-communism—Europe, Eastern. | Communism and motion pictures—Europe, Eastern.
Classification: LCC PN1993.5.E82 S26 2020 | DDC 791.430947—dc23
LC record available at https://lccn.loc.gov/2019034571

A British Cataloging-in-Publication record for this book is available from the British Library.

∞ The paper used in this publication meets the requirements of the American National Standard for Information Sciences—Permanence of Paper for Printed Library Materials, ANSI Z39.48-1992.

www.rutgersuniversitypress.org

Manufactured in the United States of America

For my parents and my sister for all the dinner-table conversations

CONTENTS

POST-COMMUNIST MALAISE

INTRODUCTION

RETHINKING POLITICAL MODERNISM AND ART CINEMA

Since the global financial crisis of 2008, Europe has witnessed the rise of far-right political parties. Though lacking in overt militarism, their rhetoric echoes the fascism of the thirties. This turn toward the right discredits the end-of-history utopia of liberal democracy promised by Francis Fukuyama after the fall of communism. Instead of liberal democracy, this new right-wing populism promotes a European identity—one that is Christian and white and that reinforces gender binaries—as an alternative to the European Union (EU). For example, Hungarian prime minister Viktor Orbán gained international notoriety when he erected border fences during the refugee crisis in 2015. In fall 2018, after being elected for a third term, his government withdrew funding from university gender studies programs, declaring that "the Hungarian government is of the clear view that people are born either men or women."[1]

While many right-wing populists seek to redefine the cultural identity of Europe, they do not challenge its fundamental belief in free-market capitalism. Several months after defunding gender studies, the Hungarian government faced protests over their so-called slave law, which mandated that companies can demand overtime from workers and delay paying them.[2] This form of capitalist populism is common throughout Europe. Consider the example of Nigel Farage in Britain. A former commodities broker and founding member of the far-right UK Independent Party in the early nineties, the Euroskeptic Farage was instrumental in the pro-Brexit campaign of 2016. Subsequently he launched the Brexit Party, which won the most UK seats in the

European Parliament elections of 2019. Though critical of immigration policy, Farage's column for the *Independent* also indicates that he is a libertarian capitalist when he characterizes the EU as a stifling bureaucracy opposed to free trade.[3]

In other instances, Europe's fascist past is evoked in the form of direct nostalgia. In March 2019, Antonio Tajani, then president of the European Parliament, sparked controversy for his comments about Benito Mussolini. According to Tajani, aside from his authoritarianism and desire for war, Mussolini accomplished positive things such as building the country's infrastructure and reclaiming lost territory. In their reporting on the story for the *Guardian*, journalists Angelina Giuffrida and Jennifer Rakin note that Tajani's opinion of Mussolini is not uncommon in Italy. They write that "Tajani's views of Mussolini's positive achievements are shared by many Italians, who yearn for a strongman leader and have long helped keep the spirit of Mussolini alive. The more recent revival of right-wing populism has also helped to dismantle the taboo."[4] Though Tajani apologized for his comments, this nostalgia for "a strongman leader" is indicative of the political deadlock facing Europe: its fascist past has become a viable political alternative to the neoliberal dystopia of its present.

It is within this context that this book politicizes art cinema from Eastern Europe and the Balkans to explore fundamental questions about film, aesthetics, and ideology. In particular, it revisits debates about political modernism from Marxism and seventies film theory in order to analyze how select cinemas from the regions offer ideological critiques of the neoliberal integration of Europe, whose failure has accelerated the growth of nationalism and right-wing populism. According to D. N. Rodowick, seventies film theory can be characterized as a "discourse of political modernism." In his succinct summary of Rodowick's *Crisis of Political Modernism*, Nico Baumbach explains that, "in his reading of film theory from the late 1960s through the early 1980s as a 'discourse of political modernism,' Rodowick grasped the extent to which 'theory' stood for a position that advocated for a new form of filmmaking practice. Ideology critique was tied to an idea of a countercinema that performed within film practice the very function of theory."[5] This notion of an aesthetic practice informed by theory has its foundations in the early twentieth-century Marxist writings of Ernst Bloch, György Lukács, Bertolt Brecht, and others who debated the political efficacy of a realist text compared with the formalist experimentation of modernism.

According to Rodowick, post-1968 film theory theorized the "possibility of a radical, political text" and representational "strategies emphasizing the material nature of language or cinematic presentation, especially in the form of an auto-critique."[6] However, as the title of his book implies, a "crisis" for theory emerges from this pursuit of a political modernist text because it "reduced the problem of meaning to film form alone," which meant that "the political force of theory" was secondary to the film text. In other words, the paradox of political modernist film theory is that it denies its own political potential "for actively constructing meaning in relation to film and for creating new positions of reading."[7] For Rodowick, this paradox is untangled by what is commonly called a "philosophical turn" for film studies. According to Baumbach, "Politics in this approach is viewed no longer as intrinsic to cinema and a necessary guiding force for film theory, but rather as a commitment that one is ethically obliged to acknowledge if and only if it informs one's methods and conclusions. Despite Rodowick's insistence that he has not abandoned the project of film theory, we are a long way from the claim—from Benjamin to Agamben, and including the seminal essays of sixties and seventies film theory—that, as [Jean-Louis] Comolli and [Jean] Narboni put it, 'every film is political.'"[8]

Baumbach concludes that Rodowick was "right to suggest that film theory in the 1970s tended to undertheorize its own position in constructing the link between cinema and politics."[9] Throughout *Cinema/Politics/Philosophy*, he responds to this claim of undertheorization by turning toward philosophers Jacques Rancière, Alain Badiou, and Giorgio Agamben in order to model a new discourse about politics, aesthetics, and cinema. Even if one disagrees with this interpretation of seventies film theory by Rodowick and Baumbach, one can still embrace the invitation to rethink the links between theory, politics, and cinema. Toward that end, *Post-Communist Malaise* argues that the political modernism of seventies film theory, in particular the belief in counter-cinema aesthetics that function as ideology critique, did not diminish because it paradoxically reduced the political force of theory itself. Rather, the waning interest in grand theories of political aesthetics coincided with the acceleration of neoliberalism in the late seventies and the eighties and the decline of leftist alternatives to capitalism. By the time of the post-communist era in the nineties, the end of history promised by Fukuyama, though now a discredited idea, was quickly internalized throughout the West into the mistaken belief that the grand ideological and political struggles of the century—the conflicts between fascism, communism, and capitalism—had been resolved. Thus, the notion that "every film is political" moved away from theorizing counter-cinema and its critiques of mass culture and ideology into a diverse array of approaches including cultural studies, which, as Rodowick notes, "opened the question of ideology and subjectivity from the side of the audience rather than that of the text in a way that better accounted for resistant, contestatory, or even outright deviant readings or appropriations of film and television."[10] In returning to political modernism, *Post-Communist Malaise* is not a critique of these subsequent approaches, which extend "the question of ideology and subjectivity" to account for the complex intersection of ethnicity, race, gender, and sexual identities. Rather, its thesis is that the aftershocks of the financial crisis—the global rise in right-wing populism, the normalization of austerity politics, and mass migration—necessitate that we also revisit the unresolved totalizing ideology critiques of political modernism and our ideas about counter-cinema. It may have seemed that capitalism scored a decisive victory over communism after its collapse in the Soviet Union and Eastern Europe, but the rising tide of right-wing populism since the financial crisis means that the grand ideological struggles of the last century have not been resolved.

By renewing political modernism, this book also reimagines art cinema as a mode of political discourse. Traditionally, art cinema has had multiple definitions. As Rosalind Galt and Karl Schoonover write in the introduction to *Global Art Cinema: New Theories and Histories*, it has always been an impure and "elastically hybrid category."[11] Its "common usage," they argue, refers to narrative cinema situated between mainstream and avant-garde productions, recognizable as "a mode of narration . . . loosened from classical structures and distanced from its representations."[12] This definition recalls David Bordwell's notion that art cinema is a "mode of film practice" defined by authorial presence, formal conventions, and narrative strategies of realism and ambiguity.[13] However, as Galt and Schoonover note, the category also invokes "elitist and conservative" notions of "seriousness" about film canons, which "both postclassical film theory and the turn to cultural studies" have deliberately avoided.[14] Consequently, they argue, "little sustained scholarly attention has been paid to refining and updating the parameters of art cinema as a category since the pioneering essays of the 1960s and 1970s."[15] In updating the category, Galt and Schoonover propose that art cinema can overcome its Eurocentric and elitist associations to convey a "complex vision of the global that is responsive to geographical complexity and, more important, susceptible to geopolitical analysis."[16] In other words, updating the category of art cinema allows us to analyze geopolitical transformations and new dynamics between the global and local. However, there is an additional purpose. As Christina Gerhardt and Sara Saljoughi argue in their introduction to *1968 and Global Cinema,* the idea of global cinema reflects more than present geopolitics and "the processes of globalization." Historically, it also implies "a longer and more nuanced understanding" that is "linked to radical politics" and aesthetics that reflect "the politics of international solidarity."[17]

Inspired by these collections, *Post-Communist Malaise* analyzes art cinemas from Eastern Europe and the Balkans to imagine a new radical politics and transnational solidarity for Europe. As Dina Iordanova states in *Cinema of the Other Europe: The Industry and Artistry of East Central European Film,* "The forced 'togetherness' of these countries led to numerous artistic interactions and mutual influences."[18] It is my argument that this "forced togetherness" creates a unique discourse of political modernism. In particular, the traditions of art cinema discussed in this book emerged in the decades after the Second World War, rejecting the dogmas of socialist realism in order to develop a dissident Marxism that critiques authoritarian communism. This political modernism evolved into a critique of the neoliberal integration of Europe during the post-communist era. Analyzing this evolution requires first an interpretation of communism as a political and aesthetic project.

COMMUNISM AND THE END OF UNIVERSAL HISTORY

Before the financial crisis, the decades after the fall of the Berlin Wall made it easy to forget the initial emotional allure of communism and its utopian impulses. The Soviet-style communism that spread across Eastern Europe and the Balkans was both the logical culmination and the terrifying perversion of the Enlightenment project to achieve political progress and liberation through the idea of universal history. While theologies with universal histories precede the Enlightenment and are found in early monotheisms, the writings of Immanuel Kant, G.W.F. Hegel, Karl Marx, and others serve as the philosophical underpinnings for twentieth-century communism. These intellectual origins are important to remember if we wish to understand post-communist identity and its complex relationship with European integration.

The allure of communism can be understood as the desire to be absorbed into a universal history, while its disappearance creates a sense of malaise. For example, in his essay "Beyond Diversity: Cultural Studies and Its Post-Communist Other," Russian philosopher and art critic Boris Groys characterizes communism as the promise of an inner transformation of identity into something more modern. He explains, "In the past, to be universal was to invent an idea or an artistic project that could unite people of different backgrounds, that could transcend the diversity of their already existing cultural identities, that could be joined by everybody—if he or she would decide to join them. This notion of universality was linked to the concept of inner change, of inner rupture, of rejecting the past and embracing the future, to the notion of *metanoia*—of transition from an old identity to a new one."[19] From the vantage point of the present, this may seem like a troubling and idealized interpretation of what it means to become universal. As numerous postcolonial theorists have argued, the category of universal history often reflects a Eurocentric world view and has provided philosophical justification for the worst crimes of colonialism. One does not have to read too far into Hegel's philosophy of history before encountering his belief in the superiority of Western European culture. Similarly, as Edward Said has observed, Marx's writings on Asia and India reflect a deeply ingrained orientalist world view. Nevertheless, Groys's insights about "inner change" and "embracing the future" are essential to understanding the allure of communism and its promise for people to become universal and more modern.

This promise is central to twentieth-century modernity and its ideological conflicts. As Evgeny Dobrenko writes in *Stalinist Cinema and the Production of History: Museum of the Revolution*, "The present was the main sacrifice of the twentieth century; all totalitarian regimes worked for the 'future.'"[20] However, not all totalitarian regimes "worked for the future" in the same manner with their cinema. Consider, for example, the differences between Nazi and Stalinist cinema. While propaganda was common, most films produced during the Nazi era were nevertheless escapist genre films such as musicals or comedies without explicit political content. Instead, social life itself was transformed into an aesthetic expression of ideology through mass spectacles in the form of orchestrated Nazi rallies with their ornamentalized pageantry. To use Dobrenko's terminology, under Nazism, the present was sacrificed through its simultaneous commitment to technological progress and rejection of the social egalitarianism of the Enlightenment for a horrific vision of romantic nationalism. Historian Jeffrey Herf notably describes this contradiction as a form of "reactionary modernism."[21] In contrast, under Stalinism, communism coalesces into a totalitarian vision of the derealization of the present. As Dobrenko argues, this creates a new temporality of the "concluded future." He explains, "The famous 'abolition' by Stalin of Hegel's law of negation of the negation left without an answer the question of what there would be 'after communism'; the horizon of expectations was directed towards the past, in so far as there was already nothing to 'expect' in the future. Stalin introduced a new temporality: the concluded future (a kind of future pluperfect). In order to free the ground for this new future, the present was shifted into the past, and the future-directed future was transformed into the present, as a result of which the present itself underwent complete derealisation."[22] The idea of the "concluded future" can be understood through the highly aestheticized imagery and plots of Soviet socialist realist cinema. This is especially true with the notorious Stalinist musicals produced throughout the Soviet Union and Eastern Europe. As the most aestheticized expression of socialist realism, the ideological function of such musicals was, to quote Lev Manovich, "to show the future in the present by projecting the perfect world of future socialist society onto a visual reality familiar to the viewer."[23] The musical *Traktoristy* (1939), which, like many films from the era, was later re-edited to remove references to Stalin, is a notable example. In the film, a soldier returns to his collective farm to find that his romantic interest, Mariana, has become an esteemed tractor driver who organizes other women to become more productive. Like many Stalinist musicals, it is primarily a romantic comedy with a highly standardized plot, though it is also intended as propaganda for mobilization since productivity with tractors is considered training for driving tanks in the war. The "concluded future" is clearly on display in its musical numbers, with happy peasants dancing and singing about the joys of labor and protecting the fatherland. The final stage of communism has already arrived in the present, and the peasants live in total harmony with the land and their labor.

Because communism already delineated the end of history, post-communist identity becomes indeterminate. If the promise of communism meant embracing universal history and living in the "concluded future," then there is no subsequent stage of development. There can be nothing new in the future in terms of economic and social relations. Thus, the aftershocks of the collapse of the communist regimes in Eastern Europe and the Balkans left no coherent or stable identity in their place other than a deferred promise of becoming European and integrating into its marketplace. For Groys this loss of identity allows the free market to supersede the universal project of communism. He explains, "The post-communist subject must feel like a Warhol Coca-Cola bottle brought back from the museum into the supermarket. In the museum, this Coca-Cola bottle was an artwork and had an identity—but back in the supermarket the same Coca-Cola bottle looks just like every other Coca-Cola bottle."[24] Coca-Cola, of course, is a recognizable signifier of American imperialism and global capitalism. Groys's comparison, therefore, structures the post-communist condition as a historical regression, a return to the marketplace determining identity and history, which is what communism promised to overcome. However, this regression into the capitalist past was itself upended by the economic crisis of 2008 and the subsequent politics of austerity, which deferred the utopia of a European common market into the future. This is why the art cinema analyzed in this book tends to imagine post-communist identity as liminal. For many in Eastern Europe and the Balkans, there is no returning to the communist past and there is no chance to accumulate wealth and capital, a deadlock that accelerates right-wing populism.

During the Cold War, Western scholarship on Eastern European cinema focused, appropriately so, on national cinemas[25] or politically committed aesthetics as a regional phenomenon.[26] Studies of national cinemas are still written today, but the transition into post-communism means a lack of definitive geopolitical identity for interpreting cinemas from the regions. This has led to innovative scholarship that interprets the regions through the lens of postcolonial theory. Influential books that establish this perspective are Larry Wolff's *Inventing Eastern Europe: The Map of Civilization on the Mind of the Enlightenment*[27] and Maria Todorova's *Imagining the Balkans*, which, inspired by Said, analyze the regions as discursive constructions of the West originating in the Enlightenment.[28] Both books convincingly show how the cultural identities of the regions are entangled with the historical legacies of the geopolitical divisions of the Ottoman and Austro-Hungarian Empires and their geographical status as the periphery of Europe. Recent cultural critics and film scholars map this postcolonial perspective onto the communist–post-communist divide and argue that the Soviet influence over the Eastern bloc was itself a form of colonialism. For example, in *Narrating Post/Communism: Colonial Discourse and Europe's Borderline Civilization*, Nataša

Kovačević carefully analyzes select writers for how they narrate the ideological borders between Eastern Europe and the "civilized" West. She posits "Eastern Europe as a postcolonial terrain" and claims that "the significance of communism to its history and the formation of its identity" should be considered "in postcolonial terms."[29] For Kovačević, a postcolonial reading of the post-communist condition is a necessary supplement to a Marxist perspective because it accounts for feelings of cultural inferiority. She writes,

> Eastern European communist legacies should not be analyzed only in terms of the degree of economic innovation upon or departure from Western capitalist practices. Indeed, if one does that, then one will conclude, like Immanuel Wallerstein (1991), that communism and capitalism are parts of the same "world system"; or, like Slavoj Žižek, that "'actually existing Socialism' failed because it was ultimately a subspecies of capitalism," used its "instrumental reason," was not radical enough. These are of course valid assertions, but what this type of approach misses is the significance of communism as a line of flight for Eastern Europeans from not only the power grids of Western nations, but also the stigma of economic and cultural inferiority, escape from the logic of capital and the logic of being the "other."[30]

This passage recognizes the complexities of identity formation in the regions. To be sure, the spread of communism was also a pragmatic response to the threat of fascism and the horrors of Nazism during the Second World War. Yet, as Kovačević convincingly argues, escaping from the cultural stigmas of the West—and its long history of projecting inferiority onto Eastern Europe and the Balkans, as detailed in the Wolff and Todorova books—helps explain the allure of communism. In other words, in addition to harboring the desire to become modern and live in the future, East Europeans participated in a universal political project in which they imagined themselves to be superior to the capitalist West precisely because they wished to escape from its dehumanizing gaze. Communist propaganda routinely expressed this superiority, which many people internalized before the grim realities of actually existing communism became obvious. Wolfgang Becker's *Good Bye, Lenin!* wonderfully satirizes this phenomenon. Late in the film, for example, the son creates a mock newsreel to convince his mother, who went into a coma before the Berlin Wall fell, that East Germany still exists and refugees from the West are arriving to escape the excesses of capitalism in the West.

While understanding Eastern Europe through a postcolonial lens reveals the nuances of identity formation and the psychologies that determine political affiliations, it also highlights the pitfalls of a totalizing analysis of ideology. In the introduction to the comprehensive collection *Postcolonial Approaches to Eastern European Cinema: Portraying Neighbours On-Screen*, the editors state their preference for postcolonial theory for analyzing cinema from the regions and disparage Marxism for its, "broadly speaking, sympathy toward the Soviet political project."[31] They write, "For Marxist scholars the Cold War and the East-West divide were less important than the issues of the global spread of capitalism and conflicts between the 'First' and the 'Third World.' Moreover, they construed the socialist part of Eastern Europe as a monolith entity, a claim which we obviously disagree with and which, in our view, betrays a colonial mindset."[32] The authors appropriately warn against a monolithic interpretation of Eastern Europe, which can result from thinking about historical totality. In contrast, *Postcolonial Approaches* focuses on how the "existence of neighbours, ethnic minorities and border territories undermined the modernist homogenizing projects of both nation states and the Soviet bloc."[33] This thoughtful injunction against monolithic thinking and "homogenizing projects" means that any attempt to revisit political modernism must acknowledge the realities of actually existing communism as well as analyze it as a utopian ideology. To be sure, in historical practice, communist identity was never completely uniform. Many communist regimes appealed to ethnicity as a shortcut for integration into ideology, such as with the "Russification" of the Soviet Union or the constitution of Yugoslavia, which formally recognized ethnic identity. Yet, far from undermining the homogenization of identity, this acknowledgment of difference is a necessary act of sublation. This is why in the Soviet socialist realist war epic *The Fall of Berlin* (1950), which absurdly fictionalizes Stalin arriving in Berlin after its liberation, soldiers from various republics shout their ethnicities to the camera as they dance cheerfully after raising the Soviet flag at the Reichstag. In other words, the policies of communism in the region were never uniform and instead produced a variety of political and cultural forms depending on the nation. Even though one should remain suspicious of the idea of universal history, it is important not to equate Soviet-style communism with colonialism in the context of Eastern Europe or the Balkans. The decolonization of the Balkans and Eastern Europe began at the end of the First World War with the dissolution of the Austro-Hungarian and Ottoman Empires, from which Western powers drew borders for new nation-states. For all its totalitarian horrors, the spread of Soviet-style communism did not represent a continuation of pre–First World War empires, nor did it compare to the economic exploitation and racist subjugation of non-Western peoples by the first-world white colonial powers.

While acknowledging the limits of universalizing projects, the task of *Post-Communist Malaise* is to engage in a totalizing critique of ideology that works through the current historical impasse, at which the neoliberal integration of Europe has provoked right-wing populism. In part, neoliberalism became the dominant ideology in Eastern Europe and the Balkans during the nineties because it successfully positioned itself as diversifying and privatizing the last vestiges of state power and authoritarian communism. The danger since the financial crisis and Brexit is that European integration stalls, with neoliberalism and right-wing populism locked in a dialectic. In order to resolve this dialectic, and to overcome the malaise generated by European integration, it is first important to reject the idea that universality and diversity are categorical opposites. As Groys writes,

> There is no real choice between universality and diversity. Rather, there is a choice between two different types of universality: between the universal validity of a certain political idea and the universal accessibility obtained through the contemporary market. Both—the modern state and the contemporary market—are equally universal. But the universality of a political idea is an openly manifested, articulated, visualized universality that demonstrates itself immediately by the uniformity and repetitiveness of its external image. On the other hand, the universality of the market is a hidden, non-explicit, nonvisualized universality that is obscured by commodified diversity and difference.[34]

In this passage, Groys continues the Marxist tradition of distinguishing between different types of universality.[35] According to him, the "openly manifested" form of communism privileges aesthetic uniformity, which makes its universality apparent. Consider how urban development in communist nations resulted in identical-looking apartment units and complexes.[36] In contrast, the free market universalizes exchanges between commodified individuals without the intervention of the state. For example, in the amusing "Share a Coke" campaign, individualism is mass-produced so one can order a bottle with one's name printed on it. Free-market capitalism requires greater internalization of its values than communism, whose uniformity is externalized in things such as its drab urban architecture. The universality of the free market is "obscured" in comparison because it depends on "commodified diversity." Thus, the transition from communism to free-market capitalism in Eastern Europe and the Balkans is not the historical progress from aesthetic homogeneity to diversity and freedom. To repeat Groys's Coca-Cola metaphor, it is the transition from an identity that participates in a universal history to one that is lost in the marketplace.

NO ALTERNATIVE

The malaise produce by post-communist identity means that the problem of capitalist realism is acutely felt in Eastern Europe and the Balkans. In *Capitalist Realism: Is There No Alternative?,* Mark Fisher defines the problem as the inability to imagine future alternatives to free-market capitalism.[37] The subtitle of his book invokes Margaret Thatcher and the phrase she would repeat in speeches, that "there is no alternative" to free-market capitalism. Her continued association with the phrase is highlighted by the humorous 2012 reports that a Russian-dubbed bootleg of *The Iron Lady,* the biopic of Thatcher for which Meryl Streep won a Best Actress Oscar, circulated in Moscow and was mistakenly reviewed by a film critic. In this version, Thatcher is dubbed as saying, "Crush the working class, crush the cattle, crush these bums."[38] Thatcher herself was skeptical about the economic viability of the EU and was opposed to a superstate that would infringe on British sovereignty, a position that still characterizes pro-Brexit conservatives.[39] While the financial crisis legitimatized her skepticism, the irony is that the EU demanded Thatcher's neoliberal market reforms for the southern and eastern spheres. Greece, for example, had to choose between exiting the union and accepting a harsh austerity program.

Capitalist realism is a response to Fukuyama's thesis in *The End of History and the Last Man* that the end of communism means the end of history and that the last man is the one whose needs would be satisfied by liberal democracy and free-market capitalism. In the years following the book's publication, Fukuyama has written several articles tempering his utopianism about the end of history. For example, in a 2014 article entitled "At the 'End of History' Still Stands Democracy," he acknowledges that the "political decay" of democratic institutions is a real problem and that many governments have performed poorly when it comes to promoting economic growth and fostering a public sphere. Political corruption, according to Fukuyama, is also a problem in the case of Bulgaria and Romania. Nevertheless, he argues that "in the realm of ideas . . . liberal democracy still doesn't have any real competitors."[40] Its failures exist only in practice and not as ideology. Seven years earlier, before the financial crash, he expressed optimism about the EU. In his article "The History at the End of History," he responds to accusations that his book promotes a neoconservative world view that serves as the intellectual groundwork for the hegemonic foreign policy of the George W. Bush administration. Instead of America, he praises the historical trajectory of Europe: "*The End of History* was never linked to a specifically American model of social or political organisation. Following Alexandre Kojève, the Russian-French philosopher who inspired my original argument, I believe that the European Union more accurately reflects what the world will look like at the end of history than the contemporary United States. The EU's attempt to transcend sovereignty and traditional power politics by establishing a transnational rule of law is much more in line with a 'post-historical' world than the Americans' continuing belief in God, national sovereignty, and their military."[41] But by 2018 Fukuyama acknowledged that the "post-historical" dream of the EU was experiencing more than just "political decay." In *Identity: The Demand for Dignity and the Politics of Resentment*, he develops the Hegelian argument about the struggle for recognition, or what Fukuyama calls identity politics, in order to explain the rising tide of nationalism, which threatens liberal democracy. This demand for identity recognition can neither be satisfied by economic means alone nor ever be fully transcended. As such, Fukuyama recommends that we create "broader and more integrative" identities formulated around "adherence to basic liberal principles,"[42] which would allow us to redefine citizenship and belonging.

While Fukuyama is correct that we cannot fully transcend the desire for identity recognition, the problem with the EU is not that it lacks a broad enough identity. Rather, its neoliberalism will never fulfill the promise of its motto to be "united in diversity." As historian Walter Laqueur describes, the fundamental error of the EU is its belief in "the mistaken idea that there could be an economic union without a political union. There was little enthusiasm on the part of the richer European countries to help get the weaker economies out of trouble, especially if these weaker ones had behaved irresponsibly, or even fraudulently. Why should Germans retire at sixty-seven so that Greeks could retire at fifty-three? In other words, with all the talk about European identity and common values, there was little solidarity. Perhaps there could not be."[43]

Thus, it is impossible for Eastern Europe and the Balkans to become "post-historical" in the manner Fukuyama initially imagined when the aftershocks of the financial crisis created political and economic instability that will last for decades. These problems cannot be solved transnationally as long as the EU privileges developing an economic union over a political union. Without an egalitarian political union, the EU cannot create transnational solidarity and will reinforce the cultural and economic divides between East and West that Kovačević describes in her book. As Laqueur argues, under the current design of the EU, there is no reason why a German worker should feel solidarity with his or her Greek counterpart, considering their cultural differences, or why the Hungarians should feel compelled to let Brussels control their border policies. Neoliberalism and the long-term repercussions of a decade of austerity policies will continue to promote cultural fragmentation rather than solidarity.

BEYOND MALAISE?

The lack of cultural solidarity between Europe's regions that Laqueur describes has been a frequent theme in art cinema from Eastern Europe and the Balkans since the early nineties. In fact, it is difficult to find optimistic representations of European integration that embrace the end of history. Though it critiques European integration, *Post-Communist Malaise* also speculates on how to work through the problem of capitalist realism and the malaise of post-communist identity. Because revisiting political modernism is central to this project, the subsequent chapters are organized around close readings of films, placing them in dialogue with film theory and political philosophy. The selection process for the films is defined entirely by how they establish this dialogue, regardless of their canonical status. To the extent that I privilege the close reading of individual films and directors' styles, I am not advocating a return to auteur criticism. Rather, my attention to authorship and style aims to mediate between traditional concepts of art cinema and a revised approach to political modernism. The intent is not to privilege regressive notions of cinematic mastery, which, too often, has been gendered as masculine throughout film history. Instead, *Post-Communist Malaise* aims to restore what Terry Eagleton calls "the futurity of the future"[44] by updating classical aesthetic categories, like art cinema, to trace the emergent possibilities for a new mass politics after communism.

Chapter 1, "Eastern European New Waves and Political Modernism," situates discourses about political modernism in the context of Eastern European and Balkan cinemas of the sixties and seventies. Marxist debates about political modernism and theories of counter-cinema from classical film theory are summarized and critiqued for establishing a binary between Hollywood and Western European art cinema. In contrast, this chapter argues that opposition between modernism and realism, which is central to a discourse of political modernism, is complicated in Eastern Europe and the Balkans because of the legacies of Stalinism and socialist realism. After the Second World War, many directors from the regions began as documentarians who grappled with the dogmas of socialist realism and developed ideological aesthetics that were critical of authoritarian communism. This chapter traces how select directors from the era evolved from documentarians into political modernists. Films by Dušan Makavejev, Věra Chytilová, and Miklós Jancsó are closely analyzed.

Chapter 2 is titled "What Happens after the End of History?" It analyzes political modernist films from the nineties that represent the transition to free-market capitalism and the violent dissolution of the former Yugoslavia. The first half contrasts the end-of-history discourses in political theory by Fukuyama, Samuel P. Huntington, and Michael Hardt and Antonio Negri with the satirical visions of post-communist Europe in the late films of Jan Švankmajer and Chytilová, both of whom were censored by the post-1968 authoritarian Czechoslovakian regime. Their late films revive the ideology criticism of their early work, with free-market capitalism becoming the target instead of authoritarian communism.

The second half of the chapter examines a variety of texts, from Hollywood to European art films, that represent Sarajevo and the dissolution of Yugoslavia, such as the late films of Jean-Luc Godard and Makavejev. My analysis focuses on films that interpret the dissolution of Yugoslavia as a form of economic disintegration rather than adhering to the common Western view that the cause of the conflict was the eruption of tribalism and "ancient hatreds" after the end of communism. In particular, Yugoslavia's collapse should be understood as the sociopolitical outcome of the country's severe economic contraction during the eighties and the neoliberal market reforms and austerity demanded by international financial organizations in order to service its unsustainable levels of debt. In other words, Yugoslavia was a casualty of the first global wave of neoliberalism during the eighties whose fate predicts one possible outcome for Europe after the financial crisis and its decade of austerity, which has accelerated the rise of right-wing populism.

Chapter 3, "Slow Cinema and the Escape from Capitalist Realism," closely reads the films of Béla Tarr and Cristi Puiu and politicizes their styles in order to complicate contemporary dialogue about international slow cinema. This chapter argues that their synthesis of cinematic realism and modernism, inspired by Andrei Tarkovsky, invites spectators to dwell on the duration of cinematic images. Both directors develop unique long-take styles that critique capitalist realism by immersing spectators in a radically materialist vision of the present. Their work also dwells on the possibility for reconciliation with the communist past, with differing conclusions. Tarr, whose films are analyzed in the first half of the chapter, denies the possibility because in his work the narratives of progress that structure communism and capitalism have been exhausted and replaced with apocalyptic expressions of historical malaise. To counter this apocalyptic malaise, Tarr proposes a humanist vision that demands compassion for the doomed and miserable characters who populate his films. In comparison, the second half of the chapter reads the films of Puiu, whose style expresses hope for historical reconciliation and spiritual transformation that overcomes the malaise produced by post-communism.

Chapter 4, "Theo Angelopoulos, Greece, and the Ends of Europe," analyzes the late films of Theo Angelopoulos, who, during a forty-year career, developed an ambitious political modernist style. In the seventies he gained an international reputation for his Marxist epics, such as *The Traveling Players* (1975), whose radical long takes chronicle twentieth-century Greece as a conflict between communism and fascism. In his later films, his aesthetic shifts toward mapping the regional identity of the Balkans through melancholy stories about borders and migration. He also explores whether cinema can help us reconcile with the past and imagine a new future politics. The first part of the chapter focuses on his films *The Suspended Step of the Stork* (1991) and *Eternity and a Day* (1998), which predict the refugee crisis of 2015 through their images of borders and exile. Both films use exile as a metaphor for imagining new forms of belonging. The second part of the chapter develops this analysis of borders and exile in relation to the self-reflexivity of *Ulysses' Gaze* (1995) and *The Dust of Time* (2008), which meditate on the ability for cinematic time to escape the malaise of post-communism.

The conclusion is divided into two sections, which summarize the preceding chapters and their arguments about communism, capitalism, art cinema, and political modernism. By drawing parallels to the collapse of Yugoslavia, the conclusion reiterates the impossibility for neoliberalism to integrate Europe. In the long term, free markets and austerity politics cannot culturally unify the continent and will instead accelerate the rise of right-wing populism that positions itself as an alternative to the economic and social failures of the EU. The book concludes by reframing the discourses of political modernism from the preceding chapters as expressions of utopian thinking and political hope. In the end, the films analyzed throughout *Post-Communist Malaise* speak to the utopian potential of the materiality of cinematic time to imagine a new political and cultural organization for Europe. Without this imagined alternative to the current union, one founded on transnational cultural and economic solidarity, the integration of Europe will continue to stall.

1 • EASTERN EUROPEAN NEW WAVES AND POLITICAL MODERNISM

THE NEW WAVES AND COUNTER-CINEMA

Eastern Europe experienced its own new waves of national cinemas in the decades following the Second World War as a new generation of filmmakers began to experiment with visual styles and narrative structures. Though often overshadowed in Western film culture by French and Italian cinemas and auteurs like Ingmar Bergman and Akira Kurosawa, many Eastern European films were internationally recognized. Most notably, the Czech New Wave produced several critical successes in the sixties with, for example, *The Shop on Main Street* (1965) and *Closely Watched Trains* (1967) winning the Academy Award for Best Foreign Language Film, while Miloš Forman's *Loves of a Blonde* (1965) and *The Fireman's Ball* (1967) were also nominated. On the European festival circuit, the films of the Yugoslav Black Wave, such as *Early Works* (1968) and *Innocence Unprotected* (1968), won major awards at the Berlin International Film Festival. Hungarian director Miklós Jancsó even won Best Director at Cannes in 1972 for his complex and lengthy sequence shots.

While many Eastern European films are safely entrenched in the art cinema canon, their contributions to discourses of political modernism have been undervalued. This is because our understanding of the concept has been filtered through the geopolitical lens of the West, with the binary between Hollywood and Western Europe structuring its meaning. For Peter Wollen, Jean-Luc Godard epitomizes the ideal of counter-cinema rather than, for example, Dušan Makavejev. In his essay "Godard and Counter Cinema: *Vent d'Est*," Wollen explains that his critical approach is to take "seven of the values of the old cinema, Hollywood-Mosfilm, as Godard would put it, and contrast these with their (revolutionary, materialist) counterparts and contraries."[1] Equating the studio systems of Hollywood and the Soviet Union is a provocative idea, but the similarities between the two are not analyzed. Ultimately counter-cinema is defined by its rejection of Hollywood rather than Mosfilm. This opposition between Europe and Hollywood is common in film theory. Recall that David Bordwell explains art cinema as a mode characterized by authorship, ambiguity, and realism in the form of characters who lack clear motivations and goals, as well as a preference for location shooting and an engagement with contemporary sociological problems. While this definition clarifies the general conventions of Western art cinema, it limits our understanding of cinema from other areas because it fails to consider how geopolitics and regional identities mediate these conventions, which is essential for updating our understanding of political modernism and art cinema.

Even when considering the regional politics of Eastern Europe, a fundamental obstacle remains. As the introduction argues, there is a tendency to reduce the former Eastern bloc to a monolithic identity. According to Jonathan Rosenbaum, this is why it was difficult for Western audiences and critics to interpret the more explicitly political new-wave films. In his essay that accompanies the Criterion Collection DVD of Dušan Makavejev's *WR: The Mysteries of the Organism*, he argues, "Between the mid-1960s and the mid-1970s, it was generally felt among Western intellectuals and cinephiles that cutting-edge, revolutionary cinema came from Western Europe, Latin America, and the United States. . . . By contrast, the wilder politicized art movies coming out of Eastern Europe at the time . . . were treated as curiosities, aberrations that wound up getting marginalized by default. The fact that they came from Communist countries made them much harder for Westerners to place, process, and understand; in most cases, an adequate sense of context was lacking."[2] Describing these "wilder politicized art movies" as marginalized is an overstatement, given the critical success of directors like Jancsó and Makavejev in the West. However, Rosenbaum is correct that their films were frequently misunderstood and their politics simplified when interpreted from a Western perspective. He explains, "Part of the problem was a certain intellectual as well as sensual impoverishment arising from the one-dimensional view of Communism fostered by the cold war, even among some of the better-educated leftists and cinephiles, which tended to lump together the Eastern European countries as if they were all part of the same stereotypical gray wasteland."[3] In other words, the issue is not simply that Western audiences lacked the necessary cultural and geopolitical information to interpret these films. The same can be said regarding art cinema from Asia, Latin America, or the Middle East. Rather, the fact that Eastern Europe is a "stereotypical wasteland" in the Western imaginary means that the "wilder politicized" films could be treated as artistic curiosities especially when compared with the more internationally popular films from the region. For example, American film critics could interpret *Closely Watched Trains* as a simple humanist statement, such as when Roger Ebert praised it as "a quiet, charming, very human film."[4] In contrast, the political modernists analyzed in this chapter, Věra Chytilová, Makavejev, and Jancsó, are more abstract and dialectical, and inclined to speculate on history and civilization instead of expressing straightforward humanism or anti-communism. Rather than singularly rejecting classical Hollywood, one reason for which Wollen champions the counter-cinema of Godard, they synthesize a range of styles, including European art cinema, Soviet montage, and socialist realism. Their work, this chapter argues, dialogues with Marxist debates about political aesthetics that began in the thirties in the writings of Ernst Bloch and György Lukács in which they argue the merits of German expressionism.

As D. N. Rodowick observes in *The Crisis of Political Modernism*, these writings inform the political modernist film theory of the seventies because they establish a binary between "modernism" and "realism."[5] For Bloch and Lukács, these are not mere aesthetic categories. They reveal a fundamental fissure in Marxist theory regarding the nature of historical totality. In "Realism in the Balance," Lukács argues that expressionism represents the worst tendencies of modernist experimentation insofar as it privileges subjective experiences rather than representing their "underlying unity, the totality, all of whose parts are objectively interrelated."[6] Lukács claims that, for both the artist and the reader, "the crux of the matter is to understand the correct dialectical unity of appearance and essence."[7] According to him, a realist like Thomas Mann achieves this balance better than a modernist like James Joyce, whom Bloch champions for his montage of inner monologue. In the end, for Lukács, expressionism and modernism are too enamored with appearance. When "followed through logically,"[8] they are antirealist, as they decadently abandon a belief in an objective external reality.

In his defense of expressionism, Bloch questions the idea that historical totality can be experienced as an objective unity. In his essay "Discussing Expressionism," he writes, "Lukács's thought takes for granted a closed and integrated reality that does indeed exclude the subjectivity of idealism. . . . Whether such a totality in fact constitutes reality, is open to question. . . . But what if Lukács's reality—a coherent, infinitely mediated totality—is not so objective after all? What if his conception of reality has failed to liberate itself completely from Classical systems? What if authentic reality is also discontinuity?"[9] The distinction, thus, between Lukács and Bloch is that the former postulates a reality that is "infinitely mediated" to form a whole, while the latter asks whether it is experienced as discontinuity. For Bloch, German expressionism mirrors the social conditions of early twentieth-century modernity. Thus, it does not dispense with an objective external reality but represents it as fragmented. Rightly so, Bertolt Brecht criticized Lukács's theory of realism as formalistic and beholden to a nineteenth-century view of literature. In other words, according to Brecht, it is Lukács who is "remote from reality"[10] because he failed to grasp the evolution of capitalist modernity.

Contextualizing this debate within Western discourses about art cinema, Bloch's defense of modernism has been more influential. For example, the political efficacy of modernist aesthetics is implicit in how Bordwell defines art cinema as the rejection of the classical narrative conventions of Hollywood in order to arrive at a greater sense of realism. It is also apparent in how Wollen privileges "reality" over "fiction" in his "seven cardinal virtues" of counter-cinema. "The cinema," as he states, "cannot show the truth, or reveal it, because the truth is not out there in the real world, waiting to be photographed."[11] In both cases, realism and "reality" are understood, structurally, as the rejection of narrative convention and the artifices of representation.

In terms of the "wilder" political films of the Eastern European new waves, the debate between modernism and realism is less settled. In particular, Lukács's rejection of modernist experimentation echoes the justifications for socialist realism that became the official artistic dogma under communism. In fact, the basic oppositions between Lukács and Bloch were articulated at the First Soviet Writers' Congress in 1934, where Karl Radek infamously described Joyce's *Ulysses* as a "heap of dung" whose stream-of-consciousness aesthetic reflected bourgeois values.[12] In contrast, the goal of socialist realism was officially defined at the congress by Andrei Zhdanov as "to depict reality in its revolutionary development. In addition to this, the truthfulness and historical concreteness of the artistic portrayal should be combined with the ideological remolding and education of the toiling people in the spirit of socialism."[13]

During the Stalinist era, socialist realist cinema privileged "ideological remolding" over historically concrete representations of "revolutionary development." For example, popular musicals such as the Czech film *Tomorrow, People Will Be Dancing Everywhere* (1952) were utopian projections of a future socialist paradise rather than accurate portrayals of daily peasant life under communism. This predominance of socialist realism meant that subsequent politically ambitious Eastern European films were required to express an aesthetic double bind. Like Godard's counter-cinema, they rejected narrative artifice and convention. However, they had to also represent the dissonance between actually existing communism and the universality of its idealism. In other words, their aesthetic strategies presumed a belief in an external reality that was discontinuous precisely because its historical totality was distorted by actually existing communism.

Given these contradictions, it is significant that two of the directors analyzed in this chapter, Jancsó and Makavejev, began as documentarians working within the constraints of socialist realism. Similarly, the early work of Chytilová resembles cinema verité. From these origins, they evolved into political modernists with complex styles. Chytilová and Makavejev, in particular, blended documentary and fiction while increasingly experimenting with intellectual montage. On the other hand, Jancsó developed a long-take style that intensified the durational aesthetics of neorealism and Michelangelo Antonioni into an abstract meditation on history. These seemingly antithetical aesthetics, montage and long takes, emerged from Eastern European documentary traditions. Understanding how they both became capable of critiquing the gap between actually existing socialism and communist propaganda requires an analysis of these traditions.

DOCUMENTARY TRADITIONS AND THE BOUNDARIES OF SOCIALIST REALISM

The rich documentary tradition that emerged after the Second World War in Eastern Europe is not well known in the United States outside regional scholarship. In comparison, its art cinema won Oscars and its animation was also internationally influential. For example, Czech puppeteer Jiří Trnka was called the Walt Disney of the East by journalists, and Zagreb Film became an internationally respected animation studio. Documentaries, however, never achieved the same recognition. To be sure, a lack of screening opportunities in the West contributed to their obscurity, though this has begun to change in recent years. In 2014 the National Gallery of Art curated the screening series *Artists, Amateurs, Alternative Spaces: Experimental Cinema in Eastern Europe, 1960–1990*, which explores the intersections between documentary, the avant-garde, and amateur productions outside the state-sponsored studio systems. According to the curators, Ksenya Gurshtein and Joanna Raczynska, the purpose of the series is to show "the variety of filmmaking and early video practices that existed in the region in the postwar period, and it sheds light on work that was made by artists and amateurs, as well as professionals, who, despite restrictions, made independent and experimental work both on their own and with the support of smaller state-funded amateur film clubs, festivals, and studios."[14] It is important to emphasize the phrase "despite restrictions" and warn against the one-dimensional view of communism that Rosenbaum argues hindered the appreciation of the more politically ambitious Eastern European art cinema. In other words, a misconception persists in the West regarding the degree of control that communist authorities would exercise over films. Because of this, Eastern European documentaries are presumed to be propaganda, even more so than the region's animation or art cinema. As Dina Iordanova writes in *Cinema of the Other Europe: The Industry and Artistry of East Central European Film*, there is a "misleading assumption" that "documentary film of the region was strictly politically controlled and mostly used for propaganda purposes. This view is incorrect: while it may be true that newsreels and documentary films were often made with propaganda in mind, it was within the documentary realm that some of the most important socially critical works materialized."[15]

To be clear, state-sponsored studios were not frequently financing "socially critical works." However, before the upheavals of 1968, which increased state suppression of the arts in some nations, politically critical documentaries were created by smaller studios and film clubs, which largely operated free from state interference. Such was the case with the Bela Balázs Studio in Hungary. John Cunningham describes the studio in *Hungarian Cinema: From Coffee House to Multiplex* as operating "with a high degree of independence, working with its own budget. Here film students could cut their teeth on their pet projects by making short films independent of both the main studios and the Film Academy. The Balázs even adopted its own cinema . . . where regular screenings of the Studio's work were often followed by discussions with filmmakers."[16]

The 1962 documentary *Gypsies* is an example of the kind of socially critical work produced by the studio. It employs sophisticated visual and aural strategies of montage in order to raise awareness about the plight of the Roma living in Hungary. It is important to stress that this was a verboten subject in communist societies. Though the utopia depicted in socialist realist films was characterized by images of happy peasants, bigotry and poverty were the norm for the Roma under communism.

A similar degree of independence temporarily existed at the Serbian studio Neoplanta, known for releasing essential films of the Yugoslav Black Wave such as Makavejev's *WR: Mysteries of the Organism*. They also produced socially conscious documentary shorts. For example, in *Black Film* (1971), director Želimir Žilnik examines unemployment and homelessness, social problems supposedly eliminated in communist societies. He invites six homeless men to his apartment so he can find them accommodations. Frustrated by local bureaucracies as he tries to help them, he stops trying and the men leave his apartment. Their fate is uncertain. The title of the documentary is sarcastic, referencing the fact that the Yugoslav Black Wave was referred to as the "black wave" or "black film." Through the film, Žilnik questions whether the new Yugoslav cinema can solve social problems. Indeed, a postscript included at the end of the credits asks whether film functions as a weapon or feeds us shit, and it leaves the audience to ponder the answer. Unlike the Bela Balázs Studio, Neoplanta eventually experienced a government crackdown. While its films were arguably more confrontational and experimental, this was not the primary reason. Post-1968, relations between the various Yugoslav republics began to fray to the point where nationalist protests occurred in 1971.[17] Within this environment, Josip Broz Tito's government asserted more control and imposed "ideological unity." *WR*, for instance, was withdrawn from distribution in the country and Makavejev went into exile.[18] Žilnik experienced a similar fate. Moreover, there is the notorious case of Lazar Stojanović, who was briefly jailed for his thesis film, *Plastic Jesus* (1971), which was banned until 1990.[19]

While *Gypsies* and *Black Film* are fascinating examples of films that directly critique communist orthodoxy, they were not the norm. Rather, the formal experiments found in the documentary traditions were more indicative of how the new generation of filmmakers worked within the aesthetic constraints of socialist realism. It was by incorporating modernist tendencies into a realist framework that they were able to examine the dissonance between actually existing communism and its ideals. This seems like a counterintuitive claim since modernism and formalist experimentation were rejected as symptoms of bourgeois decadence. However, filmmakers often found new ways to synthesize both tendencies. Consider the Latvian documentary short *Ten Minutes Older* (1978), which inspired two world cinema anthology films in 2002, *Ten Minutes Older: The Trumpet* and *Ten Minutes Older: The Cello*.[20] It consists of a single nine-minute shot, with an occasional zoom, of children watching a puppet play. The director, Herz Frank, included a subtitle, *A Tale about Good and Evil*, despite the fact that the audience is never shown the play. This offered a pretense of narrative so that the Soviet authorities would not reject it as an exercise in abstract formalism.[21] The incorporation of modernist abstraction within a realist narrative is also evident in the 1974 Hungarian documentary *New Year's Eve*, produced by Bela Balázs Studio. On its surface, it is a linear narrative about a New Year's Eve in Budapest. Throughout, however, its form echoes that of modernist city symphony films like Walter Ruttmann's *Berlin: Symphony of a Great City* (1927) or Dziga Vertov's *Man with a Movie Camera* (1929), using montage to abstract its subject into a satirical statement on modern alienation and technological mediation.

This dialectic between abstraction and concrete narrative realism also characterizes the aesthetics of the political modernists of the new wave. Though it directly emerged from the experimental traditions of Eastern European documentary, its origins can also be found in Soviet cinema of the thirties as montage directors first adjusted to the dogmas of socialist realism. In his essay "Eisenstein, Socialist Realism, and the Charms of *Mizanstsena*," Bordwell explains how directors like Eisenstein synthesized their modernism of grotesque visuals within a realist style that privileges depth of field. He writes, "Montage editing had been well suited to suggest mass movements sweeping across cities and continents. The new depth style could present more intimate scenes and focus on individual characters while also inflating them and their enterprises. In gigantic sets, looming figures enact dramas of epochal significance; deep space becomes and arena of momentous treachery and sacrifice, genius and betrayal, military strategy and struggles for the soul of the people."[22] In other words, images of lateral collective movement are replaced with deep space that mythologizes individuals and their contributions to shaping history. This is exemplified by the difference between Sergei Eisenstein's *Strike* (1924) and his later *Alexander Nevsky* (1938). In the riot sequence in *Strike*, the dynamic visual compositions privilege lateral mass movements of the peasants, primarily through the foreground of the frame. Similarly, the iconic edit from the slaughter of the cow falling to the peasants' hands rising emphasizes vertical movement through the frame. In comparison, in the later *Alexander Nevsky*, the visuals privilege an extreme depth of field and include cuts from foreground to background during its ice battle sequence, which construct an illusion of realist space. As Bordwell notes, "Eisenstein often replaces lateral staging with action that proceeds toward and away from the camera. Simple instances of this tactic can be found in the deep-space work of other Soviet directors of the period, but in Eisenstein, the spatial dynamics bursts the bonds of the single shot. Axial editing combines with depth staging to create a constantly unfolding foreground, opening up new vistas of space for the characters to hurl themselves into."[23] To summarize, "the bonds of the single shot" were overcome by incorporating modernist montage into realist spatial aesthetics. This was further developed in the Eastern European new waves by their political modernists. Rather than creating a counter-cinema that rejects codes of representation and the illusion of depth, they accelerated "the revolutionary development" of reality as demanded by the doctrine of socialist realism. In general, the Western counter-cinema exemplified by Godard aims for ideological demystification through flat images and self-referential formalism.[24] In comparison, the approaches of Chytilová, Makavejev, and Jancsó are more ambiguous and less concerned with demystifying cinema. They synthesize modernist and realist tendencies in order to open "up new vistas of space" that critique communism.

SURREALISM AND DOCUMENTARY IN DUŠAN MAKAVEJEV

Before his first feature, *Man Is Not a Bird* (1965), Makavejev directed eighteen amateur documentary and fiction shorts. Thus, he is closely associated with postwar film clubs and experimental documentary traditions.[25] In fact, the National Gallery of Art screening series *Artists, Amateurs, Alternative Spaces* includes his first fiction shorts, *The Seal* (1955) and *Anthony's Broken Mirror* (1957). Regrettably, many of these early works have been poorly archived. His first documentary, *Jatagan Mala* (1953), about life in a Roma settlement near Belgrade, is presumed lost, and the original soundtracks for the two aforementioned fiction films are missing.

Makavejev's earliest films are amateurish when compared with *WR: Mysteries of the Organism* or *Sweet Movie*, but they indicate his interest in fusing modernist experimentation with social criticism through surrealist imagery and intellectual montage. *The Seal*, for example, tells the life story of a man living in a totalitarian society. It is narrated by him after his death, through the use of Esperanto intertitles, as he waits for state bureaucrats to officially declare him dead. Visually, the film employs spatial discontinuity and includes nightmarish imagery such as having all of the state authorities and bureaucrats wear the same masks, rendering them faceless. The most playful sequence is when the man meets his wife. The two are seated on different park benches apart from each other. Makavejev cuts to an overhead long shot and uses stop-motion to show the benches moving together before merging into one. Moreover, the rapid montage during the main character's feverish deathbed scene foreshadows Makavejev's later work with its shots of faceless bureaucrats juxtaposed with images from the character's childhood and burning fields of grass.

In *Anthony's Broken Mirror*, Makavejev abandons the generic political allegory of *The Seal* for a surrealist parable of frustrated desire. The extended pre-title sequence begins in a neorealist mode with the camera moving through a city street, revealing rubble and people walking. We are introduced to our protagonist as he plays marbles with children. Once he leaves, he wanders aimlessly until he finds a store with a mannequin in the window. From here, the film transitions into its surrealist premise. The man falls in love with the mannequin. Frustrated that she remains behind the glass, he tries charming her with pantomime. In one bizarre sequence, he removes a rabbit from his jacket that he accidentally crushes against the window. A pair of soldiers disperses the gathering crowd and helps him bury the rabbit. Returning to the mannequin, the man breaks the window with a brick. He stares at the broken glass and the destroyed mannequin, realizing she was not real. The film ends with a high-angle shot of the man, alone and isolated on the street. A unique work, *Anthony's Broken Mirror* recalls Luis Buñuel's Mexican-period films in the early 1950s more than it does anything in Eastern European cinema at the time. Its clash between socially critical realist imagery and destructive desires hints at the complex fusion of Marx and Freud that will be more evident in his mature political modernist works.

Many of Makavejev's early documentaries downplay surrealism in favor of experiments with intellectual montage and humorous social commentary. *Parade* (1962), for example, gently satirizes preparations for the annual May Day Parade in honor of Tito's Partisans. Ironic juxtapositions are evident from the start, such as when a man walks his pig down the street while patriotic music is heard on the soundtrack. By emphasizing preparations instead of the parade itself, Makavejev deflates the mythologization of the event and reveals it to be a constructed spectacle. It is not surprising that the documentary was initially banned before being re-edited for release. Even more ambitious is *New Domestic Animal* (1964), a nine-minute visual essay about progress in rural areas. Throughout, Makavejev juxtaposes shots of cars with shots of animals. The musical score that accompanies the former is frequently consonant, whereas the latter is accompanied by either a dissonant score or silence. As the patterns of montage develop, a narrative emerges. The cars are replacing horses as a mode of transportation and food delivery. No longer useful, the horses are slaughtered. The documentary emphasizes a dark view of historical progress in which embracing technological innovation depends on a violent destruction of outmoded forms of life.

The dichotomies of Makavejev's early work—fiction-documentary, surrealism–social satire—are fully synthesized in *WR: Mysteries of the Organism* and *Sweet Movie*.[26] The former includes a documentary about psychoanalyst Wilhelm Reich, whose eccentric ideas about a universal libidinal energy called orgones led to legal trouble and his imprisonment. This is juxtaposed with a fictional story set in Yugoslavia, where a dedicated revolutionary named Milena meets a Soviet ice skater ironically named Vladimir Ilyich. Together the two parts of the film form a complex essay that addresses a wide range of themes, such as sex, political revolution, human freedom, and totalitarianism. If there is an overarching thesis in the film, it is that sex and communism unleash revolutionary energies that can be misdirected into totalitarianism.

Despite its suggestion that the communist revolution has failed, *WR* is never defeatist about the possibilities for establishing human freedom. Makavejev visualizes this in one of the strangest scenes in the film. Decapitated by Vladimir Ilyich, who is unable to control his orgone energy, Milena's head speaks from a coroner's table, stating that she is not ashamed of her communist past. In his British Film Institute monograph about the film, Raymond Durgnat describes this moment as follows: "Milena speaks, posthumously, for all the Communists who, murdered by other Comrades, were 'faithful unto death.' She failed, but is unrepentant, as if her effort, not her 'unhappy end,' were the truth. Her resurrection, and non-recantation, might seem religious, outside an autopsy room. Hope springs eternal even on the dissection table."[27] In essence, she expresses the contradiction in Makavejev's political modernism: Marxism has failed, so we must reanimate Marxism. As Durgnat writes, "*WR* makes perfect sense as a Marxist criticism of Marxist ideologies."[28] This reanimation is only possible if we embrace our libidinal forces but are not consumed by them. Late in the film, for example, Makavejev cuts from a close-up of a newly molded plaster dildo to a shot from a Soviet film with an actor portraying Stalin who talks about completing the first stage of communism. Next he cuts to found footage of a mental institution showing a patient banging himself against a wall. Makavejev juxtaposes this disturbing image with a folk song praising the glorious party. The metaphor created by this intellectual montage is not subtle. It suggests that the appeal of Stalin depends on misdirected and codified sexual energy. He is the symbolic phallus at the center of the madness of party politics.

In *Sweet Movie*, Makavejev continues his synthesis of Freud and Marx in order to further understand the failures of the communist revolution. Like *WR*, the film blends fiction with documentary found footage, such as of the Katyn Massacre committed by the Soviet Union in the Second World War. In particular, it intertwines two stories. The first follows Miss World, the "virgin beauty" contest winner who is forced to marry the world's richest man, a Texas capitalist named Mr. Kapital. She escapes on her wedding night and travels the world having unusual sexual encounters with absurd men like "El Macho." The second story, set in Amsterdam, is about Anna Planeta, the captain of the "revolutionary" boat *Survival*, which has a giant head of Karl Marx for its bow. The film begins with Anna singing about seeing something black on a mountaintop and wondering if it is "cow shit" or her "beloved." Her song introduces the film's central conundrum—namely, whether we can distinguish between politically transformative forms of desire and what Georges Bataille would call the "excremental forces," which can spark primal and involuntary reflexes that lead to social repression. Consider the notorious Otto Muehl commune sequence from the film. Comatose after her objectification by male characters, Miss World is delivered to the commune in a wheelbarrow to be reanimated from her sexual trauma. Their "methods" are "excremental" to say the least, as members vomit, regurgitate their food, defecate on plates, urinate, and mimic infants. Steven Shaviro describes this scene as the moment when our "inner fascist, with its fear of boundary dissolution and flows,"[29] emerges. In other words, our affective response reveals the psychic forces on which totalitarianism feeds. Yet Makavejev himself describes his intentions with the sequence as the opposite in a brief article he wrote, "*Sweet Movie*: The Gentle Side of 'Destructive Art.'" Emphasizing that the excremental imagery is presented with an innocent and optimistic spirit, he writes,

> I was sure that the "provocative content" could overcome the censorial impulses waiting at the end of our work if the excess normally considered dangerous is wrapped up in infantility, happiness and pure "joy of life." It ended, paradoxically, both ways. The film played in many countries; however, it is still banned in Canada and the United Kingdom.
>
> I think I've interpreted correctly the Commune's "destructivity" as respect for life in all its wilderness, unpredictability, freedom, pleasure. Celebration. It was clear to me that all their actions, ugly or shocking, were pure play and performance, innocently offered to both themselves and to the camera eye, and politically more than correct.[30]

His optimism that the sequence should not provoke one's "inner fascist" and we should instead accept the extreme imagery as "pure play and performance" is betrayed by Miss World's subsequent experiences. After she leaves the commune, Miss World films a commercial in which she writhes around naked in a vat of chocolate. The excremental itself is commodified and Miss World is objectified as she was at the beginning of the film. Unlike *WR*'s Milena, who refuses to apologize for her communist past, offering hope that her revolutionary energy has not been destroyed, Miss World remains objectified. Her chocolate commercial is a variation on the virgin beauty pageant that awarded her to Mr. Kapital and set her on her journey. In both she is put on display.

By its conclusion, *Sweet Movie* exhausts the "hope springs eternal" of *WR* and Makavejev's earlier films. Rather than hinting at the persistence of a utopian spirit, the reanimation of its characters heightens the film's central conundrum about whether we can distinguish between politically transformative forms of desire and primal and repressive reflexives. This sense of political exhaustion becomes more prevalent in Makavejev's subsequent, more conventional art cinema narratives, in particular *Montenegro* (1981) and *Manifesto* (1988), which satirize the notion that desire can create political change. Yet his post-communist work, which chapter 2 analyzes, returns to the essayistic montage of his political modernism, invoking new questions about history now that the communist project has ended.

FROM CINEMA VERITÉ TO MONTAGE IN VĚRA CHYTILOVÁ

Unlike Makavejev, Chytilová did not begin in the amateur film club and experimental documentary traditions. She attended the Film and Television School of the Academy of Performing Arts in Prague, the famous Czech film school. Perhaps this is why her style evolved more quickly from realism to abstract modernism, with her early work indicating a strong cinema verité influence before she developed her avant-garde style. Rather than evincing a radical break between the two modes, she progressed organically. This is because before the experimental *Daisies* (1966), she was already stretching the aesthetic boundaries of socialist realism. Her forty-minute thesis film, *Ceiling* (1962), tells the story of Marta, a fashion model who becomes increasingly alienated from her profession, which objectifies her. Chytilová adheres to a direct, observational style throughout. However, satirical commentary is clearly evident in scenes where Dixieland jazz is heard on the soundtrack as Marta prepares for a fashion show with other models. Moreover, Chytilová repeats crane shots that view Marta from a height, emphasizing her alienation. Toward the end of the film, there is also an example of the kind of intellectual montage that she develops in her avant-garde work. As Marta walks the streets after spending the night with a lover, there is a close-up of her legs and high heels. Chytilová match-cuts to a shot of mannequin legs, further emphasizing Marta's dehumanization. The end of the film finds her escaping from her life as a model as she is riding a train into the country.

Her next film, the short *A Bagful of Fleas* (1962), further breaks from the conventions of socialist realism. It is an attempt to construct an entirely first-person film, reminiscent of classical Hollywood noirs like *Lady in the Lake* (1947) and *Dark Passage* (1947). Unlike those works, the main character is not introduced with a prologue or the use of mirror shots throughout. Instead, the audience is immediately immersed in the perspective of Eva, the young woman who stands in for the camera, as she arrives to work at a textile factory. Though we sometimes hear Eva's internal monologue, the film is primarily set in the women's dormitory and often resembles a vérité documentary with observational long takes with no clear dramatic momentum. Most scenes feel loosely improvised as the young women playfully attempt to overcome the boredom of their situation. Eventually, dramatic conflict arises as another young woman, Jana, rebels and faces a committee meeting to determine whether she should be fired for her indifference to her work.

Something Different (1963), Chytilová's first feature-length film, further pushes the boundaries of vérité by introducing elements of associative montage. It tells two stories that never intersect. The first is a quasi-documentary of real-life gymnast Eva Bosáková as she reluctantly trains for the championship. The second follows Vera, a fictional housewife, who is alienated and bored because her husband ignores her, while her young son tries her patience with his tantrums. Eventually, she begins to have an affair. For the most part, Eva's narrative is presented as straightforward documentary, linearly visualizing her preparation for her last competition. Vera's narrative, on the other hand, is discontinuous and edited rhythmically to music to convey the repetitions of her daily life. Though the two strains of the film do not overlap, Chytilová associates them through montage and manipulation of the soundtrack. At one point, the piano music Eva trains along with is used as a soundtrack to Vera's narrative. During another moment, Chytilová cuts from Eva's domineering trainer to Vera's son, graphically matching them through motion. Such associations highlight the central theme of the film—namely, how the lives of both women are determined by patriarchy. In particular, both Eva and Vera are uncertain about their desires and are trapped in roles defined by men. At the end, Eva becomes a trainer after retiring from competition and Vera breaks down after learning her husband was also having an affair. She begs him to stay with her. This suggests that the choices for both women remain limited and that the "something different" of the title eludes them.

Chytilová's next two films, *Automated World* and *Daisies*, complete her transformation from cinema verité to modernist abstraction. The former is her twenty-minute short in the omnibus film *The Pearls of the Deep* (1966), which consists of five adaptions of Bohumil Hrabal stories. Similar to Chytilová's earlier work, it begins in observational cinema verité mode with shots of a wedding taking place next door to a restaurant, whose employees are shown working. However, the narrative quickly develops a dream logic. A female corpse is discovered in the restaurant, which is forced to close. The patrons remain standing outside in front of the window, voyeuristically leering inside. One of the female employees allows a man named Karl to enter. Presumably her friend, he begins to tell a strange tale about how his suicidal fiancée left him. As he continues to tell his story, Chytilová cuts to flashbacks of him creating abstract industrial art using sheet metal and a hammer. We also learn that he likes to create death masks for his friends. In a humorous scene, Karl hangs his art prints in a workers' hall that has large pictures of Karl Marx and Vladimir Lenin. When asked by the employee if the workers liked his art, he replies that the younger workers did. It is difficult not to interpret this as a satirical broadside against the dogma of socialist realism and its prohibition against modernist experimentation. However, unlike Chytilová's prior films, *Automated World* does not develop anything resembling a direct political critique. Instead, it descends into surrealism. The bride enters the restaurant and we learn that her husband was arrested for punching one of the police officers. She decides to take Karl home because she does not want to be alone. The film concludes with a perplexing sequence during a storm in which Karl tears her wedding dress apart and ties it to trees in order to strengthen them. As he strips her naked, the bride asks him to make her a death mask. Though the ending is opaque, it lends itself to a Freudian reading. When juxtaposed with the earlier scenes of Karl creating abstract industrial art for workers, the conclusion hints at the tension between artistic creation and destruction, at the darker subconscious forces, which cannot be represented by socialist realism.

Chytilová further explores the dialectic between artistic creation and destructive impulse in *Daisies*, her most famous work. Expanding on the experiments with intellectual montage from *Something Different*, *Daisies* completely abandons narrative realism and cinema verité and replaces them with a series of associations and repetitions. The brilliant title sequence establishes the motif of destruction as it rhythmically alternates between footage of bombs falling and a close-up of gears moving as militaristic music is heard on the soundtrack. Chytilová then introduces us to the main characters, Marie I and Marie II, in a black-and-white shot of the women seated in front of a wooden fence. We listen as they decide to "go bad" because the entire world has gone bad. However, the soundtrack includes nondiegetic sounds of creaking wood as the two Maries move their bodies, immediately distancing us from interpreting their rebellion in terms of any realistic psychological motivations. Indicative of this distancing, the film immediately cuts to a color image of the two women frolicking in a field containing an apple tree, a Garden of Eden reference that foreshadows the allegory of Chytilová's subsequent feature, *The Fruit of Paradise*. The narrative discontinuity establishes

Daisies as an essayistic and philosophical exploration. Indeed, the remainder is a complex experiment in aural and visual montage, as the two Maries find creative and novel ways to relieve their boredom, often with antisocial behavior at the expense of the foolish older men who take them on dates. Like *Automated World,* the film ends ambiguously without resolving its exploration of artistic creation and destruction. After destroying a banquet hall filled with tables of food, the two Maries resolve to conform and be good. However, a giant chandelier crashes down on them. Chytilová cuts back to the war footage from the opening but includes a curious dedication that is typed across the screen to the sound of a machine gun: "This film is dedicated to all those whose sole source of indignation is a trampled-on trifle." Given that *Daisies* was initially withheld from release because of its images of wasting food and subsequently banned after the Soviet invasion, the dedication predicates its own response. Under socialist realism, war and militarism are less objectionable than artistic abstraction and experimentation.

The Fruit of Paradise (1970) is Chytilová's final film of the Czech New Wave. Her most obscure work, it expands on the cynicism and associative montage of *Daisies* but also incorporates art cinema conventions throughout. The former is evident in the abstract nine-minute prologue, which closely resembles the underground American experimental cinema of the sixties rather than anything seen prior in the Czech New Wave. Recalling Stan Brakhage's prelude to his *Dog Star Man* (1961–1964) series, Chytilová presents abstract images in order to tell a creation myth. A naked Adam and Eve are imposed over shifting close-ups of leaves, flowers, and grass, which change in color. As the prologue continues, choral voices sing passages from the book of Genesis about knowledge and temptation. Eventually the film transitions into an allegorical narrative presumably set at a resort near a beach, where Josef and Eva, the modern-day versions of Adam and Eve, are staying. To the extent that there is a discernable story, it focuses on Eva's curiosity and temptation when a mysterious character named Robert arrives. We soon learn in the film that he is a murderer.

Because of its biblical parallels and narrative ambiguity, like *Automated World, The Fruit of Paradise* appears to retreat from satirical political critiques. Considering that it was released in the shadow of the Prague Spring and the Soviet invasion, its abstract images and narrative about temptation and truth telling are not political evasions. In particular, the conclusion can be interpreted as expressing self-reflexive despair over cinema's ability to tell the truth in a repressive society. Eva shoots Robert and escapes. She runs back to Josef, imploring him not to seek the truth like she did. The choral voices return to the soundtrack to sing the book of Genesis. The final desaturated image shows a field of grass waving in the wind. Its dreariness contrasts with the expressionistic color schemes that Chytilová explores throughout. The film's formalism has negated itself and its own search for the truth. In essence, we return to the opening prologue, now devoid of aesthetic possibilities for creation. This despondent ending is appropriate considering Chytilová's own fate. She was banned from filmmaking for several years as the era of political and cultural liberation ended in Czechoslovakia, though she returned to direct several films throughout the seventies and eighties. It was not until her post-communist features, analyzed in chapter 2, that she regained the political sensibility that animates her early work when she satirizes the transition into free-market capitalism.

THE INVERSION OF SOCIALIST REALISM IN MIKLÓS JANCSÓ

Like Chytilová, Jancsó was a product of film school rather than the culture of amateur film clubs. After graduating, he directed several documentary newsreels during the fifties, which he later dismissed as "all lies" and mere technical training.[31] These are rarely referenced in scholarship on Jancsó or the Hungarian film industry, and it is unclear how many survive in the archives. Mira Liehm and Antonin J. Liehm describe them in their comprehensive survey of Eastern European cinema as "in no way significantly different from films produced in the fifties, conforming to the general policy line."[32] In other words, they are likely the type of communist propaganda that Makavejev already satirized in *Parade*. Ironically, Jancsó claims the newsreels may have saved his life, as he was filming in China during the Hungarian Revolution of 1956. He believes he would have been hanged as a Stalinist.

Following the revolution, he directed his first feature film, *The Bells Have Gone to Rome* (1958), which is rarely screened and not very well known in the West. It is a standard socialist realist war drama about a heroic group of teens fighting during the last days of the Second World War. It has occasional flourishes of the visual talent that Jancsó will develop in his political modernist phase, such as the early sequence where the solders dig trenches, which incorporates long takes, fluid crane shots, and deep focus. However, it is interchangeable with any number of war films produced in the Eastern bloc throughout the late fifties. It would be four years until his next feature,

Cantata (1962), where he breaks from the narrative conventions of socialist realism and introduces the theme of alienation as a successful doctor struggles to reconcile with his peasant origins. Compared with his internationally recognized work, the film is conventional humanist new wave art cinema, heavily indebted to Antonioni in its exploration of ennui. Similarly, *My Way Home* (1964) is a transitional work. Often sentimental in tone, it tells the story of the friendship between a Hungarian prisoner of war and a Russian soldier guarding a remote outpost during the Second World War. It also introduces many of the themes and formal elements of Jancsó's mature style: geometrical visuals, group dynamics, and arbitrary exercises of power are staged via long takes on landscapes that express the cruelty of history.

With his next two films, *The Round-Up* (1965) and *The Red and the White* (1967), Jancsó emerged as an international art cinema auteur. Though his reputation declined throughout the eighties and nineties, his legacy is secure in Hungarian film history and the global art cinema canon. In recent years, his political modernist period has been critically revisited, perhaps because most of the films are finally available on DVD. It is important to remember that, at the height of his popularity, during the socially tumultuous climate after 1968, he was frequently discussed by Western film theorists. In 1969, his international reputation was such that *Sight and Sound* published a major article, and in 1970 *Cahiers du Cinéma* devoted a critical roundtable to his recent work. The latter is compelling for how it establishes the range of critical discourse that surrounds his work. The participants were Lacanian film theorist Jean-Pierre Oudart and the journal's coeditors at the time, Jean Narboni and Jean-Louis Comolli. Oudart, for example, is suspicious of *The Confrontation* (1969) because it functions too much as a "pure aesthetic object."[33] To understand this criticism, it is important to recall Wollen's virtues of "counter-cinema," where "pleasure" and "fiction" are aligned with Hollywood. On the other hand, Narboni acknowledges the fusion between form and politics in Jancsó's work, while Comolli sees Jancsó's aesthetic project as a reflection on the historical mechanisms that produce Stalinism.

This idea that Jancsó's political modernist period presents a formalist discourse about Hungarian history is the dominant interpretation of his work. While accurate, it does not historicize the formal innovations themselves, the method by which he fuses the political and the aesthetic. Makavejev and Chytilová reinvent the intellectual montage of earlier modernisms and interject them into documentary styles and vérité. However, Jancsó's experiments with complex camera movements, long takes, and depth of field are tied more directly to the conventions of socialist realism. The uniqueness of his political modernism is that it both dedramatizes and accelerates the visual grammar of socialist realism, such as the deep space that Bordwell argues emerges as a visual trait in thirties Soviet cinema. In essence, Jancsó slyly fulfills Lukács's demand that revolutionary realist art represent an "infinitely mediated" historical totality. Perhaps this explains why *The Round-Up* is one of the films praised by Lukács in his later interviews as he becomes increasingly critical of communism.[34] Jancsó's aesthetic project is, as Comolli argues, to reveal the historical mechanisms that culminate in Stalinism. Because Jancsó privileges camera movement and staging, his discourse on Stalinism is more abstract than the one Makavejev offers in *WR: Mysteries of the Organism* through montage. In *Cinema by Other Means,* Pavle Levi describes how Jancsó's inverted method for staging a scene sketches a thesis on history without the use of montage. He writes, "During the shooting of a Miklós Jancsó film it is, then, the actors who follow the elaborate tracking choreographies performed by the camera, not the other way around. The camera never simply 'covers' the events; rather, the protagonists' actions provide the content which fitted into the already patterned movements of the filming apparatus. The tracks along which the camera moves outline, as if in a diagram, a nondeterminate dynamic structure: cinema as a relational 'master code.' The filming of actual actions fleshes out this abstract matrix, giving it a variety of particular audiovisual expressions."[35] This passage is an astute description of how Jancsó's camera movements produce meaning by subverting indexicality. Recall that in classical film theory the celluloid image is presumed to be inherently indexical because of its ability to represent external reality. Within this model, the camera operates as the tool by which a profilmic event in reality is captured and translated into an image. As Levi argues, the difference in Jancsó is that the camera first diagrams a historical structure, which is then filled with profilmic content. He adds, "Jancsó does not use the camera to interpret history dialectically—to detect, in different epochs and socioeconomic constellations, instances of an ongoing struggle between classes, between the oppressor and the oppressed. Instead, he creates filmed testimonies to his Marxist conviction that History, much like the cinema, is an always already dialectical, though empty, structure."[36]

Levi is correct that Jancsó's style outlines "History" as an "empty structure." Both *Red Psalm* (1972) and *The Confrontation* diagram historical patterns and structures through the use of long takes, camera movement, and reframing.

In addition, the musical performances and dance sequences in both films read as formal inversions of socialist realist imagery and deconstructions of the codes of narrative cinema. *Red Psalm*, in particular, feels like a satire of socialist realist musicals where happy peasants build a socialist paradise.

Both films formally and thematically mirror each other in how they trace the historical logic of revolutions and their cycles of violence. The premise of *The Confrontation* can be summarized in one sentence: in the aftermath of the Second World War, a group of revolutionary communist college students visit a monastery to recruit the priests and their students to their cause. The minimal plot that emerges is revealed through complex camera movements and long takes that subdivide the communist students into different factions vying for power while they sing, dance, and debate whether they should engage in terrorism against the monastery or attempt to engage in a dialogue. All the while, the representations of state power, the police, enter and exit the frame at will, attempting to arrest people.

The closest the film has to a central character is Judit, the young idealistic communist. The first shot begins with a close-up of the back of her head, which is repeated as the film's closing image. During the confrontation with the seminary, she becomes the student leader and preaches for the necessity of antifascist violence and terror. At one point she demands that the seminary students have their heads shaved, but changes her mind when another communist reminds her that it invokes the symbolism of Auschwitz. She is, in other words, the Stalinist in the film, the revolutionary whose antifascism turns tyrannical. Though she is expelled by her fellow students, at the end of the film the police office implies that she has a bright future working for the state. The film begins and ends with similar shots of her, suggesting that her transformation from revolutionary to tyrant is a circular process.

Red Psalm intensifies the formal elements of *The Confrontation*. While the plot is similarly minimalistic, the average shot length is longer and the camera movements and mise-en-scène are more complex. Set in 1898, its story concerns a peasant revolt on the Great Hungarian Plain against their landowners. Most of the film consists of sequence shots that visualize the peasants' conflict with bailiffs and the military and the church officials who arrive to crush their rebellion. These shots diagram historical patterns that are more circular than those found in *The Confrontation*. For example, the camera maps semicircles around the chaotic action. Often the mise-en-scène itself is staged as circles: the peasants engage in traditional folk dances, the military surrounds the peasants, or the peasants surround a church. The narrative also resurrects characters, such as when a soldier is brought back to life by a peasant's kiss. Yet Jancsó ends the film with a surreal scene of violence. After slaughtering the peasants, the church and military celebrate. A peasant woman grabs a gun and shoots several soldiers on horseback, then turns to the camera and repeats a song we have heard throughout the film. She is the first peasant who is semi-individualized at the start of the film when one of the soldiers states that the bailiff would like to speak to her. By concluding *Red Psalm* with her fantastical violence, Jancsó closes his historical circle of revolution and violence. As in *The Confrontation*, the dialectic between them seems unresolvable.

POLITICAL MODERNISM UNTIL THE END OF HISTORY

The postwar era of Eastern European political modernism peaked in the middle of the seventies in several nations. The increase in repression after 1968 by communist regimes stifled national cinemas, and many filmmakers were banned or forced into exile. Formalist experimentation is less evident, and there are not as many notable examples of reimagining of the modernist montage and documentary realism perfected by Chytilová and Makavejev. To be sure, there are key exceptions, such as the innovative Polish cinema of the seventies and eighties. For example, the blending of documentary and fiction found in *Something Different* or *WR: Mysteries of the Organism* is instrumental to Andrzej Wajda's *Man of Marble* (1977), which tells the story of a young film student making a documentary about a legendary bricklayer named Birkut whose image was turned into marble statues for communist propaganda. It was followed by the sequel *Man of Iron* (1981), which dramatizes the Solidarity labor movement, cofounded by Lech Wałęsa, who appears as himself. This "cinema of moral concern," as Polish cinema from the late seventies and eighties is often referred to, produced several politically incisive films that were banned by the government, such as Ryszard Bugajski's *Interrogation* (1982), a bleak portrait of political prisons in the fifties. The also banned *A Women Alone* (1981), by Agnieszka Holland, tells the story of a single mother, Irena, whose life in Lodz is so grim and oppressive that she plots an escape to the West.

Hungarian cinema also produced internationally renowned political art films in the eighties. István Szabó's *Mephisto* (1981) became the first Hungarian entry to win the Academy Award for Best Foreign Language Film.

Though less popular, Márta Mészáros's trilogy, *Diary for My Children* (1984), *Diary for My Loves* (1987), and *Diary for My Father and Mother* (1990), is a remarkable achievement.[37] Highly autobiographical, the films follow the postwar life of a young woman named Juli Kovács as she confronts the realities of Stalinism, Hungarian communism, and the 1956 revolution. In the second film, like Mészáros herself, Juli enters film school in Moscow and is confronted with the dogmas of socialist realism when she makes a documentary about Hungarian peasants of which the authorities do not approve. Throughout, Mészáros intercuts the fictional autobiography with documentary footage of Stalin and communist parades, as well as scenes from other films, including socialist realist musicals. According to Catherine Portuges, this strategy caused *Diary for My Children* to be delayed by Hungarian censors, who demanded minor cuts. Interestingly, Mészáros was forced to remove footage from the legendary Soviet propaganda epic *The Fall of Berlin*,[38] which Makavejev intercuts into his post-communist feature, *Gorilla Bathes at Noon*.

In addition to the examples of Polish and Hungarian cinema, political modernist trends are evident in the stylistic innovations in the long take in global art cinema during the seventies, which served as the precursor to the slow cinema of the twenty-first century. Greek director Theo Angelopoulos, the focus of chapter 4, emerged in the seventies and continued the legacy of Jancsó's political modernism. Outside the Balkans and Eastern Europe, a range of long-take styles were influential during the decade, from the minimalism of Chantal Akerman to the malleable and multifaceted temporality of Andrei Tarkovksy, whose influence is analyzed in chapter 3. These long-take styles prefigured the political modernism of the post-communist era, when geopolitical shifts demanded new experiments in cinematic duration and realism in order to represent the transition into neoliberalism throughout the former Eastern bloc. To summarize, during the new waves of the sixties, the aesthetic task of political modernism was to critique the gap between actually existing communism and its utopian promises. In the neoliberal era of European integration, this evolved into a critique of the difference between "actually existing Europe" and its free-market utopia, which promised to unify the continent.

2 • WHAT HAPPENS AFTER THE END OF HISTORY?

I. FROM COMMUNISM TO CAPITALISM

The Post-Communist Order

In the decades after the Second World War, Eastern European art cinema established a political modernist discourse to critique authoritarian communism. As chapter 1 argues, working within the ideological constraints of socialist realism, this discourse incorporated formalist experimentation into realist aesthetics, with montage and long takes becoming preferred stylistic modes. In several nations, this tradition subsided by the middle of the seventies as regimes became more authoritarian and repressive, resulting in less artistic experimentation, though politically vital films continued to be produced. As communist regimes began to collapse in 1989, this aesthetic tradition established by the new-wave cinemas was reimagined. Directors censored in the seventies returned to explicitly political filmmaking, while a new generation influenced by their work made an impact on global art film culture. This revived the international reputation of cinema from the regions during the nineties. Though communism and its legacies remained a common theme, there was also a shift toward representing the instability of the new Europe. In particular, many of the political modernist art films of the decade are haunted by the existential and sociological effects of the transition to free-market capitalism and the violent dissolution of the former Yugoslavia. This chapter analyzes films that represent this transition. The first half contrasts influential political theories of the nineties about the new Europe and its post-communist order with the satire found in the late work of Jan

Švankmajer and Věra Chytilová, who were censored by the post-1968 authoritarian Czechoslovakian regime. Despite their newfound freedom from state censorship, their visions of the emerging Europe are as cynical as their representations of actually existing communism during the Cold War.

The second half of the chapter examines a variety of films, from Hollywood to European political modernism, about Sarajevo and the dissolution of Yugoslavia. Regarding the latter, the films of Jean-Luc Godard and Dušan Makavejev are highlighted. In his post-communist work, Godard has repeatedly returned to Sarajevo as a setting and a metaphor for the demise of Europe. However, his political and aesthetic discourse about Sarajevo is closer in spirit to Hollywood "message movies" in how it narrates the causes of the war. In these Western films, changes in the structure of global capitalism and the pressure to adapt to a market economy are rarely examined as a cause, a failure that implicitly imagines the Balkans as culturally backward. In comparison, nineties films from the region such as Makavejev's essayistic *Hole in the Soul* (1994) and Srđan Dragojević's *Pretty Village, Pretty Flame* (1996), which are analyzed in the second half of the chapter, emphasize images of economic and cultural disintegration over narratives of ahistorical tribalism and "ancient hatreds." Contrary to popular Western discourse, the resurgence of ethnic nationalism in the former Yugoslavia was not a by-product of "ancient hatreds" that remerged after the collapse of communism. Rather, it was a sociopolitical response to the country's severe economic contraction during the eighties and the neoliberal market reforms and austerity demanded by international financial organizations in order to service its unsustainable levels of debt. In other words, Yugoslavia was a casualty of the first global wave of neoliberalism during the eighties, whose complex federal system of ethnically divided republics quickly disintegrated after the death of Josip Broz Tito. Its fate, this chapter argues, predicted the conditions of Europe after the financial crisis, when austerity politics also fueled right-wing nationalism.

The reason why the disintegration of Yugoslavia was misunderstood and labeled as a result of "ancient hatreds" is that the end of communism promised the acceleration of the economic integration of Europe that began with the Hague Congress of 1948 and the key transnational economic treaties of the fifties, which created the European Coal and Steel Community, the European Economic Community, and the European Atomic Energy Community. In the new capitalist utopia, it was inconvincible that free-market reforms should cause social disintegration. Eastern bloc nations were eager to integrate economically into the West. Cultural and political alliances were formed in order to establish this goal. One such example is the Visegrád Group, which consisted of Hungary, Poland, and the former Czechoslovakia. It became known as the V4 once Czechoslovakia dissolved. Its website describes its achievement as follows: "All the V4 countries aspired to become members of the European Union, perceiving their integration in the EU as another step forward in the process of overcoming artificial dividing lines in Europe through mutual support. They reached this aim in 2004 (1st May) when they all became members of the EU."[1] From the vantage point of the migrant crisis of 2015, the idea that the nations of the V4 took a "step forward" toward overcoming the "artificial dividing lines" of Europe by becoming members of the EU in 2004 is wishful thinking. In response to the wave of migrants arriving primarily from the Middle East across the Mediterranean Sea, Hungary built razor-wire fences on its border with Serbia and Croatia. By 2017, it was constructing a "high-tech border fence" described as "capable of delivering electric shocks to unwanted migrants and armed with heat sensors, cameras, and loudspeakers that blare in several languages."[2] There is, of course, a glaring historical irony in Hungary building a border fence in the new Europe. In June 1989, Hungary had dismantled the electric fence on its Austrian border, signifying an end to the iron curtain and anticipating the fall of the Berlin Wall in November. In other words, in the nearly thirty-year gap between the crumbling of the iron curtain and the refugee crisis, national borders replaced ideological ones. Consider that right-wing populist Viktor Orbán, who was elected Hungarian prime minister in 2010, advocates for "illiberal democracy," which in a 2014 speech he defines as follows:

> What is happening today in Hungary can be interpreted as an attempt of the respective political leadership to harmonize relationship between the interests and achievement of individuals—that needs to be acknowledged—with interests and achievements of the community, and the nation. Meaning, that Hungarian nation is not a simple sum of individuals, but a community that needs to be organized, strengthened and developed, and in this sense, the new state that we are building is an illiberal state, a non-liberal state. It does not deny foundational values of liberalism, as freedom, etc. But it does not make this ideology a central element of state organization, but applies a specific, national, particular approach in its stead.[3]

Placed in the context of the entire speech, Orbán's objection to the "liberal state" is that it privileges individual rights and cannot protect the nation from foreign interests. Given such nationalist rhetoric critiquing the "liberal state," it is no surprise that there has been a sharp rise in xenophobia and anti-Semitism in Hungary under Orbán and the dominance of Fidesz, his far-right party. Shockingly, even further to the right is the neo-Nazi party Jobbik, which won 20 percent of the vote in the 2014 parliamentary elections by promoting rhetoric of international Jewish economic conspiracies. Symbolic of this new extremism, in 2017 the famous statue of György Lukács was removed from a Budapest park and replaced with one of Saint Stephen, the founder of the Hungarian state. According to the *Hungarian Free Press*, the removal was the idea of "a young nationalist, Marcell Tokody, a neo-Nazi Jobbik party councilor of Budapest. . . . Jobbik brought up Lukács's 'distractive' Communist past and even cooked up a bogus accusation that he ordered the execution of Hungarian soldiers in 1919."[4] Read through the lens of the popular political theories of the nineties, the end of the Cold War should have lessened nationalism across Europe as markets began operating freely across borders. Recall, for example, that Francis Fukuyama's end-of-history thesis argues that liberal democracy and its system of free markets is the endpoint of historical evolution. No greater form of human government is possible. As the introduction argues, in the years since *The End of History and the Last Man* was first published in 1992, Fukuyama has defended the EU's project of transnational law, and not the United States, as the model government for the end of history. While the violent disintegration of Yugoslavia could be dismissed as a historical anomaly by Western observers, the steady rise of nationalism throughout Europe since the financial and migrant crises has upended the neoliberal premise that markets would strengthen liberal democracy. Gaining traction instead is the "clash of civilizations" thesis, which channels economic anxiety into cultural resentments.

Arguments about clashes in values between civilizations are not new to the post-communist era. They were common in the political philosophy of the Enlightenment, such as in G.W.F. Hegel's *Philosophy of History*, where he distinguishes among "the Oriental World," "the Greek World," "the Roman World," and "the German World." The revival of this discourse in the nineties can be traced to Samuel P. Huntington's influential *Clash of Civilizations and the Remaking of World Order*. In the book, which was written in part as a response to Fukuyama, Huntington argues that clashes between civilizations, and not the spread of liberal democracy through free markets, will dominate geopolitics in the new post-communist order. He identifies several unique civilizations, including the West, the Orthodox world, and the Muslim world, that will engage in conflicts with each other in the form of "fault line wars." He argues that the disintegration of Yugoslavia was caused by a clash of civilizations:

> The war in Bosnia was a war of civilizations. The three primary participants came from different civilizations and adhered to different religions. With one partial exception, the participation of secondary and tertiary actors exactly followed the civilizational model. Muslim states and organizations universally rallied behind the Bosnian Muslims and opposed the Croats and Serbs. Orthodox countries and organizations universally backed the Serbs and opposed the Croats and Muslims. Western governments and elites backed the Croats, castigated the Serbs, and were generally indifferent to or fearful of the Muslims.[5]

This interpretation of the war is similar to the "ancient hatreds" thesis that communism suppressed natural tendencies toward ethnic conflict. However, Huntington assumes that Serbs, Croatians, and Bosnian Muslims, or Bosniaks, primarily identify as members of distinct religious civilizations—Orthodox Christianity, Western Catholicism, and Islam—more so than as unique ethnicities. In the immediate aftermath of 9/11, the Balkans receded as the primary fault line of civilizational clashes. Islam versus the West became the master narrative. Writing in the *Nation* in October 2001, Edward Said succinctly critiqued Huntington and his discourse of Islam versus the West, writing that Huntington does not have "time to spare for the internal dynamics and plurality of every civilization, or for the fact that the major contest in most modern cultures concerns the definition or interpretation of each culture, or for the unattractive possibility that a great deal of demagogy and downright ignorance is involved in presuming to speak for a whole religion or civilization. No, the West is the West, and Islam Islam."[6] Said's argument is straightforward. Imagining Islam as a monolithic entity, without distinct religious sects or conflicting national interests, is cultural imperialism. It also assumes that Islam is irreconcilable with Western values. As with the civilizational interpretation of the disintegration of Yugoslavia, cultural differences are reduced to essentialist traits, obscuring changes in geopolitics that affect identity.

No political theory on the left during the nineties was as influential as Fukuyama's neoliberalism or Huntington's theory of the clash of civilizations. In the brief period at the end of the decade when antiglobalization protests were occurring in the United States and Europe, Michael Hardt and Antonio Negri's *Empire* was relatively successful and widely reviewed for an academic book of theory, an achievement later repeated by Thomas Piketty's *Capital in the Twenty-First Century* in 2013. Yet a decade of aftershocks from the financial crisis has turned Hardt and Negri's post-Marxism into the mirror image of Fukuyama's neoliberalism rather than an accurate prediction of the post-communist order. Hardt and Negri argue that sovereignty has become uncoupled from the state and has mutated into complex networks of transnational corporate entities and international organizations that serve the interests of the few remaining dominant nation-states. This has given rise to a new form of empire that, they explain, "establishes no territorial center of power and does not rely on fixed boundaries or barriers. It is a *decentered* and *deterritorializing* apparatus of rule that progressively incorporates the entire global realm within its open, expanding frontiers. Empire manages hybrid identities, flexible hierarchies, and plural exchanges through modulating networks of command."[7]

In other words, Hardt and Negri believe that a postnational form of peoplehood called the multitude can emerge to challenge empire, creating a political space, a "living alternative," for a transnational network of opposition. This is the subject of their 2004 sequel, *Multitude: War and Democracy in the Age of Empire*, where they expand on the ideas introduced in the final chapter of *Empire*, "The Multitude against Empire." Describing how the multitude will overcome notions of peoplehood common within modernity, in the preface to *Multitude* they write,

> We should distinguish the multitude at a conceptual level from other notions of social subjects, such as the people, the masses, and the working class. *The people* has traditionally been a unitary conception. The population, of course, is characterized by all kinds of difference, but the people reduces that diversity to a unity and makes of the population a single identity: "the people" is one. The multitude, in contrast, is many. The multitude is composed of innumerable internal differences that can never be reduced to a unity or a single identity—different cultures, races, ethnicities, genders, and sexual orientations; different forms of labor; different ways of living; different views of the world; and different desires.[8]

In essence, the multitude will create a decentered network of local struggles, converging to challenge empire and the global spread of capitalism. It is here that we can see the mirror image of Fukuyama's neoliberalism. The idea that emergent forms of heterogeneous peoplehood will resist capitalism depends on a faith that the spread of free markets across the globe can sustain enough economic growth to create the conditions for its own undoing. However, in the aftermath of the financial crisis and the age of austerity politics and low growth, it is homogeneous nationalist right-wing political parties such as those in Hungary, and not Hardt and Negri's "multitude," that are gaining power with their retrograde concepts of peoplehood, anti-immigrant xenophobia, claims of civilization clashes, and border fences. They have been more successful at harnessing anti-EU sentiments than, for example, leftist parties like Syriza in Greece, whose leader, Alexis Tsipras, capitulated to the financial sector of Europe for economic survival. In essence, the 2017 French election between the right-wing Marine Le Pen and the centrist Emmanuel Macron, who won handily, represents the short-term geopolitical horizon for Europe: a choice between more neoliberal capitalism, on one hand, and the xenophobia and reactionary nationalism of the far right, on the other. Indeed, in the 2019 European parliamentary elections, Le Pen's National Front party edged out Macron's centrist En Marche party.[9]

The influential political theories of the nineties shared a general belief that the end of communism would give rise to new formations of peoplehood and democracy. For Fukuyama, the triumph of free markets enshrines liberal democracy as the most evolved form of government, while Hardt and Negri believe that the contradictions of capitalist empire will give rise to the decentered, liberatory politics of "the multitude." On the other hand, for Huntington, conflicts between civilizations and cultures will replace the ideological battles of the twentieth century. In comparison with these theories, the political modernist cinema of the nineties was less inclined to interpret the end of communism as a radical break in history with new possibilities for freedom, expressing instead uncertainty and doubt. The works analyzed in the prior chapter were animated by anti-Stalinism and antiauthoritarian aesthetics. In the post-communist films of Švankmajer, Chytilová, and Makavejev, this antiauthoritarian aesthetic shifts from critiquing communism to critiquing the destructive impulses of capitalism. A sense of historical exhaustion is palpable in the late films of these political modernists, who emerged from the new waves and the avant-garde. The new capitalist world that they depict is, in many ways, grimmer than the past. Having already chronicled the excesses of communism, they despair at the possibility of overcoming the excesses of capitalism and its destruction of social bonds and economic exploitation.

The Agitprop of Jan Švankmajer

The first great political modernist film of the post-communist era is Švankmajer's *Death of Stalinism in Bohemia* (1990). Though his career began in the sixties, Švankmajer was not associated with the Czech New Wave. As was the case with the experimental cinema discussed in chapter 1, screenings of his early shorts in Czechoslovakia were primarily limited to film clubs. These works can be described as formalist experiments in puppetry and stop-motion animation that emphasize the tactility of mechanical objects and the natural world, which are juxtaposed in unusual ways. By the late sixties, however, a politically oriented surrealism became evident in *The Garden* (1968), *The Flat* (1968), and *A Quiet Week in the House* (1969), the last of which was released after the Soviet Invasion. *The Garden,* for example, is an adaptation of a story by Ivan Kraus, a Czech writer who also stars in *The Flat.* In the film, a man travels to the countryside to visit his friend and discovers that his house is surrounded by a "human fence" of people who have locked hands together. According to Peter Hames, "The original story played on the Czech words for hedge, 'Zivy plot' ('living fence'), and clearly has totalitarian overtones. 'The people' are ignored as individuals, and are merely elements in a structure supporting the owner's comfort and lifestyle. Yet Švankmajer's film is less an attack on Stalinism than a demonstration of fundamental elements in the human situation where people acquiesce in their own oppression and manipulation."[10] *The Garden,* in other words, shares some similarities with the formalism found in Miklós Jancsó's *Confrontation* or Chytilová's *Daisies,* where the critiques of Stalinism and authoritarian communism are indirectly expressed through the aesthetic design of the film. However, Švankmajer's late sixties political turn also reflects a literary modernist influence that is less evident in other political new-wave filmmakers. Franz Kafka and Sigmund Freud cast a shadow over *The Garden* and *The Flat* more so than either Sergei Eisenstein or socialist realism. The absurdities Švankmajer visualizes in these three films—the human fence in *The Garden* and the irrational domestic spaces in *The Flat* and *A Quiet Week in the House*—are presented as manifestations of psychological and civilizational forces rather than the failings of ideology.

This politically motivated surrealism eventually led to state censorship for Švankmajer. In 1972, he was banned from filmmaking for the remainder of the decade when he refused demands by state censors. According to journalist Jonathan Jones, they objected to his attempt to mix pseudo-documentary with animation in his adaptation of the eighteenth-century gothic novel *The Castle of Otranto* on the grounds that it might cause people to question the truthfulness of television news.[11] This peculiar objection confirms how repressive the political climate became in Czechoslovakia after the Soviet invasion of 1968. Though Švankmajer did not officially work during the seventies, he did develop several ideas and scripts whose political modernism had to wait until the Velvet Revolution and the collapse of communism to be filmed. For example, the ideas for his 1992 short, *Food*, and his 1996 feature, *Conspirators of Pleasure*, originated during this ban.

Returning to filmmaking in the eighties, he gained an international reputation and entered the most commercially recognizable phase of his career. *Dimensions of Dialogue* (1982), for example, won several awards at international festivals and remains his most iconic work. At the end of the decade, he directed two micro-shorts commissioned by MTV, *Meat Love* (1989) and *Flora* (1989), as well as a music video for the song "Another Kind of Love" by Hugh Cornwell, the British singer formerly of the punk band the Stranglers. He also directed his first feature, *Alice* (1987). These works are not explicitly political, though *Dimensions of Dialogue* lends itself to an allegorical antiauthoritarian interpretation. This tendency changes with his overtly satirical short, *Virile Games* (1988). Here Švankmajer intercuts documentary footage of a riotous crowd waving Czech flags at a soccer stadium with stop-motion animation of the game itself, which quickly devolves into an absurdist series of player deaths that count toward the score. For example, a toy train is driven through the face of a player and another is cut up with scissors. The match is watched on television by a man in his apartment drinking alcohol and eating cookies. Amusingly, the soccer players and referees all share the face of the man watching television, suggesting that the spectatorships of the individual and the crowd merge into a collective fantasy of violence. Unlike the allegorical meanings found in his sixties work, here the political critique is not abstract. *Virile Games* is a warning against the destructive psychosocial aspects of nationalism. In that regard, it is a direct precursor to *The Death of Stalinism in Bohemia*, which further develops this critique.

Commissioned by the BBC, which wanted a film about the political changes in Czechoslovakia, *The Death of Stalinism in Bohemia* is subtitled *A Work of Agitprop*. In the span of nine minutes, Švankmajer encapsulates the history of Czechoslovakian communism up until the Velvet Revolution. As in *Virile Games,* he mixes documentary footage with stop-motion animation, visualizing the Cold War as clashing images of monstrous births, propaganda posters, and the formation and execution of clay workers. The ascendancy of Klement Gottwald, the first communist Czechoslovakian president, in 1948 is visualized as a monstrous cesarean birth, with Gottwald being cut by human hands from the intestines of a bust of Stalin. Gottwald emerges as a bust, which is cleaned off so it can begin giving speeches. In the sequence that follows, the same hands form clay workers with raised fists. Once they walk off the conveyor belt, the hands place nooses around their necks and hang them, a blunt image of communist progress turned into Stalinist terror. Up until this point, *The Death of Stalinism in Bohemia* is satirizing Czechoslovakian communism, highlighting the dissonance between propaganda posters about worker productivity and Stalinist terror. Švankmajer, however, concludes with a prophetic image about the emergent post-communist order. After the film shows images of Mikhail Gorbachev, Perestroika, and the Velvet Revolution, we see a large crowd waving Czechoslovakian flags. The human hands shown earlier begin painting the colors of the flag everywhere, including on the bust of Stalin it dusts off from the trash. The ending echoes the opening of the film, as the now nationalist Stalin is placed on the operating table and is cut open for a new leader to emerge. *The Death of Stalinism in Bohemia,* in other words, hints at a future of authoritarian nationalism, foretelling Czechoslovakia's dissolution in 1992, the demagogues of the Yugoslav wars, and the right-wing populists who infected Europe after the financial crash.

Švankmajer's skepticism about the Velvet Revolution and the collapse of communism opposed prevailing sentiment about Europe and its new freedoms in 1990. In "To Renounce the Leading Role," a brief companion essay to *The Death of Stalinism in Bohemia,* he argues that anthropocentrism and faith in historical progress must be rejected because they were "crowned by the industrial revolutions of the 19th and 20th centuries. And from here there is only a little step towards the ecological catastrophe before which we stand."[12] Echoing Theodor Adorno and Max Horkheimer's critique of the Enlightenment, this idea that the Industrial Revolution established human domination over nature, expressed by Švankmajer at the height of capitalist euphoria in the early nineties, must have felt like an outmoded modernism. Two decades later, though, his stubborn Freudianism and rejection of anthropocentrism are relevant in an age of economic crisis and environmental catastrophe. Scientists and academics now debate whether Earth has entered the geological age of the Anthropocene, in which humans have irrecoverably destroyed the ecosystem of the planet. In a 2012 interview, he reflects on his mind-set, which produced the film and the essay, explaining,

> *The Death of Stalinism in Bohemia* ends with Stalin, painted in national colors, giving birth. Similarly, "To Renounce the Leading Role" conveys my skepticism that the revolution would be able to change man's psyche and the paradigm of civilization. A change in the ownership of the means of production and a fairer division of material wealth are important prerequisites for the change of civilization, but they are not sufficient by themselves. Hence the attempts to bring Marx and Freud closer together that started in the 1930s and continued in the Frankfurt School.
>
> It is also necessary to shake up the illusion of anthropocentrism. . . . I think that the time is ripe for the formation of a new societal model, like it was done, for example, at the turn of the 19th century by Charles Fourier, or during the 19th century by Marx, or by Lenin in his treatise "The State and Revolution" at the beginning of the 20th century.[13]

While Švankmajer aligns himself in the interview with the Frankfurt School's tradition of synthesizing Karl Marx and Freud, the reference to Charles Fourier invokes the utopian political modernism of twentieth-century surrealism. The surrealists admired Fourier's "new societal model" and his radical vision of sexual liberation and harmonious labor. In 1947 André Breton composed *Ode à Charles Fourier*, a lengthy imagined poetic dialogue with the nineteenth-century socialist philosopher. For Švankmajer, the trouble with the Velvet Revolution and the end of communism was that it changed the means of production without establishing a new psychic relationship with civilization and discontent as advocated by Fourier, Marx, or Lenin. The authoritarian nationalism he prophesies at the end of *The Death of Stalinism in Bohemia* is thus a return of the repressed, a reconfiguration of the same psychic forces underpinning "the illusion of anthropocentrism." Unlike the patronizing interpretation that holds that the resurgence of nationalism in

Yugoslavia was caused by tribalism unleashed by the end of communism, Švankmajer's repression thesis does not assume the cultural superiority of the West because all civilizations are prone to the same regressions.

In his post-communist work, Western-style capitalism is imagined as self-destructive. As a Freudian surrealist, Švankmajer does not believe liberation from civilization is sustainable. This is the theme of his short *Food*, which is his last work filmed entirely in stop-motion animation. Its caustic imagery explores the differences between how communist and capitalist societies regulate desire and consumption. Švankmajer is especially concerned with how the transition to capitalism accelerates the destruction of social order. Divided into three parts—"Breakfast," "Lunch," and "Dinner"—the short begins by parodying the bureaucratization of consumption under communism. A man enters a dreary room for breakfast. Seated opposite him is a second man with a sign around his neck that contains elaborate instructions for how to order food. It is revealed that he has a dumbwaiter in his chest that delivers sausage, bread, and coffee. Once the first man finishes eating, he exchanges places with the second and is transformed into a dumbwaiter with a sign. The process repeats as the second man leaves and a third man enters. He, too, undergoes the same transformation once he finishes eating. The final shot of "Breakfast" is of the first man leaving as we see a long line of men waiting to enter. Throughout the first part, there is a tension between the robotic movements of the men transforming into dumbwaiters and the grotesque close-ups of them eating food, which implies how mechanized and regulated consumption has become. While all economies regulate consumption, "Breakfast" specifically parodies the idea of a centralized or planned economy, as its images of long lines and de-individualization are familiar coded critiques of communism.

"Lunch" switches to the world of capitalism. Unlike in the mechanized yet cooperative world of "Breakfast," here Švankmajer creates a surrealist comedy of class warfare. Two men are seated in a restaurant waiting for service. Their class differences are obvious. One man is well dressed and wipes his utensils with his cloth napkin, while the other man is disheveled and cleans his knife by spitting on it and rubbing it on his jacket. Unable to get the attention of the waiter, the well-dressed man eats the flowers in the vase. An absurd competition commences as the two men, ignored by the staff, proceed to eat everything: the vase, their clothes, the plate, and even the table. Finally, the wealthy man pretends to swallow his utensils, tricking the lower-class man into eating his. He then advances on the lower-class man in order to eat him. "Dinner" can be considered a coda to "Lunch," as it is also set in a restaurant. A man in a tuxedo is seated by a table with spices and sauces. He engages in an elaborate ritual of garnishing his dish. "Dinner" then turns grotesque as it is revealed that he has a wooden hand on which he attaches a fork with some nails. His meal is his severed hand. Švankmajer then whip-pans to other patrons who are consuming their body parts—a leg, breasts, and a penis. In other words, the dramatic progression in *Food* is from communism, to capitalism and class warfare, and finally to self-destruction. At sixteen minutes, it is a cleverly conceived short that suggests that post-communist freedom is self-negating since it consists of unfettered consumption that ultimately destroys itself. Švankmajer develops this idea more thoroughly in *Conspirators of Pleasure,* which also hints at a utopian possibility for a "new societal model," similar to the one the twentieth-century surrealists found in Fourier.

Conspirators of Pleasure defies simple summation. Its circular narrative resembles that of Arthur Schnitzler's *La Ronde,* though instead of exchanging lovers, its six main characters exchange sexual fetishes and rituals. We are first introduced to Mr. Pivonka, who is buying porn magazines in a shop, which he uses to construct a large papier-mâché chicken head. He engages in a strange, ritualized fetish with his female neighbor, Mrs. Loubalová. He dresses as a chicken and drives to the countryside, where he throws boulders at a mannequin of her. Correspondingly, Mrs. Loubalová dresses as a dominatrix and whips a mannequin of him. A letter that says "Sunday," presumably sent from his neighbor, is delivered to him by a mailwoman. The mailwoman has her own fetish; she chews and rolls bread into dough balls that she shoves in her ears and nostrils. We are also introduced to the shop clerk's fetish, which, echoing imagery from David Cronenberg's *Videodrome* (1983), consists of building an elaborate masturbation machine attached to a television so he can orgasm to his favorite newscaster. The newscaster, in turn, is sexually frustrated because her husband prefers touching furs and massaging his body with a wooden rolling pin that has nails and furs attached to it. The mailwoman delivers used dough balls to the newscaster, who feeds them to the carp she keeps in a large bucket of water. She trains the fish to suck her toes until she orgasms on live television while the shop clerk watches with his masturbation machine. After completing his ritual sadism against his neighbor in the country, Mr. Pivonka returns to the shop, where he exchanges a knowing glance with the clerk. Mr. Pivonka then returns home and sees the newscaster's husband, who we discover is a policeman, in Mrs. Loubalová's apartment, where a giant boulder has crashed through her ceiling, killing her. Thus, his ritual fantasy of killing his neighbor has somehow been actualized. He enters his apartment, which now resembles the setting for Mrs. Loubalová's ritual, implying that he, too, will die.

As this plot summary suggests, *Conspirators of Pleasure* is a strange film whose bizarre, provocative imagery and circular narrative elude any straightforward interpretation. The end credits state that it was inspired by Leopold von Sacher-Masoch, the Marquis de Sade, Freud, Luis Buñuel, Max Ernst, and Bohuslav Brouk, the last of whom who was a Czechoslovakian psychoanalyst affiliated with surrealist groups in the thirties. To that extent, the film is a self-conscious homage to Švankmajer's influences, reveling in Freudian themes about death drives, repression, and liberation. Yet it also hints at the kind of "new societal model" that Švankmajer, in explaining his skepticism regarding the Velvet Revolution, claims was necessary. In many ways, this new model echoes Fourier's utopian vision of sexual liberation and harmonious labor, which fascinated the twentieth-century surrealists, though he is not listed as an inspiration in the end credits. This connection is more evident in "Coming Attractions," a brief article Švankmajer wrote to accompany *Conspirators of Pleasure* that first appeared in *Time Out* magazine. Explaining his philosophy, he writes,

> The film's central motif is the sado-masochistic relationship between Mr. Pivonka and Mrs. Loubalová. This relationship, realised by means of magic and with the help of a kind of grotesque ritual voodoo, is joined by the stories of the minor characters. . . . Their obsession with pleasure (desire, freedom) makes them something of a "sect" of kindred spirits.
>
> Everything suggests that the real lives of people of this civilisation will continue to be lived more and more in something like "non-conformist sects" which grow up as a reaction to a society levelled into uniformity by advertising and consumerism. From the point of view of these masses and their manipulators, each attempt at a free, imaginative act of desire (pleasure) has to be a manifestation of perversity.
>
> *Conspirators of Pleasure* is a grotesque black comedy which reflects on this disaster.[14]

Though Švankmajer does not distinguish between the film's primary and "minor" characters in terms of the "sect" that they create, there is an important difference. Mr. Pivonka and Mrs. Loubalová's sadomasochistic ritual actualizes into death. In essence, the narrative punishes their pursuit of pleasure, and it is implied that Mr. Pivonka is about to be destroyed by the repressive forces of civilization, the police investigating Mrs. Loubalová's apartment. However, none of the secondary characters are punished, which allows for a counterreading of the film. The newscaster successfully orgasms, her husband continues his tactile fetishes, the postwoman enters a store to buy some carp, and the store clerk abandons his masturbation machine and is shown attaching chicken feathers to a rolling pin, which suggests an amalgamation of Mr. Pivonka's chicken papier-mâché fetish and the policeman's obsession with tactile objects. In other words, it is the secondary characters who successfully form a "non-conformist sect" without punishment from civilization or their death drives. They create an economic arrangement of exchanging fetishes, made possible only under capitalism. Compared with the "dumbwaiters" in the "Breakfast" portion of *Food*, their bodies are not mechanized and their consumption is not centralized and regulated. And unlike the "multitude" imagined by Hardt and Negri, they do not form a network of opposition against global capitalism. In an insightful analysis on his blog, philosopher Steven Shaviro describes their arrangement as follows:

> Švankmajer proposes a strange new sort of social bond, one that is irreducible either to Communist solidarity and communitarianism, or to capitalist atomism. There is no common interest, no togetherness; but also no competition of rationally calculating, autonomous individuals in the marketplace, and no Hobbesian war of all against all. Everything is irreducibly particular; but all these particularities are incomplete and uncontained, not to mention too compulsive and too partial to be recuperated as attributes of a "self." . . . The social bond is oblique and forever incomplete; it is embodied, not by public rituals and shows of empathy or solidarity, but precisely by the odd conjunction of private rituals, selfish passions, compulsions that can never be confessed, and that are characterized by shame and embarrassment as much as by orgasmic release.[15]

Shaviro is correct that the bond the protagonists create is "irreducible" to communism or "capitalist atomism." However, their economy of exchanging fetishes is only possible in the post-communist public sphere, where consumer capitalism accelerates. Recall, for example, the notorious Otto Muehl commune sequence from Dušan Makavejev's *Sweet Movie* analyzed in the previous chapter. A benchmark of political modernist extremity under communism, the film exposes the limits of communal belonging. Its excremental imagery elicits affective responses of revulsion and disgust at the commune's refusal of bodily privacy. In comparison, the protagonists of *Conspirators of Pleasure* express no overarching communal identity. The rituals of the secondary characters retain a sense of private interiority and fetishized individuality. However, the economy they create is not, as Shaviro observes, founded on rational autonomy and competition, the twin ideals of classical liberal capitalism. As a social bond, it echoes Fourier's *phalanstère,* his imagined building for a utopian socialist community structured around mutual sexual satisfaction, made possible under the post-communist transition to capitalism.

In his essay "Coming Attractions," Švankmajer imagines more social positives resulting from the economy found in *Conspirators of Pleasure.* He argues for the creation of elaborate masturbation machines similar to the one the shop clerk creates in the film. Švankmajer lists numerous benefits, including "a healthy, non-frustrated labour force" and "a harmonious family." He also sardonically observes that "it may be expected that this new, progressive opinion concerning the organisation of sexual life in a modern industrial society will not meet with immediate understanding, especially from the more conservative part of the nation which, as we know, unfortunately always forms the majority."[16] To be sure, the essay and the film raise a basic question of interpretation about Švankmajer's devotion to Freud and avant-garde modernism. Masturbation machines and the exchange of fetishes are obviously not intended as pragmatic political alternatives. As images and metaphors of a utopia, we can ask whether they do express a possibility for overcoming the malaise of post-communism. In posing this question, it is important to stress that Švankmajer's interest in creating tactile objects originated during his ban from filmmaking in the seventies. He explains in the introduction to the English-language edition of his book *Touching and Imagining: An Introduction to Tactile Art,*

> I occupied myself with an intensive study of touch in relation to imagination. I turned to a field of creativity that could be regarded as almost an extreme

> contradiction to the audiovisual film. Without that prohibition, the experimentation described in this book would probably have never happened; so much for the idea that totalitarian systems and censorship act as a brake on original creativity. In a sense they act in exactly the opposite way. To overcome difficulties and to get around prohibitions whips up defiance and subversion, which is inherent in all creativity worth that name; it achieves fine nuances.[17]

As Švankmajer states, his experiments with tactility are intended as subversions. The shift into individual sensation and touch reestablishes the sense of control over the imagination that is destroyed by the totalitarian censorship of public art forms like cinema. In the post-communist condition, this embrace of the pleasure principle directs this subversion elsewhere. Without a menacing state to reject, the target becomes what Švankmajer calls the "principle of reality[,] . . . the pragmatic rope which has regimented us."[18] In other words, the economy created by the secondary characters in *Conspirators of Pleasure* is a utopian rejection of commodification and use value. They establish a social bond that, as Shaviro argues, is "irreducibly particular" and allows the characters to escape from the malaise of capitalist realism.

To that extent, *Conspirators of Pleasure* is Švankmajer's most optimistic post-communist feature. The others drift into misanthropy and imagine no liberation from the shackles of civilization. In *Little Otik* (2001), a couple desperately desires to have a baby. One day the husband brings home a tree stump that looks like a baby, which the wife treats as real. The stump comes alive and grows into an all-consuming monster that eats food and humans. In her astute reading of the film, Anikó Imre argues that it explores "the conditions of late capitalism through the allegory of obsessive eating and cannibalism," an art cinema tradition popularized with Peter Greenway's *The Cook, the Thief, His Wife and Her Lover* (1989). She adds, though, that *Little Otik* is also "specific to the historical moment of post-communist European transitions."[19] In contrast to *Conspirators of Pleasure*, which depicts the utopianism of liberated desire, *Little Otik* reverts to the grim, satirical view of the transition to capitalism expressed in *Food*. Unrestrained consumption leads to self-destruction.

Lunacy (2005) offers a more sophisticated treatment of liberation and unrestrained freedom than *Little Otik*, though its implications are equally grim. Its indeterminate setting is presumably nineteenth-century France, though several technological anachronisms suggest it is set in the present with the main character believing he is in the past. It is a loose adaptation of two Edgar Allan Poe stories, "The Premature Burial" and "The System of Doctor Tarr and Professor Fether," that also includes quotations from de Sade texts. It tells the story of Jean, who encounters an insane Marquis, based of course on de Sade, in an asylum managed based on principles of total freedom by the inmates, who have overthrown the staff. Jean, however, frees the doctors, who reestablish their totalitarian control. In a strange prologue to the film, Švankmajer appears in front of a white backdrop and explains, "The subject of the film is essentially an ideological debate about how to run a lunatic asylum. Basically there are two ways of managing such an institution, each equally extreme. One encourages absolute freedom, the other the old fashioned, well-tried method of control and punishment. But there is also a third one that combines and exacerbates the very worst aspects of the other two. And that is the madhouse we live in today."[20] The two methods, Sadean transgression and totalitarian control, are vividly imagined throughout the film. However, their dialectical synthesis—the "very worst aspects" of both—is only clarified during the final shots of the film. Once Jean is taken away in a straitjacket, Švankmajer cuts to a tracking shot along the meat aisle in a supermarket, over which we hear funeral music on the soundtrack. The final shot is a steak breathing in its cellophane package, the Sadean freedoms of the flesh transformed into a supermarket commodity. The idea recalls Adorno and Horkheimer's *Dialectic of Enlightenment* and their argument that de Sade's novel *Juliette* is the logical outcome of Kantian philosophy and the Enlightenment's project of reason. Both are expressions of domination. In the context of post-communism, it is an image of a deadlocked civilization incapable of progress. It is not surprising that Švankmajer's subsequent film, *Surviving Life* (2010), reverts to a mostly depoliticized surrealism as its middle-aged protagonist, Eugene, tries to understand his reoccurring dream of a woman as he escapes into his fantasy world. While *Conspirators of Pleasure* sees Švankmajer working through the contradictions of post-communism to imagine new social bonds, *Lunacy* and *Surviving Life* suggest no such alternatives.

In the funding campaign for his final film, *Insects*, released in 2018, Švankmajer describes the work as "very misanthropic."[21] It is about a small troupe rehearsing the brothers Čapek's absurdist 1922 *The Insect Play*, in which a narrator dreams of insects with human characteristics. Scenes from the rehearsal are interspersed with behind-the-scenes footage of Švankmajer directing the film and his crew creating some of the animation. At times, the meta structure of the film purposefully blurs reality and representation. One of the troupe members eats another, a giant ball of dung chases the beetle character, and a woman is stabbed during performance and gives birth to a baby that quickly ages. As with *Lunacy* and *Surviving Life*, Švankmajer personally introduces the film. He notes that *The Insect Play* foretells the rise of Hitler and Stalin, but he assures us that his film carries no such meaning. He claims that he devised it as an exercise in automatic writing. However, Švankmajer is being typically coy. The distancing effect of including behind-the-scenes footage means *Insect* never arrives at pure imagination divorced from meaning or content. Rather, the film implies that even in our imaginations we behave like insects, which is the precondition for the next dictatorships to emerge. In the final shot, Švankmajer looks to the camera and says, "I told you so!"

Rejecting Post-Communist Patriarchy in *Traps*

Chytilová's career also stalled for several years during the seventies, though she was not officially banned like Švankmajer was for his refusal to acquiesce to the demand of censors. Rather, after her formalist experiments with montage in *Daisies* and *The Fruit of Paradise*, she was unable to develop new projects. In a 1994 interview for French television, she states that she was allowed to direct *The Apple Game* (1976) on the condition that her films must be more "realistic."[22] Given such a demand, it is not surprising that she reverted to her earlier cinema verité in films such as *The Prefab Story* (1979), though this lack of formalist experimentation still did not appease state censors. The critical documentary realism of *The Prefab Story*, which tells the story of the inhabitants of an unfinished apartment complex, caused the film to be banned shortly after its release. Consequently, in the eighties, she dabbled in a wider range of styles and genres, directing horror films, comedies, and documentaries. The one constant after her return to filmmaking was that she persisted in her criticisms of how patriarchy represses women. In the comedy *The Apple Game*, for example, Anna is a nurse who becomes pregnant after sleeping with the womanizing Doctor John. In the end, she rejects him and gives birth alone.

In her post-communist films, Chytilová does not temper her critiques of patriarchy. In fact, they are intensified. For her, the end of communism, with its promises of market-oriented freedoms, has not liberated women. *Traps*

(1998) masterfully visualizes a world in which patriarchal market and government forces converge to destroy women. In other words, like Švankmajer, Chytilová rejects the utopian prognosis that the end of history has arrived with the transition to capitalism. This skepticism is first established in her 1992 comedy, *The Inheritance.* Conventional compared with her modernist experiments, it contains broad humor and stars popular Czech actor and playwright Boleslav Polívka, who coauthored the script. It was popular domestically and a financial success. According to Hames, its importance is that "it was one of the few films to cast a jaundiced eye on the excesses of the 'new capitalism.'"[23] In its rags-to-riches plot, Polívka portrays Bohus, a lazy man who lives on a small village farm with his aunt. A lawyer informs him he has inherited money and businesses from his father. Bohus behaves drunkenly and decadently, spending money on a funeral for his goat, prostitutes, and a carnival ride for the village. He loses his inheritance when it is revealed that his "father" was actually his stepfather. However, in an absurd plot twist, he is rescued from poverty again when the death of his real father in Argentina leaves him another inheritance.

The film has numerous innocuous jokes about the new Europe and the transition to capitalism in Czechoslovakia.[24] Before his first inheritance, a village official visits Bohus and complains that nobody wants to apply for home gas delivery, stating, "We fought for it under communism and no one wants it!" Similarly, early in the film, Bohus and his friends see wealthy Germans on horseback and he observes, "Two years after the revolution and Krauts are everywhere." This image is repeated later in the film when the wealthy Bohus rides on horseback past villagers who complain he has not bought anything for the village. However, the screwball plot and broad comedy of *The Inheritance* masks a darker view of the transition to capitalism, which is revealed in the film's final shot. After learning of his second inheritance, Bohus looks around at the people in the local bar. In a close-up, he stares into the camera and ominously declares, "Now I can buy you all." In other words, his newfound wealth has transformed his affable drunkenness into a desire for domination. Chytilová's next feature, *Traps,* explores this darker desire for domination.

Traps is an approximate translation of its Czech title, *Pasti, pasti, pasticky,* which is a pun on an old Czechoslovakian children's song. Not well known in the West, the film was finally released on DVD in 2015 after Chytilová's death. As Carmen Gray argues in her excellent essay for the DVD booklet, the mixed to negative reaction from international critics likely hurt its chances for wider distribution outside of a few film festivals. Gray highlights one review that accuses the film of "bitterness," "hatred," and "cheap political satire."[25] Another review, by Andrew James Horton, a critic who writes frequently on Eastern European cinema, complains that it was "depressingly reactionary" and sent "conflicting signals to the viewer."[26] Based on such criticisms, it seems that Chytilová's rape revenge comedy, with its satirical tone and narrative shifts, provoked moral revulsion. It tells the story of Lenka, a veterinarian who castrates pigs. One day her car breaks down. She is picked up by Petr, an advertising executive, and Dohnal, a corrupt government minister. Petr subdues her while the minister rapes her in the forest and then knocks her unconscious. Once awake, she pretends to have amnesia, convincing the men to drive her home. The minister agrees, hoping he can rape her again. Lenka drugs and castrates them. The film then becomes an absurdist comedy as the men are desperate to reattach their testicles and invent stories about what happened. Dohnal, for example, convinces people that he was assaulted by unknown men who castrated him. In the most grotesquely humorous scene, he comes home to his wife and places his testicles in the freezer in a lunch pail. The drunken friend who drove his wife home the previous night and slept on the couch wakes from his hangover and makes himself breakfast, eating the minister's testicles with eggs. Lenka, however, has no humorous scenes. She is despondent and besieged by nightmares. Her fiancé exposes his own misogyny when he "forgives" her for being raped. Petr and Dohnal are not legally punished for their crimes. Lenka is arrested by the police when she tries publicly confronting the minister.

Based on this incomplete plot summary, it is understandable why critics rejected Chytilová's film on moral grounds. Moreover, as Gray argues, *Traps* denies the subversive pleasures of American exploitation cinema like *I Spit on Your Grave* (1978), the notorious rape revenge film, where violence and vengeance are affective substitutes for justice. Moral objections, however, obscure the clever satire of patriarchy in the film and ignore Chytilová's return to the modernist aesthetics of her sixties work. Indeed, the montage sequence that begins *Traps* recalls the numerous castration jokes visualized in *Daisies*. After shots of pigs copulating and close-ups of Lenka castrating them, Chytilová cuts to a close-up of Petr's back as he has sex with his girlfriend, who we learn wants to have a baby. After he argues with his girlfriend, the film crosscuts to Dohnal and his wife. Apparently, he cannot orgasm unless his wife recites Rudyard Kipling's classic poem "If." It is tempting to dismiss this opening as an obvious statement that the men are pigs. Yet the visual connections Chytilová establishes between the men and Lenka through the film suggest the opening is also a sly allusion to the final sentence of George Orwell's *Animal Farm*, in which the pigs and men resemble each other in their authoritarian impulses. In other words, the new Europe has replaced the tyranny of the state with that of the market. After all, Lenka's rapists, Petr and Dohnal, are symbols of the new European economy. Working for an advertising agency, Petr's expressed goal is to make lots of money. His current assignment is to create billboards for Bach Balls, chocolate balls named after a wealthy businessman with the absurd slogan, "The sweetest suck of all." Dohnal, on the other hand, is a sexually frustrated environmental minister who engages in crony capitalism. At a lavish party for Bach, Petr sees Dohnal and recognizes him as a former classmate. He drives him around to look at billboard sites for Bach Balls, which is how they encounter Lenka.

Traps conveys a darker vision regarding the transition to capitalism than most other nineties Eastern European art cinema from directors who began in the communist era. For example, Krzysztof Kieślowski's *White* (1994), the middle work of his *Three Colors* trilogy, presents a more palpable mockery of the new Europe. Returning from France, the main character, Karol, discovers that capitalism has come to his native Poland, symbolized by his brother buying a tawdry neon sign for his hair salon and characters repeating that "these days you can buy anything," including a corpse. Karol transforms into a scheming capitalist in order to get revenge on his French ex-wife. Similarly, István Szabó's *Meeting Venus* (1991) gently satirizes the idea of cultural unity for post-communist Europe through its story of a director who desperately tries to stage a transnational production of Wagner's opera *Tannhäuser*. Compared with such films, however, *Traps* is unique for how Chytilová offers a feminist perspective that presents patriarchy as an elementary problem in the new Europe. Yet Chytilová has denied that she is a feminist in an interview for a profile for the *Guardian*. This interview from the year 2000 has stirred controversy as critics have sought to understand Chytilová's rejection of feminism. For example, Gray references it in her essay for the *Traps* DVD, and Dina Iordanova discusses it in her book *Cinema of the Other Europe*. At the root of the controversy is this passage:

> Her most recent film, the very black comedy *Traps,* was celebrated by a handful of hardcore feminists, but regarded elsewhere as a cruel depiction of post-communist Czech society. In a country whose ex-play wright president, Vaclav Havel, once described women's rights as "dada and meaningless," and where feminism is regarded as a problem, Chytilova's radical attitude sits uneasily. . . .
>
> So does Chytilova consider herself a feminist, and if so, how does this affect her film-making? "Is your newspaper a serious one?" She peers over her large sunglasses. "You ask pointless and primitive questions."
>
> Her steam rising, she explains that she does not believe in feminism per se, but in individualism. "If there's something you don't like, don't keep to the rules—break them. I'm an enemy of stupidity and simple-mindedness in both men and women and I have rid my living space of these traits."[27]

In the context of the profile itself, it is difficult to discern how seriously the reader should interpret Chytilová's rejection of feminism since it also might merely reflect her irritation with the interviewer, whose article offers limited insights. Given the bad pun of the title, "Bohemian Rhapsodist," and the implication that one must be a "hardcore feminist" to appreciate *Traps,* Chytilová's irritation with the interviewer is justified. However, as Iordanova notes, Chytilová is not the only Eastern European female director to reject "feminism" when asked about it in interviews. According to Iordanova, Eastern European directors like Chytilová or Márta Mészáros, who has also rejected being labeled, are reacting to "the somewhat aggressive importation of Western feminism in the immediate aftermath of 1989," meaning that they are skeptical of adapting solutions to the social and economic problems of post-communism for women.[28] While this may be true, the determining principle may also be a refusal to reduce their work to prepackaged labels, which is implied by Chytilová's declaration of "individualism." Moreover, Eastern European women directors are not unique in denying their "feminism" despite the fact that the revolutionary content of their films indicates the appropriateness of the label. Chantal Akerman, who directed the revolutionary feminist film *Jeanne Dielman* (1975), would often reject the use of "isms" to describe her work.[29] Perhaps the tepid critical response to *Traps* justifies Chytilová's antagonism toward labels. One wonders whether the film, if it were directed by a man, or if it were not satirizing patriarchy, would be accused of "bitterness" or described as "depressingly reactionary."

Chytilová's subsequent feature, *Expulsion from Paradise* (2001), was met with similar critical disinterest. The film reunites her with Polívka, who co-scripted and starred in *The Inheritance*. In *Expulsion* he stars as a Rosta, a pompous director trying to create an experimental work about Adam and Eve called *Paradiso*, which is a self-referential premise since Chytilová herself made *The Fruit of Paradise*. However, his producer wants the film to be erotic exploitation, while the screenwriter is interested in making grandiose statements about humanity. Rosta struggles to direct the nudist extras on the beach location and encounters various personal problems. While the idea of a male director in existential crisis may seem like a clichéd topic for Chytilová, *Expulsion from Paradise* has more in common with the surrealism of David Lynch's *Inland Empire* (2006) than it does with its art cinema precursor, Federico Fellini's *8½* (1963). Its low-resolution digital video cinematography, transferred to 35mm celluloid, creates a hyperreal aesthetic. Moreover, it is not always discernable whether we are watching a scene from *Paradiso* since Rosta also has a small role as a doctor. As Dora Viceníková astutely writes in her brief analysis, "Chytilová combines two stylistic tendencies which had already appeared at the beginning of her film career," the cinema verité tendencies of her earliest work and the symbolism of her late sixties films.[30] The strangeness of *Expulsion from Paradise* is that it deadlocks these two tendencies. In other words, it does not attempt to synthesize its realism with its modernism. Thus, the scenes that are clearly about Rosta struggling to direct *Paradiso* or manage his personal life are presented in a handheld vérité style, while the footage from his film, with its repetition of nude bodies dwelling on the beach, portrays the abstract landscapes Chytilová herself visualized in *The Fruit of Paradise*. At the conclusion of *Expulsion from Paradise*, diegetic levels of reality seem to collapse and the film becomes inscrutable. It appears Rosta has hired a cameraman who rides on a Jet Ski, shown earlier, to capture more naturalistic reactions from the nudists. Thinking the man is spying on them, the nudists unintentionally drown him and carry his body ashore. Rosta screams at everyone and clears them away. But once they leave, the cameraman inexplicably stands up and walks toward the water with Rosta. The final image is an extreme wide-angle shot of the two of them standing at the edge of the shore talking. Its status is indeterminate, impossible to interpret as part of *Paradiso*, Rosta's life, or his fantasy. The image ends Chytilová's experiments with political modernism with an unresolvable tension between the need to capture external reality on camera and the desire to simultaneously express the symbolic interiority that structures that reality. Her final film, *Pleasant Moments* (2006), is a comparatively apolitical comedy-drama about Hana, who is a psychologist, and her patients. Told in an aggressively naturalist handheld style, it is largely composed of narrative vignettes. Though it lacks the overtly satirical impulses of her other post-communist features, it is an observant film about Hana's attempts to balance her professional life and personal life with her husband, who is more interested in suggesting threesomes. As with the female protagonists in Chytilová's other films, Hana's spirit is constantly stifled by the patriarchy that surrounds her. As such, it is an appropriate final film.

II. FROM CAPITALISM TO NATIONALISM

Sarajevo: From Hollywood to Godard

For the earlier generation of political modernists like Švankmajer and Chytilová, the end of communism was not a cause for celebration. They were critical about the new Europe, relying on their Freudian, Marxist, and feminist perspectives to analyze the destructive impulses of capitalism. The other problem that haunted art cinema of the nineties was the bloody dissolution of Yugoslavia. It proved more elusive and difficult to translate into precise political discourse. Representations of the conflict often struggled to understand its causes. This is especially true of Western films from the decade, which framed it as a depoliticized battle between barbarism and humanism with Sarajevo as a central metaphor. The British production distributed by Miramax, *Welcome to Sarajevo* (1997), is a significant example of Western strategies for representing the conflict. Directed by Michael Winterbottom, it is adapted from *Natasha's Story*, the 1994 book by war correspondent Michael Nicholson about his journey to adopt a Bosnian orphan. Though well received by critics internationally, *Welcome to Sarajevo* is ultimately more interested in its Western characters, its journalists and aid workers, than it is in establishing a historical narrative for the conflict. An even more egregious example is *Savior* (1998), which stars Dennis Quaid, who regains his lost humanity while in Bosnia. He is an American mercenary fighting for Bosnian Serbs because years ago he witnessed his wife and son killed by Islamic terrorists. He lets go of his hatred when he tries to deliver a pregnant woman to safety. This tendency to reduce Bosnia to a backdrop for Western characters and their melodramas can also be found in mainstream Hollywood movies that incorporate the conflict into the plots of action blockbusters such as *The Peacemaker* (1997) and *Behind Enemy Lines* (2001). The latter is noteworthy for its highly fictionalized account of American pilot Scott O'Grady, whose jet was shot down over Bosnia. The film's divergences from reality were such that O'Grady himself sued the producers for defamation of character and for telling his story without permission.[31]

The clichés of these depoliticized Western films about the Bosnian War reach their apex in Angelina Jolie's *In the Land of Blood and Honey* (2012). It exemplifies the "ancient hatreds" thesis that dominated political discourse during the nineties, rendered more absurd because the film was released two decades after the war, indicating how little has changed in the Western imaginary. Set during the Bosnian War, it tells the story of a pair of doomed lovers, the Serbian Danijel and the Muslim Ajla. Danijel is a reluctant soldier with the Yugoslav army, where his father is a general. He is a guard in a prisoner camp where Bosnian Muslim women are routinely raped. Once Ajla is placed in the camp, Danijel arranges for special treatment and protection for her. In her attempt to raise awareness about rape and war crimes committed against women, Jolie creates a generic message about searching for humanity in wartime, with no concern for understanding the causes of the country's disintegration. As Croatian philosopher Srećko Horvat argues, the problem with the film is that

> the only cause it can find for the conflict is ethnic hatred (and sexual lust). Yet at the time of its Croatian premiere, the minister of finance was announcing new austerity measures and privations, not only in healthcare and social security but in prisons. The same goes for the rest of the ex-Yugoslavian region, where "war tycoons" first used the chaos created by the war to rob ("privatise") state companies and industries. . . .
>
> What is finally needed for all ex-Yugoslavian countries is a land not of blood and honey but a *Land of Blood and Money*: a film that would show how the atrocities were carried out not only in the name of the Nation or Ethnic Belonging but—as always—in the name of Money.[32]

Building on Horvat's argument, one could create a more honest version of Jolie's film. Instead of a reluctant nationalist under the thumb of his father's ideology, Danijel should be a mercenary who rapes women because he is paid well to loot the population and commit war crimes in an economy that has completely collapsed. Indeed, during the nineties, the archetypal Serbian war criminal was not the reluctant civilian torn between desire for the other and national affiliation. It was Željko Ražnatović, otherwise known as "Arkan," a career international criminal who robbed banks in Western Europe before returning to Yugoslavia in the eighties. He formed a paramilitary group that was active in Croatia and Bosnia during the war. Afterward, he was a popular crime boss in Belgrade before his assassination in 2000 in an apparent turf dispute. Such a story, however, would not appeal to the Western gaze and its romantic vision of a backward region where ancient hatreds erupt without economic cause.

To a lesser extent, political modernists from the West also tended to depoliticize the complexity of the wars in Yugoslavia. In several of his post-communist works, Godard uses Sarajevo as a metaphor for his reflections on modernity, culture, and the death of cinema. References to the Bosnian War can be found throughout his work. His features *For Ever Mozart* (1996) and *Notre Musique* (2004) are set in Bosnia, and he has directed two shorts about Sarajevo, *Je Vous Salue, Sarajevo* (1993) and *Bridge of Sighs* (2014), the latter of which is one of thirteen shorts in the omnibus *Bridges of Sarajevo* (2014) about the meaning of the city for Europe. Of these four works, *Je Vous Salue, Sarajevo* is the most compelling since it encapsulates Godard's thoughts about the city and the war. In its brief two minutes, it shows the infamous 1992 photograph taken by journalist Ron Haviv that was published in *Time* magazine and sparked an international discussion. It is a horrifying image of Arkan's Serbian paramilitary forces kicking the corpses of Muslim civilians they have massacred. Godard reveals the picture in fragments before zooming out to show it in its entirety. On the soundtrack, he reads a text whose relevant excerpt is the following: "Culture is the rule, and art is the exception. Everybody speaks the rule; cigarette, computer, t-shirt, television, tourism, war. Nobody speaks the exception. It isn't spoken, it is written; Flaubert, Dostoyevsky. It is composed; Gershwin, Mozart. It is painted; Cézanne, Vermeer. It is filmed; Antonioni, Vigo. Or it is lived, then it is the art of living; Srebrenica, Mostar, Sarajevo. The rule is to want the death of the exception. So the rule for cultural Europe is to organize the death of the art of living, which still flourishes."[33] As Des O'Rawe observes, this text reappears in two other Godard films from the nineties. In the voice-over for *Je Vous Salue, Sarajevo,* it is situated between quotations from French author Georges Bernanos and French poet Louis Aragon.[34] This aesthetic approach is indicative of Godard's late work, where he creates a montage of images overlaid with dialogue or narration from literature, philosophical texts, or other films. The voice-over for *Je Vous Salue, Sarajevo* directly expresses a repeated theme in these later works, which is whether cinema and images can resist a European culture that spreads uniformity and death. Echoing Adorno, Godard suggests that the historical path of European culture evolves toward fascism and the death of the "art of living" in the Bosnian cities he mentions. This is why Holocaust footage repeats in much of his work since the late eighties. For him, the twentieth century is defined by its conflicts and the multiplication of its horrors. As he states in an interview, the century "didn't invent horror, it just churned out thousands of copies."[35] Western culture commodifies these "copies" of horror, which explains why Godard has repeatedly criticized Steven Spielberg and *Schindler's List,* calling it "Max Factor," meaning that Spielberg was incapable of representing the historical facts of Oskar Schindler's story and instead conveyed a "phony" sense of reality by shooting the film in black and white.[36] Moreover, his feature *In Praise of Love* (2000) contains several criticisms directed against Spielberg and Hollywood. For example, two children circulate a petition to have *The Matrix* (1999) dubbed into the Breton language, and a group of arrogant American film producers represent "Spielberg and Associates," who are hoping to buy the story rights of an old woman who was part of the French Resistance.

As a critique of European modernity, Godard's binary between culture and art has some validity and shares a philosophical vision with other political modernists like Švankmajer. The failing, however, is that it articulates nothing historically specific about Sarajevo or the Bosnian War. As with *In the Land of Blood and Honey,* Godard's Sarajevo films could be set elsewhere and their meaning would not change. In other words, they fail to function as the counter-cinema that he epitomized in the early seventies for political modernist critics. Given his objection that *Schindler's List* turns the Holocaust into Max Factor without proper consideration for historical facts, it is ironic that he is guilty of a similar evasion in his visions of Sarajevo. This is especially evident in his misguided *For Ever Mozart,* which repeats his theme of the conflict between art and culture. Separated into four sections, it intertwines two related stories. In the first, an older director named Vicky tries to complete his art film, *The Fatal Bolero,* which is financed by a man who runs his business in a casino, a crass metaphor for the capitalist culture that Godard rejects. The second story concerns Camille, Vicky's daughter, who decides to go to Sarajevo to stage an Alfred de Musset play. She is accompanied by Jamila, her family's maid, and Vicky's assistant, Jerome. Vicky accompanies them at first but turns back to continue directing his film. Jerome and Camille are killed by Serbian guerrillas while Vicky completes *The Fatal Bolero,* which reflects on war. In an amusing scene, Vicky attends the premiere at a multiplex. The audience in line grows skeptical, wondering whether there will be nudity and claiming they will leave if it contains poetry or if it is in black and white. Finally they abandon the line to go see *Terminator 4,* a prophetic joke considering Hollywood produced a fourth film in the franchise in 2009.

Though humorous, the premiere of Vicky's film highlights what is so misguided about *For Ever Mozart.* Despite its occasional satirical insights about Westerners ignoring the horrors of Bosnia, ultimately the conflict in Bosnia is treated as a backdrop for Godard's sour views of art destroyed by commerce. The scenes set near Sarajevo are likely to strike spectators from the region as unintentionally comical and ridiculous, as the Bosnia depicted in the film obviously resembles the Swiss countryside seen in other late Godard films. The Serbian guerrillas who rape and murder Camille and her companions resemble the generic barbarians seen at the end of his *Weekend* (1967) rather than the militias captured in the photo in *Je Vous Salue, Sarajevo.* The point is not that the film lacks sufficient realism or authenticity in its representations of Bosnia given that Godard is interested in conveying a deliberate sense of artifice. War, as Godard reminds us, is another expression of commodified culture. Rather, the problem is that his notion of "the art of living" destroyed in Sarajevo is too ahistorical. Without an account of why Yugoslavia dissolved into warfare quickly in the post-communist age, "the art of living" becomes a general critique of European modernity without a narrative of how its logic unfolds locally.

Godard returns to Sarajevo in *Notre Musique,* a more complex work than *For Ever Mozart,* which benefits from being filmed in Sarajevo and nearby cities like Mostar. It is divided into three distinct narrative segments, which reference Dante's *Divine Comedy.* The first is titled "Kingdom 1: Hell" and consists of ten minutes of an aggressively nonnarrative montage of fiction films and documentaries depicting wars, genocide, and violence. The second section, "Kingdom 2: Purgatory," is the lengthiest and is set in Sarajevo.

Godard, who plays himself, has arrived for an international conference titled "European Literary Encounters," where he delivers a lecture on the relationship between text and image in cinema. A variety of other characters attending the conference are introduced, including a group of Native Americans; Judith, an Israeli journalist who interviews a French ambassador and a Palestinian poet; and Olga, a French Russian Jew who intends to commit suicide. This section of *Notre Musique* functions as an extended metaphor for historical reconciliation after war and colonialism. Asked why she has traveled to Sarajevo, Judith answers, "Because of Palestine," and states that she wanted "to see a place where reconciliation seemed possible."[37] Similarly, Olga visits the famous Mostar Bridge, which was still not rebuilt by the time *Notre Musique* was in production. She encounters the Native Americans from the conference there. In one shot, edited to suggest her mental perspective, she imagines them dressed in traditional outfits, as if they have emerged from a Hollywood western. This blunt image expresses Godard's analysis of cinema and its relationship to colonial violence. Yet it also highlights the limitation of *Notre Musique*. Its discourse about historical reconciliation after war and violence avoids sustained reflection on whether the Serbians, Croatians, and Bosniaks who actually live in the country have overcome their past. There is a powerful scene where Godard and other conference attendees take a taxi from the airport and drive through former Serbian front lines, discussing the lasting scars of violence, and another scene set in the ruins of a library. However, Godard is more interested in commenting on the conflict between Israel and Palestine than in exploring the causes of the dissolution of Yugoslavia. Despite the formal complexity of its sound design and montage, *Notre Musique* does not engage with the question of reconciliation in Sarajevo or its integration into Europe. This is evident in the film's conclusion. At the end of the "Purgatory" section, Godard returns home and receives a phone call informing him that Olga has gone into a cinema in Jerusalem, threatening to blow herself up and looking for another Israeli willing to do so for the cause of peace. *Notre Musique* concludes with the brief "Kingdom 3: Paradise," where Olga, presumably in the afterlife, wanders to a forest near a lake. It appears to be an idyllic setting where Olga encounters other young people reading and relaxing, though it is soured by the fact that the lake is guarded by American marines and a chain-link fence. The Americans have colonized heaven, Godard seems to suggest. It is at once a bluntly satirical image and elliptical ending, casting doubts on whether the historical reconciliation that the film seeks is possible and, if it is, proposing that it must be found in purgatory and not hell or paradise.

Dušan Makavejev and the End of the Third Way

Of all the post–Second World War political modernists to achieve international recognition during the sixties and seventies, Makavejev was best positioned to represent the dissolution of Yugoslavia. Born in Belgrade and a key director of the Yugoslav Black Wave, he possessed a cultural familiarity with the region that gave him an advantage over the remoteness too evident in the Godard films about Sarajevo. Equally important is his style of modernist montage, which examines the dialectic between social revolution and terror. Though he never directed an entire film about the dissolution of Yugoslavia, references to the conflict in his nineties films link the breakup of the country to the legacies of communism and the social and economic malaise generated by the transformation into market capitalism. In these final works, he returns to the essayistic mode of his iconic films analyzed in the previous chapter. This is in contrast to his films of the eighties, *Montenegro* (1981), *The Coca-Cola Kid* (1985), and *Manifesto* (1988), which more closely resemble conventional European art cinema in their narrative form and political discourse. Like Švankmajer's and Chytilová's, Makavejev's career was stunted by censorship during the seventies. The controversies generated by *Sweet Movie,* and his exile from Yugoslavia, led to a seven-year gap before his return with *Montenegro,* a Swedish black comedy that became a popular international art film. While his eighties films are more conventional in form than his early and late work, they are not without merit as political discourse. *Montenegro* has received critical praise, but *The Coca-Cola Kid* and *Manifesto* have been comparatively ignored, notably by Lorraine Mortimer in her excellent monograph on Makavejev because she considers them "less rich" than his other films.[38] Both films warrant more detailed consideration, but for the purposes of this chapter, *Manifesto* will be the focus since it introduces many of the themes found in his post-communist work.[39]

Despite their more conventional narratives, *Montenegro* and *The Coca-Cola Kid* are not radical departures from his earlier work in terms of their political discourse. Like *WR: Mysteries of the Organism* and *Sweet Movie,* they investigate whether sexual liberation can be channeled into social revolution. In *Montenegro,* for example, Marilyn is an American housewife who lives in Sweden. The banality of domestic life has depressed her. She is losing her grasp on sanity, as suggested by the bizarre scene where she tells her daughter they are in a movie. Moreover, Makavejev establishes visual connections between her domestic entrapment and the caged monkey at the zoo she visits. The opening title credit states, "A little girl questioned a monkey in a zoo: Why do you live here? Isn't it nicer where you come from?" As the plot develops, Marilyn is sexually liberated by her encounters with the exiled Yugoslavs who operate a nightclub. She begins an affair with a young man named Montenegro. However, like Anna Planeta in *Sweet Movie* or Vladimir Ilyich in *WR: Mysteries of the Organism,* she is unable to contain the psychic energy unleashed by her liberation and resorts to violence. She murders her lover and poisons her family. Ultimately, *Montenegro* successfully translates Makavejev's political modernism and its dialectic of liberation and terror into the more conventional framework of European art cinema. His next film, *The Coca-Cola Kid,* is less complex. It is primarily a farcical comedy about a Coca-Cola executive named Becker who travels to Australia to discover why sales are so poor in a remote region. He discovers that T. George McDowell, a local cola producer, has controlled the market for years. The film is blunter in its politics when judged by the standards of Makavejev's earlier work. Its anticolonial and anticorporate satire is largely subsumed by the conventional plot, in which Becker falls in love with Terri, the daughter of the local cola producer. After having sex with her, he is liberated from his corporate mentality. The only hint of Makavejev's trademark irony is the onscreen text at the conclusion of the film, which informs us that one week later a new world war will begin, undercutting the happy ending by reminding the audience of the geopolitical tensions evident during the decade.

Manifesto is a much darker film that predicts the malaise depicted in his post-communist work. While *Montenegro* and *The Coca-Cola Kid* retain Makavejev's interest in sexual liberation and revolution, *Manifesto* suggests that the revolutionary potential of communism has been exhausted, the opposite of the sentiment expressed in *WR: Mysteries of the Organism* in the iconic scene where Milena's reanimated head says she is not ashamed of her communist past. The film begins with a sardonic text introducing the setting and its theme of failed revolutionaries: "Central Europe 1920: after the fall of great Empires new governments appeared, taking themselves very seriously. Life became hard for revolutionaries. However, ice-cream was sold and enjoyed as if nothing changed." Loosely inspired by Émile Zola's story *For a Night of Love,* the film is set in a small town expecting a visit from the king. It begins with a scene on the train where Svetlana, a revolutionary plotting to assassinate the king, is returning home. She flirts with Avanti, a member of the secret police arriving in town to arrest suspected revolutionaries. The first person detained is Rudi Kugelhopf, whom Svetlana has seduced for her cause. Later in the film, Rudi's colleague Lily Sacher is also arrested by Avanti, though she is not a revolutionary. She discovers him in the woods having sex with Tina, the underage teenage orphan girl who sells ice cream in town. Thus, Avanti wants her to disappear.

Makavejev expresses multiple ironies with the arrests of Rudi and Lily. Both are subjected to torture by a scientist named Doctor Lombrosow. He explains his methods by referencing Marx's famous phrase about how communism will satisfy all social needs: "My method of reeducation is based on scientific insight into human nature and personalities which means from each according to his ability, to each according to his need."[40] Moreover, the name Lombrosow invokes the nineteenth-century Italian criminologist Cesare Lombroso, who believed he could detect criminal proclivities through physiognomy. Through such references, Makavejev satirizes scientific communism as totalitarian and dehumanizing. First introduced by Friedrich Engels, it has a complex history in Marxist theory and in governmental practices, but in essence its idea is that communism has discovered the scientific laws of history, economics, and nature. It is also a rejection of the utopian socialism of thinkers like Fourier who influenced Švankmajer and Wilhelm Reich. Ironically, the commitment to scientism under Stalinism meant that the state would promote pseudoscientific theories, as in the notorious case in which they embraced Trofim Lysenko's alternative genetic theory because Gregor Mendel's ideas reflected a bourgeois capitalist world view. Thousands of biologists were imprisoned.

Doctor Lombrosow employs his "permanent revolution rotor" on Rudi, which is a giant hamster wheel designed to "harness" the revolutionary energy of its subject. Once inside, Rudi runs exuberantly, declaring his commitment to the revolution and the forward movement of history, shouting that "the wheel of history cannot be turned back." Doctor Lombrosow responds by pulling a lever that rotates the wheel backward. Undeterred at first, Rudi continues to run while still shouting his slogans. Eventually, however, his revolutionary energy is exhausted and he prefers life in his hamster wheel. Given a chance at his freedom by Lily, who has escaped, he demurs by stating that they serve hot food in the lab and that the movement could use a martyr. Rudi is granted his wish when Lily unintentionally sets fire to the lab. The doctor's torture device is an allusion to Leon Trotsky's idea of a permanent revolution of socialism occurring internationally rather than in one nation. In other words, Makavejev reminds spectators that Stalin's vision of national communism, or "socialism in one country," defeated Trotsky's world revolution and created an authoritarian party apparatus with an ideology of scientism that centralized the Soviet state. This victory is also dramatized in the film by Lily, who replaces Rudi in Svetlana's plot to kill the king. Doctor Lombrosow's torture conditioned Lily into a Stalinist revolutionary demanding immediate action. At the end of the film, her heroics on the top of a moving train in pursuit of Avanti imply a mechanical commitment to violence and killing rather than the pleasures of utopia in which the affable Rudi believes.

Makavejev incorporates footage from *Manifesto* into his final short film, *Dream,* included in the omnibus film *Danish Girls Show Everything* (1996). Given his legacy as a major political modernist in world cinema, it is unfortunate that *Dream* should languish in obscurity because *Danish Girls Show Everything* has never been widely distributed internationally. *Dream* is a four-minute essayistic montage that dwells on a variety of topics, such as the end of revolutionary politics, the Bosnian War, and the triumph of scientism and its victory over utopian humanism. Unlike his earlier work, the tone of *Dream* is ominous and its imagery is apocalyptic and contains none of Makavejev's absurdist sense of humor. The bleakness of its message is conveyed through the juxtaposition of the film's images and its voice-over. Echoing Chris Marker's strategy of using a female narrator as an authorial substitute, *Dream*'s female narrator describes Makavejev's disjointed, surreal dream:

> I dreamt last night about reality. What a relief when I woke up. Animals are watching us. What do they see? How do we appear to them? What do they think of us? An English lady, a murder mystery writer, became famous for inventing unusual murders. One of her perfect crimes took place on a train between Zagreb and Belgrade. All eleven partners in crime were related to the victim. The *Orient Express*: exquisite food, superb wines and scenery that will capture your heart. Sixty years later, in exactly the same place, a chain of real murders began. All victims and their killers were also related. A hungry chicken. A curious kitten and a human brain. Shoulder to shoulder, a bird and a man run to advance the science of life.[41]

Makavejev's associative montage links *Manifesto* to Agatha Christie's *Murder on the Orient Express* and the civil war in Yugoslavia. In particular, he links shots from *Manifesto* of Svetlana adjusting her garter belt while talking to Avanti on the train with cover art to Christie's book and graphic photos of people murdered in Yugoslavia with animals wandering among the corpses. This string of associations depends on a familiarity with the plot of *Murder on the Orient Express*. The detective Hercule Poirot deduces that the victim, Mr. Ratchett, otherwise known as Lanfranco Cassetti, who kidnapped a child heiress in the United States, was stabbed in revenge by twelve friends and relatives of the child, all of whom are aboard the train. Read in isolation, the reference to the plot and setting of *Murder on the Orient Express* implies that tribalism and vengeance are endemic to the former Yugoslavia, which would align the film with the dominant theories in the West about the historical backwardness of the Balkans and its contiguity with the Orient rather than civilized Europe. However, in the context of the complex associations woven throughout *Dream*, the reference recalls the idea expressed by Godard in *Je Vous Salue, Sarajevo* about culture and "the art of living." Makavejev, though, is not issuing a blanket indictment of all of European modernity and its culture of death as Godard does. Rather, he obliquely parallels the dissolution of Yugoslavia to the triumph of scientism and progress over utopian humanism. If the particular crime in *Murder on the Orient Express* can only occur on a train, a technological symbol of how modernity reconfigures our perceptions of space and time, then the war crimes of Yugoslavia are similarly made possible through the reorganization of life according to the "scientific" market principles of progress. This is further established through the rhythmic juxtaposition of images that accompany the voice-over, which include a man jogging, a chicken wandering in the snow, footage from *Manifesto*, and two women leading an emu into a building. The montage concludes with an image of the emu running on a treadmill with an apparatus attached to its face, while two female scientists keep it moving forward. As the camera pans right, we see a man with a breathing apparatus attached to his face, also running on a treadmill. The voice-over states, "Shoulder to shoulder, a bird and a man run to advance the science of life." In other words, Makavejev's final image is one where the energies of life are measured and quantified. If, in his earlier political modernism, such life energies were celebrated as vital for the eruption of social revolution, then *Dream* suggests their defeat, transformation, and reification into scientific data. The fact that the most joyful subversive of Eastern European political modernism concludes his career on a melancholy note is indicative of the disillusionment he felt over the collapse of Yugoslavia, which is a topic he explores in his brilliant autobiographical essay film, *Hole in the Soul,* made for the BBC in 1994.

Though only fifty minutes, *Hole in the Soul* has a complex associative structure. We follow Makavejev in Los Angeles, where a film festival is honoring him. He meets with his agent to discuss his inability to find funding for his next project; visits with his friend Dennis Jakob, who was a creative consultant on *Apocalypse Now*; and has a scripted encounter with a guru who explains that Makavejev lost his soul in a country that no longer exists. These moments are interspersed with scenes in Belgrade, where he reunites with former collaborators, visits his family, and tours the Church of Saint Sava. To that extent, *Hole in the Soul* self-consciously echoes the structure of *WR: Mysteries of the Organism,* which is also set in Belgrade and the United States. However, the exploration of revolutionary energies in the earlier work becomes a melancholy rumination on Makavejev's own artistic obsolescence and the death of Yugoslavia. The former theme is introduced in the Los Angeles scenes, where Makavejev includes shots of iconic Sunset Boulevard and narrates, "This Boulevard, for instance, was directed by Billy Wilder. So I see myself going down white stairs straight into an ambulance, passing Erich Von Stroheim, floating in the pool face down, successful, and dead."[42] This reference to Billy Wilder's misanthropic film about Hollywood is amusing since Makavejev identifies both with the Norma Desmond character, the forgotten silent-screen star, and with Joe Gillis, the failed screenwriter whom she kills. Though not destroyed by a studio system adapting to new sound technologies, Makavejev does visualize his obsolescence when he cuts to a billboard for Arnold Schwarzenegger's 1993 film *The Last Action Hero* while a news reporter informs us that the film failed to turn a profit on its hundred-million-dollar budget. In other words, he implies that the victory of free-market principles has destroyed his ideals of cinema, a reversal of fortune from the seventies, when *WR: Mysteries of the Organism* made such a significant international impression that Francis Ford Coppola famously approached Makavejev to direct *Apocalypse Now*. After he is denied access to shoot footage in the Directors Guild of America building, Makavejev returns to the *Last Action Hero* billboard, zooming in on the bottom of Schwarzenegger's boot. A quick cut to a close-up of Makavejev staring at the boot suggests an allusion to George Orwell's *1984* and the famous moment when O'Brien tells Wilson that the imagined future will be a boot crushing a face forever. Yet the scenes of Makavejev in Los Angeles are presented with absurdist humor, such as when he interviews, in a movie theater lobby, an animal wrangler and her pig that was in a theatrical production of *Li'l Abner* and shares a birthday with Stalin.

It is when Makavejev visits Dennis Jakob in his office that *Hole in the Soul* turns melancholy and the themes of Makavejev's obsolescence and the demise of Yugoslavia intertwine. The scene begins with Jakob describing the sixties generation of new-wave filmmakers to which Makavejev belonged as engaging in a Nietzschean "slave revolt" against cinema values. Chastising him, Jakob adds, "Now I hear from your wife that they even have festivals and things in your honor in Russia. When you were banned in Russia, once you were something. You were a threat to somebody. But now [you are] winning a festival or some kind of program in your honor. Dušan, you are now like Flaubert—a bourgeois living the bourgeois life and you're trying to be an artist."[43] Makavejev's voice-over responds by saying, "If I have to choose between Nietzsche and Flaubert the Frenchman seems to me a better choice," as he cuts to a scene in Belgrade in which Milena Dravić, star of *WR: Mysteries of the Organism*, and Eva Ras, from *Man Is Not a Bird* and *Love Affair*, visit Makavejev and his mother-in-law. As the scene develops, Makavejev cuts to a title card that states, "Dennis Sees No Future for Me," doubling back to his conversation with Jakob, who says, "All the stuff that used to work no longer works. You are no longer funny." Jakob also reiterates that Makavejev needs to be perceived as a threat, especially in his own country. This becomes the central sequence in *Hole in the Soul* as Makavejev creates complex connections between the past and present and the personal and the artistic. He critiques Jakob's romanticized opposition between aesthetic revolution and bourgeois values. One cannot be banned from a country that no longer exists, as Makavejev once was in the early seventies after *WR: Mysteries of the Organism*. Moreover, in a country torn apart by warfare, the bourgeois ritual of dinner and wine becomes an act of mourning for the destruction of the past. Tellingly, Eva Ras has brought a bottle of wine from Mostar, stating, "Mostar is no more but the wine is still there," and adding that it may be the last prewar wine. Consequently, Makavejev inserts into the dinner scene archival footage of children diving from the Mostar Bridge into the river Neretva. Later in the film, he will show footage of its destruction during the Croatian and Bosnian conflict.

This associative montage hints that the destruction of the past is not a virtue, which is how Jakob describes the aesthetic revolution of the new-wave cinemas. Makavejev himself has always been interested in working through the past rather than radically breaking from it. In *Innocence Unprotected* (1968), he juxtaposes a documentary of stuntman Dragoljub Aleksić, director of the first Serbian sound film in 1942, with German and Soviet propaganda, creating a complex essay about historical loss and political naïveté. Made during the Nazi occupation, Aleksić's film was censored by the Nazis, and after the war he was charged and acquitted by Yugoslav authorities as a Nazi collaborator and war profiteer for directing the film. Significantly, Makavejev recycles footage from *Innocence Unprotected* at the beginning of *Hole in the Soul* while he describes his childhood during the war. This footage is used to investigate his own historical loss and political naïveté—namely, his belief in Yugoslavia and his commitment to creating antiauthoritarian aesthetics. Thus, *Hole in the Soul* is about coming to terms with the failure of both in a world that values the box office earnings of *The Last Action Hero* as a marker of success. The film ends with Makavejev riding a boat with some friends down the Sava River. Asked about his next project, he expresses his desire to make a film about the history of Yugoslavia and its collapse into civil war. His friend, satirical Serbian rock star Rambo Amadeus, makes a comic plea for funding by looking directly into the camera and asking the "bastards" and "rich producers" for "a couple of hundred million dollars." As the boat moves into the sunset, Makavejev cuts back to Los Angeles as we see the pig that shares Stalin's birthday waddle down the Hollywood walk of fame.

On a deeper level, the associative montage of *Hole in the Soul* connects the excesses of nationalism and capitalism. The scenes in Los Angeles thematically rhyme with those in Belgrade. In particular, the *Last Action Hero* billboard scene echoes the moment when Makavejev's friend visits a street market and talks to a man selling and bartering bundles of money. To understand this scene, it is important to note that the rate of inflation in the then Federal Republic of Yugoslavia—formally comprising Serbia and Montenegro—"peaked in January 1994, when the official monthly inflation rate was 313 million" percent.[44] In both cases, Makavejev emphasizes money as a destabilizing force, artistically and socially. In other words, unfettered capitalism is the cause of the notorious failure of *Last Action Hero,* whose excessive marketing campaign included painting its logo on an unmanned space rocket.[45] However, the most important insight of *Hole in the Soul* is that it also associates the destructive excess of capitalism with the symbols of the new nationalism in the former Yugoslavia.

In the sequence following the street market scene, Makavejev visits the Church of Saint Sava in Belgrade. Construction of the church first began in the thirties and was halted by the Nazi invasion. It resumed again in the late eighties, when its massive dome with gold crosses and copper plates was finished. In the film's voice-over, Makavejev describes its construction as follows: "Recently, in a burst of nationalist euphoria a huge concrete edifice was suddenly raised only to be abandoned again. Like in a dream gone wrong energy originally used to build a road to heaven went to creating a hell on earth." The meaning of this poetic voice-over becomes clear when Makavejev and his film crew visit the roof of the dome, which overlooks Belgrade. Scanning the cityscape, he asks his crew, "Show us the house Arkan is building. We want to be trendy, to see the latest developments, right?" As explained earlier, Arkan was the notorious war criminal whose paramilitary group pillaged and looted the countryside in Croatia and Bosnia. Sardonically describing him as "trendy," Makavejev suggests that nationalist euphoria and capitalist excess share a similar spirit. To understand this parallel, it is important to note that during the Cold War, Yugoslavia was a founding nation of the Non-Aligned Movement, along with India, Indonesia, Egypt, and Ghana. As such, Yugoslavia perceived itself as offering a "third way" between Western capitalism and the Soviet Union. According to Richard Byrne, Makavejev has spoken frequently about his identification with Yugoslavia and its "third way" ideology. Byrne writes, "In the new countries carved from Yugoslavia's remains—where linguists busily invented new words to differentiate their languages from the common one they once had shared—Makavejev was forced to shed that identity with which he so closely identified himself. Geographically, he is now a Serbian filmmaker, and not a Yugoslav filmmaker. Or maybe not, if one chooses simply to disappear. One can then, perhaps, remain eternally Yugoslav."[46] Makavejev's political modernism ends with him mourning the death of the alternative to both Stalinism and Western capitalism. However, this mourning avoids the trap of passive nostalgia since it also allows Makavejev to critique the post-communist present by associating the new nationalisms with the excesses of capitalism. For him, the end of the "third way" means the ascendency of tent-pole movies, megachurches, and gangster-capitalist war criminals. This distinguishes *Hole in the Soul* from Western films about the Yugoslav wars, such as Angelina Jolie's *In the Land of Blood and Honey*, which imagine ethnicity as an immutable identity, or Godard's post-communist work, which depoliticizes the conflict and reduces Sarajevo to an abstract metaphor for reconciliation. This vision of "blood and money" instead of "blood and honey," to paraphrase Croatian philosopher Srećko Horvat, elevates *Hole in the Soul* above the more popular nineties art cinema about the former Yugoslavia that promoted the "ancient hatreds" thesis. The persistence of this thesis repeats historical misconceptions about communist societies, and Yugoslavia in particular, that need to be corrected.

Yugoslavia: The Neoliberal Ogre Awakes!

As chapter 1 argues, the new-wave cinemas from Eastern Europe were undervalued for their political modernism compared with their Western counterparts. Jonathan Rosenbaum observes that these films were more difficult to interpret because Western audiences and critics "tended to lump together the Eastern European countries as if they were all part of the same stereotypical gray wasteland."[47] A similar assumption exists concerning the realities of nationalism and ethnic identity under communist regimes. In other words, the idea that "ancient hatreds" erupted at the end of history presumes that communist governments repressed all forms of nationalism and ethnicity. This is not the case in either Stalin's Soviet Union or Tito's Yugoslavia. In the former, in practice, some forms were encouraged, such as the promotion of Russian nationalism during the Second World War, despite official communist dogma that nationalism was a bourgeois identity.

In Tito's Yugoslavia, on the other hand, the relationship between communism and nationalism was even more complicated. As the country was less centralized than the Soviet Union, its "third way" ideology meant that successive Yugoslav constitutions granted more legal autonomy to its various republics and autonomous regions, which had prominent ethnic majorities. At the same time, a federal "Yugoslav" identity was promoted by authorities and new forms of national belonging were also acknowledged. For example, in 1968 Bosnian Muslims were granted legal status as a nation. In 1983 political philosopher Ernest Gellner observed the complexity of this phenomenon in his classic study *Nations and Nationalism* when he wrote,

> In Bosnia the ex-Muslim population secured at long last, and without arduous efforts, the right to describe themselves as Muslim, when filling in the "nationality" slot on the census. This did not mean that they were still believing and

> practicing Muslims, and it meant even less that they were identifying as one nationality with other Muslims or ex-Muslims in Yugoslavia, such as the Albanians of Kosovo. They were Serbo-Croat speakers of Slav ancestry and Muslim cultural background. What they meant was that they could not describe themselves as Serb or as Croat (despite sharing a language with Serbs and Croats), because these identifications carried the implications of *having been* Orthodox or Catholic; and to describe oneself as "Yugoslav" was too abstract, generic and bloodless.[48]

The question becomes, If Yugoslavia encouraged new expressions of national identity, how can we explain the persistence of the "ancient hatreds" thesis in the Western imaginary and European art cinemas? Most art films and political analyses sought no other explanations for the disintegration of Yugoslavia. A notable exception regarding the latter is the comprehensive five-hundred-page study *Balkan Tragedy: Chaos and Dissolution after the Cold War* by Susan L. Woodward, which provides a detailed analysis of Yugoslavia's rapid economic disintegration during the eighties. As she argues, "To explain the Yugoslav crisis as a result of ethnic hatred is to turn the story upside down and begin at its end."[49] To be sure, beginning at the end of the story has its obvious ideological benefits. It alleviates Western capitalism of any guilt for the causes of Yugoslavia's disintegration. While Woodward's book is too complex for a detailed summary, in essence her argument is that Yugoslavia was forced to implement harsh austerity measures for a decade before its disintegration. Since the country was not aligned with the Soviet Union, it was integrated into the Western financial system, which meant the economic shocks of the seventies—the oil crisis, inflation, and skyrocketing interest rates—spiked its foreign debt levels, pegged in U.S. dollars, causing it to become unsustainable. Similar to present-day Greece after the euro crisis, Yugoslavia experienced a precipitous decline in standard of living as it was forced to impose neoliberal market reforms to service its debt. The reforms continued to fail and strain the social fabric. As Woodward observes,

> By 1985–86 the preconditions of a revolutionary situation were apparent. One million people were officially registered as unemployed. The increasing rate of unemployment was above 20 percent in all republics except Slovenia and Croatia. Inflation was at 50 percent a year and climbing. The household savings of approximately 80 percent of the population were depleted. . . . This

> leads to economic and social polarization. While most people were preoccupied with making ends meet under the austerity program and the dominant mood was that of localism, personalism, scapegoating against minorities (ethnic and women), and antipolitics, independent political activity and new civic groups were also bubbling up.[50]

Given Yugoslavia's complex constitutional order, which guaranteed self-determination for its various republics, the "social polarization" that emerged as a result of economic collapse readily took the form of international and interethnic scapegoating. According to Woodward, this meant that the wealthier republics, such as Slovenia, which was the first to succeed, were incentivized to privilege their own economic interests over reforming the federation. In addition to the economic chaos of the eighties and the subsequent battles for political reform, the end of the Cold War meant that Yugoslavia no longer had a privileged geopolitical status as a nonaligned communist country, so it no longer functioned as a potential ally against the Soviet Union. As such, the nationalism that emerged in the eighties was normalized by the time the country descended into war in the early nineties. Bosnia, the most ethnically heterogeneous of the republics, would see the most horrific fighting, which became a three-sided conflict between Bosniaks, Serbs, and Croats.

Not many nineties films from the former Yugoslavia attempted to dramatize its social and economic collapse in the previous decade. For example, *Before the Rain* (1995), which was nominated for an Academy Award, tells the story of doomed interethnic lovers and imagines the Macedonian countryside as trapped in circular patterns of history. It resembles *In the Land of Blood and Honey* more than it does *Hole in the Soul.* Moreover, the theatrical cut of Emir Kusturica's *Underground,* which spans the years 1941–1992, leaps from an extended montage of Tito's funeral in 1980 to the onset of the Bosnian War in 1992, suggesting its inevitability. One notable exception to this trend of treating the war as a historical inevitability is Srđan Dragojević's *Pretty Village, Pretty Flame* (1996),[51] which tells the story of the disintegration of the friendship between Milan, a Bosnian Serb, and Halil, a Bosnian Muslim. Told from Milan's perspective while he lies wounded in a hospital in Belgrade, it employs a range of political modernist aesthetic techniques: nonlinear narration that alternates between different time frames, faked newsreel footage, and other distancing devices. These techniques force the viewer to piece together answers to the central question of the film: How does Milan evolve from a reluctant participant in the Bosnian War, at one point even shooting other Serbs who loot Halil's home, into a psychotic nationalist who, at the end of the film, tries to murder a Muslim with a fork in a hospital? As the film's nonlinear narrative progresses, it primarily focuses on an incident in the war in which Milan and his squad, led by a Tito-loving former communist, are trapped in a tunnel by Muslim soldiers, including his former friend Halil. Milan came to be trapped in the tunnel, Dragojević suggests, as a result of the economic disintegration of the country, which sparked interethnic rivalry, a theme that is established in the film's mock opening newsreel.

This mock newsreel introduces the tunnel that entraps Milan during the Bosnian War as the "Brotherhood-Unity Tunnel." Dated 1971, the newsreel is a clever mockery of the type of communist propaganda newsreel that extols the virtues of central planning and public works, which Makavejev was already satirizing in the early sixties. At first, Dragojević aims for realism as a narrator celebrates communist progress and the workers who have overcome nature to build a tunnel that will create socialist unity among the peoples of Yugoslavia. However, as the mock newsreel continues, Dragojević floods the screen with bright colors and employs slow motion. A Yugoslav Communist Party official named by the voice-over as Džemal Bijedić has arrived for the ribbon-cutting ceremony. This is an important historical allusion since Bijedić was prime minister of Yugoslavia from 1971 to 1977 and was instrumental in securing the constitutional rights of Bosnian Muslims to declare themselves a nationality. As he cuts the red ribbon in front of the tunnel, he accidentally slices his thumb. Uncertain of how to respond, another party official covers his thumb, causing blood to comically spurt, and signals the musicians to play a song. Everybody begins to dance frantically.

After the newsreel and a brief title sequence, the film cuts to 1980 as Milan and Halil stand in front of the same tunnel, which has become completely dilapidated. In less than a decade, it has already been transformed into a ruin of the communist past. The young boys are afraid to enter because they believe an ogre sleeps inside who, when woken, will burn down all the villages. They agree to return when they are better armed. The "ogre in the tunnel" becomes the primary image in the film for explaining the disintegration of Yugoslavia. In his excellent *Disintegration in Frames: Aesthetics and Ideology in the Yugoslav and Post-Yugoslav Cinema,* Pavle Levi analyzes the ogre as follows: "Fulfilling the role of the central metaphor in the film, the tunnel thus functions as a black hole that, during Yugoslavia's communist years, stored everything that was repressed from the surface of the sociopolitical reality so that the country could maintain its image of the peoples' solidarity. The somehow timeless and transhistorical interethnic animosity (the Ogre) was supposedly also building up underneath the surface of multiethnic happiness, and it erupted in the most violent manner with the collapse of the Yugoslav federation."[52] In other words, Levi interprets the ogre as a metaphor for repressed interethnic hatred that is unleashed. This would mean *Pretty Village, Pretty Flame* is yet another cinematic example of the "ancient hatreds" thesis that dominated Western understandings of the conflict. However, the uniqueness of *Pretty Village, Pretty Flame* is the excess of meaning that it assigns to the ogre metaphor. In addition to the thesis of interethnic animosity, the film supports the idea that the ogre represents the financial debt that fueled the growth of Yugoslavia and whose repayment unraveled the country in the eighties. Indeed, money and debt are central metaphors throughout the film. Following the scene with the young boys in 1980, we see Milan arriving at the military hospital in 1994. The film immediately cuts to 1992. A subtitle informs us it is the first day of the war. Milan and Halil play a game of liar's poker, and Halil explains that they can choose from the German, Croatian, and Serbian money that he has. He also asks whether there will be a war, to which Milan jokingly says yes. This game of liar's poker is repeated later in the tunnel when the two encounter each other again after Milan's Bosnian Serb army squad is able to escape from the tunnel. Moreover, throughout the film, Dragojević links images of money and private poverty to interethnic unity and conflict. For example, a key sequence employing a flashback and flash-forward structure shows how Milan and Halil, who bond over liar's poker, start an auto-repair shop, which is looted during the war by Milan's squad, though he tries to prevent it.

In *Pretty Village, Pretty Flame*, ethnic hatred, sparked by lies and deception, is expressed as a Hobbesian battle over property and resources. This is emphasized during the sequences when Milan's squad is trapped in the tunnel and the film explains in flashbacks why the other soldiers joined the Bosnian Serb Army. In addition to Milan, the soldiers represent a broad range of classes and cultural statuses. They include the Captain, a former officer in the Yugoslav People's Army who loved Tito; two Serbian brothers-in-law; a professor; a thief; and a junky. A foreign female journalist is also trapped with them. Looking for a war story, she hides in the back of a truck driven by

Speedy, the junky soldier, who tries to rescue the squad before it breaks down. The squad members' primary bond is the perceived threat of Muslims, whom they despairingly describe as "Turks." The only soldier who joined the army for outright nationalist reasons is Laza, and the film mocks his motivations. In flashback, he is shown watching television with his extended family. The Serbian propaganda onscreen warns about "raging hordes" of Muslims and the return of Croatian fascism as threatening their livelihood. Disgusted, Laza stands up and decides to join the army. His decision, though, is immediately satirized. He hitches a ride with a truck driver and monologues about how he must protect the Serbian people from genocide by Turks and Germans. Laza, however, does not realize that the truck driver is Turkish, as indicated by the music he plays and the star-and-crescent jewelry hanging in the cab. In fact, he seems to think he is Swedish. Later in the film, we learn that his brother-in-law, who is nicknamed Fork, joined the army to ensure Laza's safety. As they depart for training, a vendor is shown trying to sell nationalist emblems to the soldiers.

The story of how Velja, the thief, came to be part of the squad is where *Pretty Village, Pretty Flame* most explicitly argues that the war in Bosnia was primarily caused by greed and debt. A flashback shows him bringing gifts to his mother and brother when the army arrives to take his brother, who has been ignoring his conscription notices. Later, in the tunnel, he argues with Gvozden, the Captain, who is nostalgic for the communist era, which he believes had more honesty and integrity. Velja engages in a lengthy rant: "You people and your honesty. You were always full of that crap. Do you think one single enemy house we burn or vice versa was honestly bought? You talk such crap. If they were, they wouldn't be so easy to burn. As long as Tito stuffed US dollars up your arse you did pretty well blathering about Brotherhood and Unity and smiled at each other. Then the time came to settle the bill. Fine, but why didn't you do it earlier? You jerked off for 50 years, drove fancy cars and screwed great girls."[53] Velja's ideas are a vulgarized version of Woodard's argument that Yugoslavia began to unravel once its foreign debt became unsustainable and the Communist Party, accustomed to a higher standard of living compared with its Eastern European neighbors, could not reform its complex legal system of "Brotherhood and Unity" to adjust to the first wave of neoliberal austerity in the eighties. In other words, this is the ogre in the film, which unleashes ethnic hatred: the final integration into a market system that incentivizes competition and greed. Thus, the most evil character in *Pretty Village, Pretty Flame* is Slobo, the patriarch from Milan's village. He lies to Milan, telling him that Halil's squad killed his mother. As an interior shot of his house suggests, Slobo radicalizes Milan so that he can continue looting and profiteering, as shown by all of the personal items he has accumulated. His name, perhaps deliberately, suggests that of Slobodan Milošević. Like Slobo in the film, Milošević's own nationalism was a means to an end for accumulating capital and wealth. A communist who rose to power during Yugoslavia's disintegration in the eighties, Milošević exploited tensions between Serbs and Albanians in Kosovo, positioning himself as a reformer who would protect Serbs everywhere. Notably, in his book *Origins of a Catastrophe: Yugoslavia and Its Destroyers*, Warren Zimmerman, the last ambassador to the country, describes Milošević as a political opportunist rather than an authentic nationalist.[54]

When viewed two decades later, the ending of *Pretty Village, Pretty Flame* is prophetic compared with other nineties films about Bosnia. Echoing the opening, Dragojević concludes with another mock newsreel, a flash-forward to 1999. As the narrator explains, the "Brotherhood-Unity Tunnel" has been renamed the "Tunnel of Peace" and rebuilt according to European and world standards. Repeating the conclusion of the opening mock newsreel, the final shot of the film is of a politician slicing his thumb during the ribbon cutting. A new cycle of conflict begins. In other words, the conclusion of *Pretty Village, Pretty Flame* prognosticates the disintegration of Yugoslavia as the disintegration of Europe itself. The first mock newsreel about the "Brotherhood-Unity Tunnel" satirizes Yugoslav communist propaganda and its claims of social progress—progress that quickly devolves once the economy deteriorates. As the film shows, a decade after the opening ceremony for the tunnel in the seventies, it has already fallen into ruin. Another decade of austerity measures during the eighties will push Yugoslavia toward civil war. This is where the parallels with the "Tunnel of Peace" imagined in the closing mock newsreel become apparent. The EU's motto, "United in diversity," echoes the old Yugoslav communist motto of "Brotherhood and unity." In both cases, unity lasts only as long as financial debt is sustainable. Once the ogre of austerity is unleashed to appease global markets, social disintegration, nationalism, and xenophobia are normalized. To counter these logics of austerity, we need a political modernism that imagines an alternative to the malaise produced by capitalist realism.

3 · SLOW CINEMA AND THE ESCAPE FROM CAPITALIST REALISM

I. THE MATERIALITY OF CINEMATIC TIME FROM ANDREI TARKOVSKY TO BÉLA TARR

Slow Cinema and the Legacy of Andrei Tarkovksy

Two developments in Eastern European and Balkan art cinema in the twenty-first century are significant for discourses of political modernism and representing the new geopolitics of Europe. The first is the emergence of the Romanian New Wave in the middle of the decade. With Cristi Puiu winning the Golden Bear at the Berlin Film Festival for his 2004 short, *Cigarettes and Coffee,* and the Un Certain Regard at Cannes for his 2005 feature, *The Death of Mr. Lazarescu,* Romanian art cinema entered an era of international critical recognition and wide distribution. Many of these Romanian New Wave films embrace Puiu's long-take style. For example, *4 Months, 3 Weeks and 2 Days* (2007) became the first Romanian film to win the Palme d'Or at Cannes and the first to be nominated for a Golden Globe. Other works, such as *Police, Adjective* (2009), *Tuesday after Christmas* (2010), and *Beyond the Hills* (2012), also achieved global recognition. The second development is the ascendancy of Hungarian director Béla Tarr into the canon of global art cinema auteurs. Though he began his career in Hungary working within the conventions of socialist realism during the late seventies, Tarr's films became increasingly stylized as he incorporated deliberate artifice—such as chiaroscuro lighting, shooting on black-and-white film stock, and formalist camera angles—into his long takes. After the release of his seven-hour *Satantango* (1994), he became a cult figure. He achieved wider recognition with his subsequent films. By the time of his final feature to date, *The Turin Horse* (2011), retrospectives of his career were common and his filmography was readily available on home video.

This chapter focuses on how Tarr and Puiu uniquely synthesize codes of cinematic realism and modernism. It is important to distinguish them from the earlier generation of modernists such as Dušan Makavejev, Věra Chytilová, and Jan Švankmajer, who returned to directing explicitly political films in the nineties. As chapter 2 explains, freed from the shackles of state censorship, these directors embraced earlier strategies of intellectual montage in order to critique the transition to free-market capitalism. This transition entered a new phase in 2004, which marked the largest single-year expansion of the EU, with ten member states joining the union, seven of which were from the former Eastern bloc and the Soviet Union.[1] As such, their formal integration into Europe necessitated a different political modernist style, one that could envision an escape from capitalist realism, which was complicated in the regions because of their communist past. This chapter argues that the durational aesthetics of Tarr and Puiu represent two modes of reconciling with the communist past while overcoming the problem of capitalist realism.

By politicizing their styles, my aim also is to complicate recent discourse about slow cinema, which is how critics categorize Tarr and Puiu. The term *slow cinema* became popular in 2010 when critics Jonathan Romney and Nick James described it as a subgenre of art cinema that privileges mood over narrative and that has become the default style on the international film festival circuit to distinguish itself from Hollywood.[2] For both critics, *slow* is not inherently negative, though it is meant as a description of how art cinema can develop its own set of stylistic clichés and mannerisms. It does, however, become a term of derision in the 2011 *New York Times Magazine* article by American critic Dan Kois titled "Eating Your Cultural Vegetables." In the controversial piece, Kois confesses to struggling with "slow films" such as Kelly Reichardt's *Meek's Cutoff* (2010). He explains,

> As a viewer whose default mode of interaction with images has consisted, for as long as I can remember, of intense, rapid-fire decoding of text, subtext, metatext and hypertext, I've long had a queasy fascination with slow-moving, meditative drama. Those are the kinds of films dearly loved by the writers, thinkers and friends I most respect, so I, too, seek them out; I usually doze lightly

through them; and I often feel moved, if sleepy, afterward. But am I actually moved? Or am I responding to the rhythms of emotionally affecting cinema? Am I laughing because I get the jokes or because I know what jokes sound like?[3]

As this passage suggests, Kois's article has a self-deprecating tone about his own "aspirational viewing" and his inability to enjoy "slow" movies. The problem, however, is that he also implies that spectators claiming to appreciate such films are guilty of performing their enjoyment in order to arbitrate cultural taste. Kois tells a story about how, as a college student, he lied to a friend about enjoying Andrei Tarkovsky's *Solaris* even though he had fallen asleep during it. The implication is that while slow-cinema fans feel culturally obligated to appreciate such movies, Kois at least honestly admits his limitations. He writes, for example, "I feel guilty to be still reaching, as an adult, for culture that remains stubbornly above my grasp. My guilt isn't unique, even if my particular aspirational viewing is my own. (Surely there are die-hard Hou Hsiao-hsien fans out there who grit their teeth every time a new Pixar movie comes out.)"[4] Despite his confessions of guilt, critics and cinephiles were justifiably angered by his suggestion that they were enjoying slow cinema in bad faith. The *New York Times* ran two responses to his article by film critics Manohla Dargis and A. O. Scott, "In Defense of the Slow and Boring"[5] and "Sometimes a Vegetable Is Just a Vegetable,"[6] the latter a roundtable that included Kois. There were numerous other responses by bloggers and critics.

The debate between film critics and cinephiles in response to Kois's article unfolded in predictable patterns, with accusations of philistinism. Academics have adapted the term to understand recent aesthetic trends in art cinema, with monographs and essay collections published in recent years. In particular, there is a critical tendency to defend slow cinema as an aesthetic challenge to the fastness of global capitalism. In *Slow Movies: Countering the Cinema of Action*, Ira Jaffe, who describes his book as an analysis of the "elements besides plot that make certain movies both slow and compelling," contextualizes slow cinema in relation to other "slow movements," such as "slow gardening," "slow food," and even "slow sex." He notes that, "if advocates of slowness lean in a political direction, it is probably to the left, given their critiques of globalisation and capitalism as well as of haste."[7] Similarly, in the introduction to their collection *Slow Cinema*, editors Tiago de Luca and Nuno Barradas Jorge expand on the relationship between slow aesthetics and the speed of global capitalism. They acknowledge that "if, however, reaction to an increasingly fast world and cinema alike may provide some points of entry for ruminations on the ideological underpinnings of contemporary slow cinema, such underpinnings still fail to explain the material and institutional conditions that make such a cinema de facto possible." In other words, their collection situates "contemporary slow cinema" within a complex network of discourses that include globalization, digitalization, and film festival culture. Ultimately they describe the politics of slow cinema as "a mode of engagement with images and sounds whereby slow time becomes a vehicle for introspection, reflection and thinking, and the world is disclosed in its complexity, richness and mystery."[8]

Not all critics accept the notion that the politics of slow cinema invite spectators to reflect on the complexity of the world and challenge the pace of global capitalism. The virtues identified by Jaffe, de Luca, and Barradas are seen by some critics as politically regressive. For example, Steven Shaviro, author of *Post-Cinematic Affect,* which analyzes postcontinuity cinema and digital media, argues in a blog post that

> it's very consoling and self-congratulatory for old-line cinephiles (a group in which I fully include myself) to tell ourselves the story that the current cultural landscape's insistence on rapidity and speed and instantaneous gratification is a monstrous aberration, and that we are maintaining truer values when we strive to slow everything down. But this is a lie. You cannot change a situation if you are unwilling to have anything to do with it, if you are so concerned with keeping your hands clean and avoiding complicity that you simply retreat into fantasies of the good old days. To my mind, this is what slow cinema is doing.[9]

If what unites slow cinema is its aim to flee from the rapidity of global capitalism through a more authentically slow experience, then regressive nostalgia is indeed ingrained in its mode of aesthetics. This is the inherent flaw with the concept. While critics like Nick James are correct that a style that privileges slowness as an aesthetic virtue exists on the international film festival circuit, it is a simplification to categorize works from across the globe as slow solely because of their rejection of the rapidity of Hollywood style. Doing so erases important geopolitical distinctions and repeats the limitations of the theory of counter-cinema articulated by Peter Wollen, which privileges Western European art cinema conventions. In other words, the concept of slow cinema obscures a diverse range of political and aesthetic discourses that do not position Hollywood as a master signifier to be rejected. To be sure, de Luca and Barradas acknowledge this limitation in the introduction to their collection with its subtitle, "From Slow Cinema to Slow Cinemas." In the case of Tarr and Puiu, one cannot understand how their styles imagine an escape from capitalist realism without also understanding their attempts to work through the historical legacy of communism, which motivate their films more than their rejection of Hollywood style.

This critical tendency to group together films that are slow by Hollywood standards does not begin with the discourse about slow cinema. In his book *Figures Traced in Light: On Cinematic Staging,* David Bordwell argues that film theory has long undertheorized cinematic staging. The reason is straightforward. He explains, "As film journalism developed in the 1910s and 1920s, many of the best writers sought to prove cinema was a distinct art, owing nothing of consequence to theater. Film staging seemed 'theatrical,' whereas the emerging technique of editing seemed 'purely cinematic.' . . . To this day critics praise a virtuoso piece of editing while remaining oblivious to far more subtle and powerful passages of staging. Some film theorists call cutting 'invisible,' but for both ordinary moviegoers and film experts, cinematic staging remains a truly imperceptible art."[10] In other words, Bordwell claims that editing, more so than staging, is considered to be the essence of cinema. However, he overstates his case regarding the absence of theories of staging or mise-en-scène. Realist film theorists from André Bazin to Siegfried Kracauer have explored these questions. Moreover, Gilles Deleuze's books on cinema and Tarkovsky's *Sculpting in Time* are frequently cited. Tarkovsky, in particular, is important for understanding the political implications of Tarr and Puiu and their long-take style. The passage in *Sculpting in Time* that best defines his aesthetic is when he explains that he rejects "the principles of 'montage cinema' because they do not allow the film to continue beyond the edges of the screen: they do not allow the audience to bring personal experience to bear on what is in front of them on film."[11] Traces of this idea can be found subsequently in Iranian director Abbas Kiarostami's description of his work as "unfinished cinema."[12] It also prefigures Tarr's belief that cinema should follow the "logic of life" rather than tell stories and Puiu's belief that "life is more important than cinema."[13]

It should be emphasized that in rejecting "montage cinema," Tarkovsky critiques Sergei Eisenstein and not Hollywood. He claims that Eisensteinian montage results in intellectual formalism because "the construction of the image becomes an end in itself."[14] The iconic Alexander Kerensky sequence in *October* (1927) is one example. This charge of formalism is ironic considering that both directors would run afoul of the Soviet state for diverging from the dogmas of socialist realism. Tarkovsky, however, is not a proponent of realism in cinema, at least not in the sense defined by the dogmas of socialist realism or the version György Lukács presents in his writings when he critiques German expressionism for its "subjectivist war on reality and all its works."[15] In *Sculpting in Time,* Tarkovsky argues for a synthesis between modernism and realism. For him, the fundamental distinction in cinema is between a style that sculpts time impressionistically to invite subjective spectatorship and a style that creates an intellectual experience through montage that forces authorial intent on spectators. Yet the uniqueness of this first kind of cinema, according to him, is that it also necessarily establishes an external reality for spectators when it sculpts time impressionistically. In a key passage of *Sculpting in Time,* he writes,

> If one compares cinema with such time-based arts as, say, ballet or music, cinema stands out as giving time visible, real form. Once recorded on film, the phenomenon is there, given and immutable, even when the time is intensely subjective.
>
> Artists are divided into those who create their own inner world, and those who recreate reality. I undoubtedly belong to the first but that actually alters nothing: my inner world may be of interest to some, others will be left cold or even irritated by it; the point is that the inner world created by cinematic means always has to be taken as reality, as it were objectively established in the immediacy of the recorded moment.
>
> A piece of music can be played in different ways, and can therefore last for varying lengths of time. Here time is simply a condition of certain causes and effects set out in a given order; it has an abstract, philosophical character. Cinema on the other hand is able to record time in outward and visible signs, recognisable to the feelings. And so time becomes the very foundation of cinema: as sound is in music, colour in painting, character in drama.[16]

As this passage suggests, cinematic time for Tarkovsky is inherently dialectical. By re-creating the rhythm of an "inner world," cinema also establishes an objective reality because it represents the "outward and visible" signs of the recorded moment. As he says, "The point is that the inner world created by cinematic means always has to be taken as reality." This is the defining aspect of Tarkovsky's aesthetic. Images of the four elements reoccur in his films to mark the passage of time. These images frequently blend with the interior time and mental images of the characters—their dreams, memories, and fantasies—obliterating the boundaries between the two realms. Consider, for example, the final image of *Nostalghia,* which tells the story of Andrei, a Russian writer in poor health, who is in Italy to research an eighteenth-century composer. He is homesick and is alienated by the beautiful Tuscany countryside. In the final shot, the deceased Andrei sits in front of his Russian home, which we see throughout the film during his dreams and fantasies but is now shown inside the Abbey of San Galgano in Italy. Thus, this image blends Andrei's interior life—his nostalgia for home—with the reality of his death in Italy. During these moments of Tarkovskian synthesis, the spectators experience time subjectively because the images invite them to project their emotions onto the screen and identify with the inner life of the characters. And yet, time is relentlessly externalized as the elements of nature frequently overtake the mise-en-scène. Thus, at the end of *Nostalghia,* the ruins of the abbey overtake Andrei's home as the camera keeps pulling back. This recalls the conclusion of his adaptation of *Solaris* (1972), where we see that Kelvin's homecoming is re-created on an island on the planet Solaris. Similarly, in the lengthy long take at the end of *The Sacrifice* (1986), images of fire, land, and water dwarf Alexander, who has burned his house down.

This synthesis of interior, mental time and external time is why Tarkovsky's style is frequently described as mystical by critics. While it is accurate to say that his films embrace the mystical elements of Eastern Orthodoxy, such a description obscures the political implications of his work. Consider, for example, Fredric Jameson's analysis in *The Geopolitical Aesthetic: Cinema and Space in the World System,* where he writes, "The deepest contradiction in Tarkovsky is then that offered by a valorization of nature without human technology achieved by the highest technology of the photographic apparatus itself. No reflexivity acknowledges this second hidden presence, thus threatening to transform Tarkovskian nature-mysticism into the sheerest ideology."[17] Given the passages quoted earlier from *Sculpting in Time,* Jameson misinterprets Tarkovsky by claiming he lacks self-reflexivity about cinema or technology. Similarly, he simplifies the political implications of Tarkovsky's aesthetics. According to Jameson, Tarkovsky's mysticism amounts to "sheerest ideology," implying that he is an aesthete disinterested in ideological critique. But this too is incorrect. In several passages in *Sculpting in Time,* Tarkovsky critiques capitalist modernity. For example, discussing his motivations for his final film, *The Sacrifice,* Tarkovsky explains,

> And the more clearly I discerned the stamp of materialism on the face of our planet . . . the more committed I felt to this film as the most important thing in my life. It seems to me that the individual stands today at a crossroads, faced with the choice of whether to pursue the existence of a blind consumer, subject to the implacable march of new technology and the endless multiplication of material goods, or whether to seek out a way that will lead to spiritual responsibility, which ultimately might mean not only his personal salvation but also the saving of society at large: in other words, to turn to God. He has to solve this dilemma for himself, for only he can discover his own sane spiritual life.[18]

For Tarkovsky, consumer capitalism and technological progress are at the root of the spiritual malaise of modern life. While his antidotes, art and religious devotion, may seem politically inadequate for Marxists, Tarkovsky does provide the aesthetic framework for the ideological critique that Tarr and Puiu employ in their films. They develop his cinematic language to represent the post-communist era, when "the stamp of materialism" has colonized the planet and the free market has encompassed all aspects of life. As Slavoj Žižek explains, Tarkovksy's innovation is that he invokes the "material spectrality of capital" while advancing a spirituality that "simultaneously involves the return to the heavy material inertia of the earth."[19] Thus, the contradiction in Tarkovsky's aesthetic is not, as Jameson misinterprets, returning to nature without recognizing how technology mediates it. Rather, it is that we can escape the spiritual malaise produced by capitalist realism by embracing the "heavy material inertia of the earth" and the existential weight of time on it. This also explains why Tarr can develop Tarkovsky's aesthetic without advancing his religious mysticism. As Jonathan Rosenbaum writes in his review of *Satantango,* the film's style suggests a "despiritualized Andrei Tarkovsky."[20] In other words, though they do not share religious beliefs, Tarr nevertheless intensifies the materialism that, according to Žižek, is the core of Tarkovsky's political aesthetic.

Béla Tarr: Capitalist Realism and the Apocalypse

Though Tarr's late films emphasize the elements of nature, in interviews he has denied that his style is influenced by Tarkovsky. When asked about

Rosenbaum's description of his work as "despiritualized Tarkovsky," Tarr responded that the difference is that Tarkovsky was religious whereas he and his collaborator and editor, Ágnes Hranitzky, are not.[21] Despite his professed secularism, his films since *Damnation* (1988) are overloaded with apocalyptic imagery and themes. As several film critics have noted, his final film before retiring, *The Turin Horse,* is structured as a reverse Genesis story, its minimalist narrative spanning the last six days of the end of the world. Like Věra Chytilová, Tarr is often a difficult interviewee and disengages when pressed about the intentionality behind his work. He has denied that his films are apocalyptic or that they contain a bleak world view. Instead of *bleak,* Tarr often employs the phrase "the logic of life" to describe his work. In denying that there is such a thing as the apocalypse, he distinguishes himself from Tarkovsky. In Tarkovsky's final film, *The Sacrifice,* the apocalypse is circumvented through faith and personal sacrifice, but for Tarr the world ends with a "whimper" because time inevitably exhausts the energies of life. There is no transcendence. Though Tarr presents himself as a depoliticized existentialist in interviews, there are clear sociopolitical elements to his vision. Indeed, his late films are populated with false prophets of capitalism who promise an escape from the misery of the present. Consider the mysterious Prince character in *Werckmeister Harmonies* (2000), who incites the men of the town to riot and destroy a hospital as an antidote to the meaninglessness of life. Similarly, film noir plots about money are common. This is the case with *Damnation,* whose story of smuggling intertwines with a love triangle. In *Satantango,* the residents of a dilapidated collective farm are defrauded by Irimiás, another false prophet, who promises to build a new utopian community. Similarly, in *The Man from London* (2007), a railroad worker is devastated by guilt when he finds a suitcase of money from a crime he witnessed. In these films, the promise of money unravels the already perilous social order of the present. Yet, in contrast to this unrelenting gloominess about history, Tarr's haptic visual style conveys the necessity of preserving human dignity during the collapse of social order. This tension between pessimism and humanism is the defining aspect of his late work.

Through this tension, Tarr's late films subvert the problem of capitalist realism and its fetishization of apocalyptic imagery. By way of comparison, consider the numerous apocalyptic superhero blockbusters released in the twenty-first century, which privilege special effects and spectacle. For example, in *Avengers: Infinity War* (2018) and *Avengers: Endgame* (2019), billions of people die. This growth of apocalyptic blockbusters is a symptom of our anxieties about capitalism. In his speech to the Occupy Wall Street movement in 2011, Žižek explains this connection as follows: "Look at the movies that we see all the time. It's easy to imagine the end of the world. An asteroid destroying all life and so on. But you cannot imagine the end of capitalism."[22] According to Mark Fisher, the reason why we cannot imagine the end of capitalism is that the belief in the end of history has become part of the cultural unconscious in the West. In his book *Capitalist Realism: Is There No Alternative?*, he explains, "This malaise, the feeling that there is nothing new, is itself nothing new of course. We find ourselves at the notorious 'end of history' trumpeted by Francis Fukuyama after the fall of the Berlin Wall. Fukuyama's thesis that history has climaxed with liberal capitalism may have been widely derided, but it is accepted, even assumed, at the level of the cultural unconscious."[23] According to Fisher, this cultural unconscious means that popular genres like science fiction can only express malaise rather than imagine alternatives to capitalism. He highlights *Children of Men* (2006) as an example, claiming that "the world that it projects seems more like an extrapolation or exacerbation of ours than an alternative to it."[24] This insight suggests the paranoid interpretation that the numerous apocalyptic blockbusters of recent years are intentional affirmations of the neoliberal principle that life can only be organized according to the market. This is how Hollywood and its culture industry function in the twenty-first century. Rather than selling products, they market apocalyptic imagery to promote the idea that there can be no alternative to capitalism at the end of history.

In contrast to such spectacle blockbusters, Tarr's late films reject capitalist realism. In them, progress is advocated by false prophets who advance the destruction of the present for a capitalist utopia of the future. In other words, his late films reject belief in historical progress, a foundational myth of Western modernity. Though this disavowal of progress suggests that Tarr's films are nihilistic, the tension in his films since *Damnation* is that they also express a straightforward message about maintaining human dignity after the failure of the communist past and the false promises of the capitalist future.

Against Stories and Progress

Tarr's rejection of progress is tied to his belief that films should follow "the logic of life." Though he generally resists explaining his work, in the brief artistic statement he wrote during the production of *Damnation* called "Why I Make Movies," he does define the intentionality behind his aesthetic: "I despise stories, as they mislead people into believing that something has happened. In fact, nothing really happens as we flee from one condition to another. Because today there are only states of being—all stories become obsolete and clichéd, and have resolved themselves. All that remains is time. This is probably the only thing that's still genuine—time itself: the years, days, hours, minutes and seconds."[25] Scholars and critics of Tarr frequently cite but misunderstand this passage in an attempt to contextualize his work historically. For example, in *Slow Movies: Countering the Cinema of Action*, Jaffe interprets this passage as follows: "Tarr's remark about time's importance privileges no one interval, not even that in which we await death. Instead, he regards time as a singular continuum more genuine than any specific action or condition."[26] Jaffe's analysis is difficult to reconcile with the actual narrative structure of *Satantango*, whose circularity does privilege and repeat concrete intervals and instants of time. It is more accurate to say that in his late films Tarr, like Tarkovsky, synthesizes realist and modernist forms of cinematic duration to convey the materiality of time.

Tarr's rejection of stories echoes Bazin's famous praise of *Umberto D* (1952), in which he explains Vittorio De Sica's aesthetic breakthrough: "The narrative unit is not the episode, the event, the sudden turn of events, or the character of its protagonists; it is the succession of concrete instants of life, no one of which can be said to be more important than another, for their ontological equality destroys drama at its very basis."[27] By way of example, Bazin praises the extended sequence where Maria the Maid wakes up and makes coffee in the kitchen. Tarr's first two features, *The Family Nest* (1979) and *The Outsider* (1981), operate in a similar mode. Their vérité style closely follows the everyday lives of characters who struggle with economic and personal circumstances. In the former, a family struggles with internal conflicts exacerbated by the failures of communist housing policies. The latter follows the life of András, whose musical talent is wasted within the confines of his working-class existence. The "instants of life" in these films are staged primarily through long takes that structure the drama as opposed to a conventional story arc that is imposed on the material.

Beginning with *The Prefab People* (1981), Tarr diverges from this neorealist conception of "instants of life." Narrative time and concrete instants become recursive as Tarr tries to represent the hollowing out of daily life by the menacing totality of progress—or "cosmic" perspective, as he has repeatedly described in interviews. In his excellent monograph *Béla Tarr, the Time After,* French philosopher Jacques Rancière explains this shift that emerges in Tarr's work with *The Prefab People.* He writes, "The unfolding of the narrative already points to the great distance between official planning—of production and of conducts—and the reality of lived time, the expectations, aspirations, and disenchantments of the men and women of the young generation. The tension between these two temporalities does not only indicate the break [*l'écart*] with the official vision of the present and the future that the young Béla Tarr would allow himself."[28] As Rancière argues, there are "two temporalities" present in the film: the bureaucratic time of communism—of rational progress, planning, and economic distribution—which conflicts with the "lived time" of the characters and their desires. However, *The Prefab People* does not merely expose the disjunction between communist propaganda and social reality like Tarr's first two films. Its circular plot and its elliptical narrative also invite an abstract reflection on time itself and how cinema represents it. In short, this is where Tarr begins his criticism of the idea of progress. The shift from neorealist narrative duration to an abstract meditation on time emerges during the opening of *The Prefab People.* The credit sequence begins with a circular camera movement, in close-up, of a brass band performing in the streets in front of apartments. Quick edits to static shots of people looking out their windows at the band eventually reveal the family whose story the film tells. Tarr then cuts to a circular shot of a bird flying above the apartments. The visual rhythm here spatializes time recursively: we move progressively from ground to sky but also laterally in a circular manner. This is the formalist tension the remainder of the film's narrative explores as it dramatizes the irreconcilable conflict between the official teleology of communism and the repetitions of daily life. For example, in the first scene following the credits, Tarr places the audience in the middle of an argument in which the husband, Robi, packs his belongings to leave while his wife, Judit, tries to stop him. It is a four-minute take that resembles the docudrama style of *Family Nest* or *The Outsider.* However, Tarr breaks his long-take rhythm with a sudden transition from a close-up of Judit crying after Robi leaves to a medium shot of him grabbing bottles of liquor from the cabinet as they have drinks in their apartment for their nine-year anniversary. The interval between the two moments is indeterminate, as are those between most scenes in the film, which give no clear sense of how much time has passed. Scenes abruptly end and then begin anew.

Later we learn that Robi has been offered the opportunity to work abroad in Romania for two years, which would double his salary. Trying to convince the reluctant Judit, he promises that they will have a car within a year and a house possibly by the second year. His vision of consumerist progress is unconvincing and echoes the earlier, satirical scene where he and his oldest son are watching a roundtable discussion on television about communism. Robi tries to explain to him the historical progress from primitive society, to feudalism and capitalism, and ultimately to socialism and communism. Yet he is unable to articulate the differences between socialism and communism, defining the latter as follows: "With communism, everyone will get everything they need,"[29] which is a blunt simplification of Marx's "From each according to his ability, to each according to his need." Robi, apparently, needs a new car and, as shown at the end of the film, a new washing machine. However, Judit is not swayed by his promise of new consumer goods and tells him to reject the offer to work abroad because she does not want to be left alone.

After showing a failed attempt at sex in their bedroom, Tarr returns to a variation of the earlier scene where Robi leaves. It appears he has decided to take the job abroad, which is why he is leaving. And yet, it is easy to miss on first viewing that this is not the same scene. On close comparison, it is a different take, runs longer, and contains variations in dialogue. This raises the question, Has Robi left and returned multiple times? Tarr provides no narrative answers and creates more temporal gaps by cutting to a shot of the couple in a small department store purchasing a washing machine after the repeated scene of the separation. It is not clear whether he is on vacation from working abroad or whether two years have passed. His dream of progress, to make more money to purchase consumer goods, only reinforces the circularity of their condition. The final shot is a three-minute take of the couple on the back of a truck with their new washing machine. They sit silently, looking unhappy, as the credits roll. There is nothing to suggest that their new purchase will improve their existential condition.

Following *The Prefab People,* Tarr stages the tension between the recursive nature of everyday life and the linear, abstract time of progress with increasingly complex trajectories. However, his next feature is the odd experiment *Almanac of Fall* (1984). It replicates the circularity found in *The*

Prefab People, beginning with a quote from Aleksandr Pushkin's 1830 poem about a demon leading one in circles. Stylistically, it diverges from Tarr's earlier vérité films or subsequent collaborations with screenwriter László Krasznahorkai, both of which explored the durations of the lived reality of their characters. Instead, its long takes, rigidly designed color scheme, and oblique and "impossible" camera angles, such as from underneath the floor, persistently convey a sense of artifice. If there ever were a Tarr film that should be called "bleak," then *Almanac of Fall* is it. It is set entirely in a large apartment where its plot of betrayals and shifting emotional bonds between the five characters unfolds in a circular manner. The two temporalities that Rancière articulates in his analysis of Tarr are nowhere to be found, which creates a lack of social reality as no externality or temporality outside the claustrophobic apartment registers in the film. Yet the introduction of deliberate artifice is significant since it foreshadows Tarr's post-communist work, which seeks to create a humanist cinema that rejects the myth of progress.

Tarr's aesthetic imagines a humanism that is antiprogress and against stories. His work rejects the idea that rationality can advance human progress, which is a central Enlightenment ideal. This explains the critical tendency to draw comparisons among Tarr, Krasznahorkai's screenplays, and the philosophy of Friedrich Nietzsche. For example, as András Bálint Kovács explains in his article on *Satantango,*

> It seemed that Krasznahorkai provided the answers to Tarr's problem of the treatment of time. The answer was the Nietzschean eternal return. Monotonous repetition, and infinitely slow and ruthless seclusion can raise even the most earthly, most worn down, most extreme and most unique-seeming world from its concrete historical and social situation and create a whole world from it. So it became possible for Tarr to bring back his naturalistic world-portrayal, while standing on the borderline between artificiality and reality. This was the most important characteristic of the human world portrayed by him. Krasznahorkai saw in the world the same thing as Tarr did: endless destruction and misery disguised as redemption and elevation.[30]

Kovács's passage is an astute description of Tarr's late films, especially how they return to the naturalism of his early work while "standing on the borderline between artificiality and reality." Nevertheless, Tarr's circular narrative time in a film like *Satantango* does not resemble Nietzsche's eternal return. Depending on one's interpretation of Nietzsche, the eternal return is a cosmological description of the nature of the universe, an ethical perspective that celebrates fate and affirms existence, or some combination of both. While one can argue there is fatalism in the cinematic world of Tarr and Krasznahorkai, there is also a substantial divergence from Nietzsche. The eternal return is woven through Nietzsche's thought, including his rejection of pity and compassion, which is something Tarr and Krasznahorkai will critique in *The Turin Horse*. They instead present the audience with a vision that rejects social progress but affirms human dignity.

That may seem like an incoherent world view until one considers that both capitalism and communism depend on myths of social progress. For example, political philosopher John Gray has offered some of the most sustained critiques of the belief in progress in his books *Straw Dogs: Thoughts on Humans and Other Animals*, *Black Mass: Apocalyptic Religion and the Death of Utopia*, and *The Silence of Animals: On Progress and Other Modern Myths*. He is an eccentric thinker whose political leanings have mutated over the years, including a period in the eighties in which he supported Margaret Thatcher. In *Black Mass* he offers a grim explanation of why social progress is a myth. He writes,

> Believers in progress—whether social democrats or neo-conservatives, Marxists, anarchists or technocratic Positivists—think of ethics and politics as being like science, with each step forward enabling further advances in future. Improvement in society is cumulative, they believe, so that the elimination of one evil can be followed by the removal of others in an open-ended process. But human affairs show no sign of being additive in this way: what is gained can always be lost, sometimes—as with the return of torture as an accepted technique in war and government—in the blink of an eye. Human knowledge tends to increase, but humans do not become any more civilized as a result. They remain prone to every kind of barbarism, and while the growth of knowledge allows them to improve their material conditions, it also increases the savagery of their conflicts.[31]

Gray's criticism should not be misunderstood. He argues that scientific and technological advances do not translate into "additive" social progress. In other words, the utopian "new man" of communism and the "last man" of neoliberal capitalism that Fukuyama promised are historically impossible. We are no more "civilized" than our historical predecessors because we "remain prone" to regressing into barbarism once our material conditions decline, a barbarism whose social manifestations are intensified by our technological progress. Gray's rejection of additive social progress and the discourse of "becoming civilized" has drawn criticism from across the political spectrum. For example, in his review of Gray's *Straw Dogs*, Marxist scholar Terry Eagleton begins his criticism with this hostile assessment: "John Gray's political vision has been steadily darkening. Once a swashbuckling free-marketeer, he has, in his recent studies, become increasingly despondent about the state of the world. With the crankish, unbalanced *Straw Dogs*, he emerges as a full-blooded apocalyptic nihilist. He has passed from Thatcherite zest to virulent misanthropy."[32] For a Marxist like Eagleton, it may appear that the rejection of "additive" social progress makes one a "full-blooded apocalyptic nihilist." Yet this diagnosis of nihilism is misguided. It is a belief in additive progress that devolves into apocalyptic despair during prolonged economic crises that appear unresolvable. When one can only judge the present by how it must evolve into the future, a dystopian and apocalyptic imagination becomes inevitable. In other words, the rejection of social progress is not nihilistic if it is transformed into a precondition to escape the malaise of capitalist realism.

To understand this transformation, it is important to consider the implications of Tarr's rejection of stories and progress. In *Béla Tarr, the Time After*, Rancière offers a detailed interpretation. He explains that in Tarr's films,

> stories are stories of liars and dupes, because the stories are themselves lies. They lead us to believe something of what we have waited for has come to pass. The communist promise was only a variation of this much older lie. This is why it is pointless to believe the world will become reasonable if we keep harping on the crimes of the last liars, but also grotesque to insist that from now on we are living in a world without illusion. The time after is neither that of reason recovered, nor that of expected disaster. It is the time after all stories, the time when one takes direct interest in the sensible stuff in which these stories cleaved shortcuts between projected and accomplished ends.[33]

While Rancière references communism in this passage, the same promise has existed for free-market capitalism since the fall of the Berlin Wall. They are both stories about the end of history. In the former, the contradictions of capitalism give way to a new age when all needs will be met and labor exploitation will end. In the latter, markets and liberal democracy create free individuals unfettered by the totalitarianism of the past. Tarr's films ask audiences to reject such historicizing, to replace teleological politics with what Rancière calls the "time after," which is when all the elements of life, the total environment of the present, are prioritized over the false hopes of progress. As cynical as the stories of Tarr's films may seem in their rejection of additive social progress, his visual style does not convey a sense of resignation. His images and camera movements demand the audience have empathy and compassion for his damned characters, who maintain their dignity while their material conditions decline. The films that most clearly articulate this demand are his short *Prologue* from the omnibus *Visions of Europe* (2004) and *The Turin Horse.*

Compassion at the End of the World

After completing *The Turin Horse,* Tarr retired from directing.[34] For a few years he administrated a film program at the Sarajevo Film Academy that closed down in 2017. *The Turin Horse* seems to have been consciously designed as a final statement. In it, the aesthetic characteristics of his other post-communist collaborations with Krasznahorkai—stark black-and-white cinematography, harsh weather, and long takes—are further purified and the apocalyptic themes of the previous films are foregrounded. *The Turin Horse* has its origins in a Krasznahorkai's brief essay "At the Latest, in Turin," whose English-language translation can be found in the collection *The World Goes On.* In fact, both the opening voice-over in the film and the first paragraph of the essay reference the apocryphal story of Nietzsche's mental breakdown after witnessing the flogging of a horse:

> Well over a hundred years ago, in 1889, on a day like today in Turin, Friedrich Nietzsche steps out of the gate of the house at number 6, Via Carlo Alberto, perhaps to go for a walk, possibly to pick up his mail at the post office. Not far away, or by then all too far away from him, a hackney cab driver is having a difficult time with his—as they say—intractable horse. When after some goading the horse still refuses to budge, the driver—Giuseppe? Carlo? Ettore?—loses patience and starts to beat the animal with his whip. Nietzsche arrives at the crowd that has presumably gathered, and with this the cruel performance of the cab driver, doubtless frothing at the mouth with rage by now, ends; for the gentleman of gigantic stature with the bushy mustache—to the barely disguised amusement of the bystanders—unexpectedly leaps in front of the driver

> and sobbing, flings his arms around the horse's neck. Eventually Nietzsche's landlord takes him home, where for two days he lies motionless and mute on a sofa, until he utters the obligatory last words ("Mutter, ich bin dumm"), after which he lives on, a harmless madman, for ten more years, in the care of his mother and sister. We do not know what happened to the horse.[35]

In the film, the dryness of the voice-over conveys a sardonic tone. This is emphasized by the fact that though the narrator claims not to know the fate of the horse, Tarr cuts to a six-minute shot of a man, whose name we later learn is Ohlsdorfer, riding the horse home. The film contains no further explicit references to Nietzsche or his philosophy. This invites the question of why *The Turin Horse* begins with the apocryphal story of Nietzsche's descent into madness when the remainder of the film follows six days in the life of Ohlsdorfer and his daughter. One answer is suggested by Krasznahorkai's own interpretation of Nietzsche's collapse in his essay "At the Latest, in Turin," where he writes, "The demonic star of living philosophy, the dazzling opponent of so-called 'universal human truths,' the inimitable champion, the nearly breathless naysayer to pity, forgiveness, goodness, and compassion—hugging the neck of a beaten horse? To resort to an unforgivably vulgar but inevitable turn of phrase: why not hug the cab driver's neck?"[36] According to Krasznahorkai, the story of Nietzsche's collapse is the recognition of "a tragic error" whereby "after a lengthy and tormenting struggle, Nietzsche's very being said nay to a chain of thought in his own philosophy that was to be particularly infernal in its consequences."[37] While this is a reductive interpretation of Nietzsche's philosophy and its historical impact, Krasznahorkai is not alone in highlighting the irony in the story of his collapse. In *Straw Dogs*, for example, Gray writes, "It is ironic that Nietzsche's breakdown should have been triggered by the sight of an animal being cruelly treated. Against Schopenhauer, Nietzsche had often argued that the best people should cultivate a taste for cruelty." Gray further explains that in *The Birth of Tragedy*, Nietzsche argues "that pity—the supreme virtue according to Schopenhauer—should not be allowed to destroy the joy of life."[38] This critique of Nietzsche is important for understanding *The Turin Horse*. If Nietzsche's mental collapse was caused by an uncontrollable outburst of compassion despite his philosophy, which espouses the opposite, then *The Turin Horse* makes a similar demand on its spectators. As Rancière argues, the film is about "the capacity of the most mediocre beings to affirm their dignity."[39] Whether spectators themselves can affirm that character dignity is the ethical demand of Tarr's work, which, like Tarkovsky's and Kiarostami's, presents them with an "unfinished cinema" in which their experience of cinematic time is defined by their subjective response to the long takes onscreen.

The Turin Horse represents Tarr's most aesthetically refined version of this "unfinished cinema." After the introduction about Nietzsche's collapse, it follows six days in the life of Ohlsdorfer and his daughter. Despite the narrator claiming, "We do not know what happened to the horse," *The Turin Horse* is about what happened. After Ohlsdorfer rides the horse home, it refuses to work. Banal signs of the apocalypse begin to emerge. The woodworms stop eating at night and an unrelenting wind howls outside. The horse also stops eating, and soon Ohlsdorfer's well goes dry. In an extended sequence, he and his daughter try to leave their home but are unsuccessful. In this nearly nine-minute sequence, divided into two shots of almost equal length, we watch them prepare and pack to leave. As they struggle to traverse the bleak and windy landscape, they finally disappear into the distance past a single tree. After the camera lingers on the tree, they return without saying anything. It seems as if the world around them is literally disappearing. The oil lamps that provide the only light eventually stop working. The film ends in darkness while the father urges his daughter to eat what remains of their cold potatoes.

Tarr and his cinematographer, Fred Kelemen, visualize the daily routine of Ohlsdorfer and his daughter with complex camera movements and precise framings that spatially dissect their house and the barn from different angles. For example, in four sequence shots where the characters eat potatoes, Tarr and Kelemen emphasize a circular pattern around the kitchen table and their eating. The first shot begins with a close-up of the potatoes boiling. Eventually the camera follows the daughter as she enters from the left of the frame and places the potatoes in the middle of the table. She then wakes her father from his nap and the camera follows him to the table, settling in on a close-up of his hand and face for nearly two minutes as he tries to eat without burning himself. During the second shot, the camera trails Ohlsdorfer as he walks from the right of the frame to the table. As the daughter serves, the camera settles in on a medium close-up of her as she eats much slower than her father. The third and fourth shots mirror each other. They are frontal angles from opposite sides of the table. The rest of their routine is presented in a similar manner with slight variations of angles as they take turns staring out the window or as the camera follows the daughter as she goes outside to the well.

In one of the lengthiest takes in the film, a neighbor arrives to purchase some alcohol from them because he is unable to go into town. The shot begins with a close-up of the back of the head of the father, who has been staring out the window, as he turns to look at the door opening. After the neighbor asks to purchase alcohol and hands over an empty bottle, the camera temporarily follows the daughter as she fills it. Next, the camera slowly returns to the neighbor, stopping in close-up, as he talks with Ohlsdorfer, who asks why he did not go into town. The neighbor replies that "the wind's blown it away," cryptically adding, "It's gone to ruin." When the father asks why, the neighbor launches into a nearly five-minute monologue about human history and the elites who degrade the world. It reaches a crescendo with, "This is the way it was until the final victory. Until the triumphant end. . . . Even things we think they can't reach, but they do reach, are also theirs. The heavens are already theirs, and theirs are all our dreams. Theirs is the moment, nature, infinite silence. Even immortality is theirs, you understand? Everything, everything is lost forever!"[40] For a film with minimal dialogue, the neighbor's speech may seem entirely out of place. However, Tarr's late films often contain extended speeches. One can find similar moments in *Damnation* and *Werckmeister Harmonies*. The neighbor's philosophizing teases us with an explanation of events and may seem like a direct authorial statement to the audience from Tarr himself. After all, the neighbor discounts the possibility for human progress and claims history is a succession of misery. However, Ohlsdorfer's response to the lengthy rant is to curtly declare it "rubbish," to which the neighbor shrugs his shoulders and leaves. The camera moves up to the window and lingers on him as he walks up the hill, occasionally stopping to have a drink. Though the sequence shot ends anticlimatically, it does highlight a key theme of the film: whereas the neighbor constructs an elaborate philosophy with vague Nietzschean themes about fate and crafts a story to explain the apocalypse, Ohlsdorfer and his daughter can only helplessly experience it without any understanding. The same holds true for the audience. There is nothing in the remainder of the film that validates or negates the neighbor's explanation. We are given no evidence for the causes of events. As much as anything that happens in *The Turin Horse*, the horse's refusal to work can be interpreted as the trigger for the end of the world. Without any narrative explanations, we are left to ponder our affective response to the father and daughter. If spectators demand that the film advance a story or express a belief in progress, then *The Turin Horse* is a grim experience. However, if spectators can accept, to quote Rancière, "the capacity of the most mediocre beings to affirm their dignity," then Tarr's aesthetic can help us untangle the deadlock of capitalist realism.

Prologue to a New Europe

In their dialectical rejection of progress in order to affirm compassion and the temporality of lived reality, the late films of Tarr operate as the type of speculative cinema that Mark Fisher argues has disappeared, replaced by films that dispiritedly cannot imagine alternatives to capitalism. He observes that, "once, dystopian films and novels were exercises in such acts of imagination—the disasters they depicted acting as narrative pretext for the emergence of different ways of living."[41] This may seem like a counterintuitive reading since *The Turin Horse* is not science fiction and it does not project a futurity that allows us to alter the course of the present. Yet it untangles the deadlock of capitalist realism by demanding that affect and compassion ground us when confronted by the inevitable collapse of capitalist ideology and its social system. Tarr thus belongs to the European tradition of pessimism beginning with Arthur Schopenhauer, who advocates that we address each other as fellow sufferers, or the minimalism of Samuel Beckett, whose characters maintain their determination in the face of hopelessness. The crucial distinction is that Tarr offers more than an existential outlook for how to survive the meaninglessness of life. Despite what he contends in his interviews, the compassionate miserabilism of his late films offer more than an abstract meditation on the cosmic condition of humanity. They also present a geopolitical aesthetic. Such is the case with his 2004 short, *Prologue*. It is included in the omnibus *Visions of Europe*, which consists of twenty-five short films from the then member states of the EU. To understand the full impact of *Prologue*, however, it is important to contextualize briefly the ideological fantasy of Europe in 2004 before the era of austerity and financial crisis.

Coinciding with the 2004 expansion of the EU, it was common to read triumphalist narratives about post-communist Europe that argued that its integration placed it on a historical path to surpass American economic and political power. One example of this is the work of social theorist Jeremy Rifkin, author of multiple books and a consultant to many European member states. His hyperbolically titled *The European Dream: How Europe's Vision of the Future Is Quietly Eclipsing the American Dream* provides unique insight into the ideological fantasy about the EU and its legal architecture before the financial crisis. Rifkin argues that the "European Dream" is the antithesis to the decaying American Dream. He devotes considerable energy to contrasting the social and economic ills of America with the hopes represented by the EU. Ultimately, for him, the European Dream represents a new narrative of progress, a story of how European values of postnationalism and socialism blended with capitalism will design a better future. He explains in his introduction,

> The European Dream takes over where post-modernity trails off. Stripped to its bare essentials, the European Dream is an effort at creating a new historical frame that can both free the individual from the old yoke of Western ideology and, at the same time, connect the human race to a new shared story, clothed in the garb of universal human rights and the intrinsic rights of nature—what we call a global consciousness. It's a dream that takes us beyond modernity and post-modernity and into a global age. The European Dream, in short, creates a new history.[42]

It is clear that this has failed as prophecy. In light of the debt crisis, austerity, and rising xenophobia, Europe will not be creating a global consciousness anytime soon. Released in 2004 during this era of EU triumphalism, Tarr's *Prologue* expresses a different tone. A five-minute short, it consists of a single Steadicam shot with a score by Mihály Víg. *Prologue* fades in to a medium close-up of faces standing in front of a wall. They are waiting in line, and their facial expressions suggest their desperation. They are presumably the homeless and the hungry. The camera then moves laterally and leftward for nearly three minutes. The effect recalls Jean-Luc Godard's relentless tracking shots in *Weekend* (1967), where the shallow depth of field creates a flat image and a world without dimensionality. However, Tarr does not flatten the image for satirical purposes. He does so in order to intensify voyeurism. We can only see the faces and the longing of the people in line. Eventually the camera stops at a window, which a woman opens as she begins to pass out bread rolls and coffee. That is the entire short. No other story emerges. We witness only the conditions of hunger and desperation. While other shorts in *Visions of Europe* express some skepticism about the EU as imagined in 2004, the starkness of

Prologue is distinct. It foreshadows the austerity politics that will take hold. The film encapsulates the political modernism of Tarr's cinema. Far from advocating nihilism, his rejection of progress and stories forms a negative dialectic that frees the future from teleology. In other words, in his last films, ideologies of progress, such as communism and free-market capitalism, which sacrifice the present for the future, are replaced with a radical immanence that demands that we have compassion for his characters, who cannot escape their present circumstances.

II. CRISTI PUIU BETWEEN SLOW CINEMA AND TRANSCENDENTAL STYLE

History, Realism, and Transcendental Style

Unlike Tarr's, Puiu's career belongs entirely in the post-communist era. He directed his first feature a decade after the Romanian revolution. Born in 1967, however, he was old enough for the collapse of communism to register as a formative historical experience whose aftershocks he would represent in his films. This uniquely positions Puiu within the discourses of political modernism of Eastern European cinema. The new waves of the fifties and sixties explored the dissonance between official communist ideology and its actually existing social structures. Directors such as Chytilová and Makavejev critiqued the system from feminist and Marxist perspectives. They were subversives who developed a political modernism to represent this dissonance. Constrained by state and market censorship during the seventies and the eighties, this subversive spirit was revitalized with their post-communist films, which were critical of the new Europe.

Puiu exhibited an aesthetic development similar to that of the aforementioned filmmakers. He began as a documentarian working in a critical realist mode who then developed a precise formalist style. As a post-communist filmmaker in his early twenties during the waning years of Romanian communism, his relationship to traditions of cinematic realism differed from those of the earlier modernists. This complicates an analysis of the political implications of his style. In particular, Puiu is skeptical of theories of cinematic realism. Given his associations with international slow cinema and his status at the forefront of the Romanian New Wave, this rejection is significant since his work is commonly described as realism. In an interview with Monica Filimon, he explains,

> There are critics who associate me with André Bazin. I heard of Bazin in school, and I read a few of his articles, but I never read What Is Cinema? in its entirety: I was not interested in it. I am a direct consequence of the communist system, of the fall of communism, of the University Square, and of everything that followed. I have had a direct, unmediated connection with History, with what it means, with the real, happening, history. And I reacted to it: I reacted to the lies. My cinema is not an intellectual pursuit. I never lived in an Ivory Tower; I went to The University Square and I screamed against communism until I got sore.[43]

Puiu's rejection of Bazin is simplistic. He associates him with the "Ivory Tower" and an "intellectual pursuit." Yet if we contextualize his comments within the political aftershocks of the Romanian revolution, then his opposition between history and realism is important for understanding the malaise of the post-communist condition. It is important to note the motivations for the University Square protests of 1990. The organization that seized control after overthrowing Nicolae Ceauşescu was the National Salvation Front. It acted as an interim government and was in control of the state media when it became a formal political party so it could run in the first elections in May 1990. This sparked a massive protest by students who demanded that the former communists who populated their party leadership be barred from running in elections. Despite this, the National Salvation Front, led by Ion Iliescu, won the first election in a landslide.

Puiu's belief that participating in the protests reflects an "unmediated connection" with history distinguishes his political modernism from Marxist orthodoxy, for which there can be no "unmediated" social relations. Labor, commodities, and capital mediate our relationship to society and history to varying degrees. The foundational Marxist philosophical texts of political modernism from the thirties analyzed in chapter 1 debate how history is mediated through aesthetic forms and whether modernist or realist aesthetics best represent historical totality. In contrast to this classical debate and its binary between realism and modernism, Puiu opposes realism and history. As he learned during the anti-communist protests in the University Square, narratives of history can no longer be trusted. Rather than offering realism, Puiu explains to Filimon that cinema must express this disillusionment with history because "it is impossible to recuperate—through words or images—what you have lived."[44] As Tarr does in his late films, Puiu positions spectators within the "time after," defined by Rancière as "the time after all stories, the time when one takes direct interest in the sensible stuff" of material reality because one no longer believes in historical progress. Unlike in Tarr's work, however, this "sensible stuff" is not the elements of nature, which convey the malaise of living in the "time after" history. Rather, in *The Death of Mr. Lazarescu* (2005), *Aurora* (2010), and *Sieranevada* (2016), the first three films of Puiu's intended series "Six Stories from the Outskirts of Bucharest," this historical malaise is expressed within domestic and institutional spaces. In *Aurora* and *Sieranevada,* for example, the camera dwells in hallways, observing characters through partially closed doors as they enter and exit rooms, often in long takes whose duration exceeds their narrative function. Thus, rather than staging a realist mise-en-scène, Puiu employs a style that is more accurately described as formalist and self-reflexive, as it calls attention to its own framing of shots. This formalism is how his films articulate post-communist malaise and attempt to transcend it. *Transcend* is the operative word here because Puiu's aesthetic goal, unlike Tarr's, is to invoke a spiritual dimension as an antidote to the post-communist condition. As Filimon argues, "His cinema seeks to inspire, in viewers, what he terms the 'ineffable,' or sense of the sacred dimension of the profane world."[45] He does so, I argue, by accentuating the dramatic and material absences of the narrative produced by the fixed camera. This aesthetic impulse originates in the fact that, to quote Dominique Nasta, Puiu was "initially trained as a painter who wanted to fill the frame with striking, albeit ordinary details."[46] As such, Puiu's aesthetic is a minimalist variation on Tarkovsky in which the roving camera externalizes time outward to establish a spiritual alternative to the material world.

Puiu's interest in conveying the spirituality of the mundane suggests that he is, despite his protestations, a realist in the vein of Bazin or Kracauer, who believed that cinema could redeem physical reality. However, his aesthetic more closely resembles a post-communist version of what Paul Schrader famously calls "transcendental style" than it does the neorealism of *Umberto D* that Bazin applauds and that is a foundational text for international slow cinema. In the introduction to his new edition of *Transcendental Style in Film,* "Rethinking Transcendental Style," Schrader argues, "Transcendental style is not slow cinema. It's one of several precursors to slow cinema. Bazin's neorealism was another. As were Antonioni's soulful meanderings. Transcendental style evolved as 'time-image.' Film-makers in different places and different traditions understood they could slow movies down to create a new reality, to explore memory, to beget contemplation, and in some rare cases simulate transcendence. Transcendental style as I described it forty-five years ago still exists, although it's as rare now as it was then."[47] For Schrader transcendental style is defined by its representation of the harshness of everyday reality, from which emerges a disparity in the form of a passionate commitment. This disparity ultimately reveals the transcendent within everyday life. According to him, the directors who best represent this style are Yasujirō Ozu, Robert Bresson, and Carl Dreyer. While "transcendental style is not slow cinema," as Schrader argues, the two modes intersect in multiple ways. He analyzes these intersections by examining the diverse range of film techniques found in both. Though he does not mention Puiu by name, he does reference the style of the Romanian New Wave. Of the twelve techniques that he highlights that "create a dissonance between time and narrative" within and between shots, Schrader's analysis of the "static frame" is most applicable to Puiu's films beginning with *The Death of Mr. Lazarescu*. He writes, "Static frame. A locked-off camera position is often employed in conjunction with the long take. . . . In *Ida,* (2013), Pawel Pawlikowski used a static 1:33 frame but composed for the lower half of the frame. Cristian Mungiu (*4 Months, 3 Weeks and 2 Days,* 2007), like a number of his fellow 'New Romanian' directors, pushed the action to the edges of a frozen frame, leaving the center vacant."[48] By emphasizing the many techniques by which directors disrupt the unity of time and narrative, Schrader establishes formal terminology for more nuanced readings of the ideological effects of slow cinema, which complicates the argument that slow cinema primarily offers "slow time" as a rejection of the rapidness of global capitalism and Hollywood. Such use of Schrader's ideas is counterintuitive considering that the primary limitation of *Transcendental Style in Film* is precisely its schematic approach to the ideological and cultural differences between Ozu, Bresson, and Dreyer. Ozu, for example, exemplifies "the transcendental style in the East," whereas Bresson exemplifies "the transcendental style in the West."[49] However, in invoking the idea of transcendental style as intersecting with slow cinema to characterize Puiu's work, my purpose is to explain how the aesthetic problem of countering post-communist malaise invites a spiritual discourse about cinematic form. To understand why, Puiu's artistic development must be situated within the context of Romania's transition into neoliberalism.

Romania Embraces Neoliberalism

From 1992 to 1996, Puiu attended art school in Geneva, where he first studied painting before switching to cinema. It was during these years that Romania transitioned into neoliberalism. In *Ruling Ideas: How Global Neoliberalism Goes Local*, economist Cornel Ban describes the process:

> Policy elites in postcommunist Romania embraced neoliberalism late, but when they did, most went all the way down, giving birth to a policy regime and economic system that leaves few tools to embed markets into progressive societal demands. Indeed, Romania's policy regime went from a synthesis of neoliberalism and the developmental state in the early 1990s to a neoliberalism with marked libertarian tendencies during the 2000s mainly because this is how the elites du jour understood the conventional economic wisdom of the day. Specifically, during the first half of the 1990s electoral outcomes brought to power political elites who had a large conflict-prone relationship with the advocates of neoliberal ideas and policies. This changed after 1996 when the levers of power went to the domestic advocates of various flavors of neoliberalism.[50]

Embedded in Ban's description of Romania's transition into neoliberalism is a historical irony. The University Square protest in 1990, which Puiu describes as formative to his artistic development, was driven by the belief that Ion Iliescu and his political party were former communists who were intent on hijacking the Romanian revolution. The unintentional side effect of this narrative is that neoliberalism came to be seen throughout the Eastern bloc as pragmatic anti-communist reform, with its privatization schemes dismantling the last vestiges of communist state power, rather than being seen as the ideological reshaping of society through market reforms. In the midst of the end-of-history euphoria of the nineties, this may have seemed like the necessary path for the future. Yet this belief in the pragmatism of neoliberalism as the only viable way to transcend the past and unify Europe has laid the groundwork for the anti-Europe right-wing populist backlash since the financial crash. A Europe unified primarily by the interests of private capital creates a public sphere of competition that exacerbates resentment during periods of austerity and low economic growth. The irony, then, is that in the case of Romania it is the ex-communists who tried to moderate against neoliberalism by offering what Ban describes as "a synthesis of neoliberalism and the developmental state in the early 1990s." But this synthesis was doomed to fail. In addition to the anti-communist sentiment that was common in the former Eastern bloc, Ban explains that "cooperation between Washington and Brussels generally had the effect of locking in a neoliberal policy regime in Romania so that, by the early 2000s, even the ex-communists folded and 'social Europe' could go only as far as the Third Way."[51] Thus, by the time Puiu finished film school in Geneva and returned to Romania, its economy had fully transformed.

Puiu's first film after returning to Romania is a documentary titled *July 13th–July 19th 1998, Craiova, the Retirement Home,* which he codirected with Andreea Păduraru, who received a grant for the project. As its title suggests, it takes place across six days in the retirement home. The documentary mixes modes and is roughly divided into two parts. The first part is expository and explains the daily operations of the home, while the second part is more participatory and includes interviews with the elderly inhabitants. There is also a coda about an invalid man washed by a nurse in his bed. This structure allows Păduraru and Puiu to encapsulate the history of Romania from its post–Second World War communism to its transition into neoliberalism during the present.

Accompanied by still images of the city of Craiova, the documentary begins with Păduraru's opening narration, which explains that the home for retirees and the chronically ill opened in 1976 and expanded in 1991. She also states that the facility has 475 patients and the monthly fee is the equivalent of thirty-seven dollars a month, which is deducted from the patients' pensions. After several scenes that detail operations at the retirement home, from doctor visits to the bread baked on site, the documentary returns to the question of pensions and fees. It is here where Păduraru and Puiu emphasize the deleterious effects of neoliberalism on formerly state-run institutions. We learn that July 17 is the day on which pensions are paid. Over a still image of retirees waiting in line, Păduraru's explains that sixty-eight patients receive no pension because the state pays their bill. She adds that the highest pension is sixty-eight dollars, while the average is forty-five dollars, and that the pensioners immediately pay their monthly bill. After relaying these facts, *The Retirement Home* follows the day of Mr. Nedelcu, one of the wealthier pensioners, who earns sixty-five dollars a month. Once he pays his monthly bill, he walks into town to buy some margarine and spices since presumably they are not provided by the retirement home. He also buys some chocolates in case his grandsons visit. Next, in one of the more depressing sequences in the film, Păduraru interviews him as he scratches two lottery tickets. It is here where the documentary conveys the human cost of Romania's full embrace of neoliberalism as described by Ban. Mr. Nedelcu describes his financial difficulties since the monthly fee for the home was raised in March from fifteen dollars to thirty-seven.

By following the daily routine of Mr. Nedelcu, *The Retirement Home* shifts away from its expository part about the daily operations of the home to its second part, where the inhabitants of the home are interviewed and tell their personal stories of the Second World War and life under the Ceauşescu regime. This allows Păduraru and Puiu to contrast the communist past with the ruinous neoliberal present. Two of the inhabitants tell stories about the dignity they felt about their work, and one man mentions how he was paid well, which implicitly contrasts with the pension-day routine of Mr. Nedelcu shown earlier in the documentary. There is one direct reference to the Ceauşescu regime. An elderly woman tells a story about how she worked for one of the county government councils, a position that required her to attend party meetings in Bucharest every few months. She explains how Elena Ceauşescu, Nicolae's wife, who held increasingly powerful administrative positions in the regime, would treat people poorly. The woman describes how she finally stood up for herself, quit her position, and confronted Elena, which frightened her and caused her to call for Nicolae, who diffused the situation. She even credibly mimics Nicolae's notorious crooked smile while narrating the encounter. She concludes her story by mentioning she eventually found another job.

The Retirement Home ends with a coda that prefigures Puiu's subsequent Bucharest stories. In her voice-over Păduraru informs us that it is the last day of filming at the home. In a stark visualization of human frailty and decay, we watch as a nurse washes an elderly invalid man in bed. This is a jarring conclusion to a documentary focused on the daily operations of the home and histories of the retirees. However, Puiu explains to Filimon that for him the "entire documentary is about this one moment at the end."[52] In particular, he describes the influence this scene had on *The Death of Mr. Lazarescu*, which introduced him to international audiences and situated him within the slow cinema movement. He states that while filming *The Death of Mr. Lazarescu*, he "showed Oleg Mutu [the cinematographer] and Ioan Fiscuteanu (Mr. Lazarescu) how the nurse washed the old man." He continues, "Fiscuteanu's wife, who played one of the nurses in *Mr. Lazarescu,* mimics the gestures of the nurse. I could have not invented that. Anyway, *The Retirement Home* was, in a sense, at the roots of this film."[53] In other words, Puiu's transcendental style emerges from the ending of *The Retirement Home,* where the inevitability of death is tempered by the nurse's humane gesture of washing the man without wearing gloves. This explains why his Bucharest films are all dramatically structured around death. Mr. Lazarescu's fate is inscribed in the very title of *The Death of Mr. Lazarescu.* In *Aurora,* Puiu himself portrays Viorel, a divorced, middle-aged man who murders his in-laws, while in *Sieranevada,* a family gathers in an apartment to commemorate their father's death. Within these stories of death, Puiu seeks moments of transcendence visible in everyday life.

From Neoliberalism to the Spirituality of Everyday Life

Once Puiu began directing feature films, it took a few years for him to develop his transcendental style as an alternative to post-communist malaise. His first feature, *Stuff and Dough* (2001), notably lacks the complex formalism of his Bucharest films. While it is critical of Romania's transformation to capitalism, it does not successfully invoke transcendence as a counterpoint. Like many post-communist films from the late nineties and the turn of the century, it relies on the figure of the patriarchal gangster to represent the new Europe, which limits its ability to understand how the transformation into market capitalism disrupts personal relationships. It tells the story of Ovidiu, an unemployed young man who lives with his parents, who operate a small store. One morning Mr. Marcel, the gangster in the film, arrives with an offer of employment. Ovidiu is to deliver medical supplies to Bucharest. After this inciting incident, *Stuff and Dough* hybridizes the road movie and the gangster film as the plot explores the chaos caused by Ovidiu's lapses in judgment, such as inviting his friend Vali and Bety, Vali's girlfriend, on the delivery. The film's realist handheld camera style is most compelling when Puiu restricts spectators to the claustrophobic space of the car, suggesting the detached perspective that he will fully explore in *Aurora* and *Sieranevada.*

In *Cigarettes and Coffee,* which won the prestigious Golden Bear award for shorts at the Berlin Film Festival in 2004, Puiu purifies the handheld style of *Stuff and Dough* into a rigorous formalism that observes the social codes of neoliberalism. The short has a minimalistic plot: an older man, Mr. Tomescu, meets a younger man, Vlad, in an upscale café to give him cigarettes and coffee. Puiu reveals that they are actually father and son, which is a shock considering the cold demeanor of the son. *Cigarettes and Coffee* begins with a long take, the camera positioned inside the café, observing the father as he first walks past the address before entering. He sits down with his son and the two have an uneasy conversation. We learn why the father has brought cigarettes and coffee: He has been laid off and needs to find two more years of work so he can retire with a full pension. The cigarettes and coffee are a bribe for the son's boss, who will fix the problem. The symbolism for audiences who lived under communist regimes is obvious. As rare luxury items, cigarettes and coffee were frequently used as bribes to help negotiate the regime's bureaucracy. Significantly, the father mistakenly purchases instant coffee since he does not know the difference. His son chastises him, explaining that now he will need to buy real coffee. The father, in other words, is not attuned to the new symbolic codes of power. In her brief analysis of the film, Alina Haliliuc explains,

> The "coffee and cigarettes" which Mr. Tomescu has brought are the inducement his son will use to try to secure the job. These objects, and the corresponding stock phrase captured by the film's title, reference a communist-era custom of "gifting" such "incentives" to a state employee so as to pave the way for a favor. Bribe was a function of an economic and political system in ruin, which survived on the back of a subterranean economy of informal exchanges. Today, the cigarettes and coffee have lost their value of rare black-market luxury items, but they still fulfill important social functions that have been codified under communism. . . .
>
> In a neoliberal society where the state shrunk its support even more than it had during the last years of communism, where people are left to rely on families to supplement their economic precarity (like Mr. Tomescu) or on carefully crafted interpersonal relations to bolster a volatile security (as in Vlad's case), knowing these codes is a vital skill.[54]

This is what elevates *Cigarettes and Coffee* above *Stuff and Dough* in its critique of neoliberalism. The gangster film genre tropes and the caricature of the "new Balkan gangster" found in it and several other Balkan films obscure the fact that neoliberalism replicates itself socially through "interpersonal relations" that "bolster a volatile security." Rather than the stereotypical gangster who criminally accumulates wealth, it is Vlad who symbolically expresses how neoliberalism upends social relations in post-communism. Though his father cannot discern the difference between instant and real coffee, he does observe that "nothing has changed. It's like the old times, with coffee and cigarettes." Vlad repeats what his father says, then pays the bill and gives him some money for his mother's medicine. This conclusion works as a retelling of the classic communist-era joke that the difference between capitalism and communism is that under capitalism man exploits man, while under communism it is the opposite, which aligns with Puiu's general skepticism about narratives of history. However, the gestures of the father and son suggest that there is an essential difference beyond the fact that one now bribes a private boss rather than an important Communist Party member. While the father is nervous, affable, and talkative, Vlad is aloof and transactional. Under the totalitarianism of communism, one could maintain an internal distance in opposition to the centralized power of the state and the party. The bribe of cigarettes and coffee under communism rejects the centralized system and redistributes commodities through a black-market economy that requires personal interactions not sanctioned by the state. Under the new neoliberal order, however, personal relations are transactional and privatized. Bribery can no longer function as a form of resistance against a centralized economy. Instant coffee may have sufficed as a bribe in the communist era; thus, Vlad's argument that he requires real coffee for his boss means that he understands the depersonalized nature of commodity fetishism, something his father cannot grasp. This explains Vlad's aloof affect and why he speaks in the same tone to his father and the waiter. He understands that survival in the new capitalist order depends on treating all human relations as transactional even when offering financial support to his ailing mother and finding a job for his father.

The Death of Mr. Lazarescu further develops the formalist aesthetic of *Cigarettes and Coffee* while returning to the spiritual component introduced at the end of *The Retirement Home*. It is the first feature of the Romanian New Wave to achieve success on the international festival circuit. It was loosely inspired by the real-life case of Constantin Nica, a fifty-two-year-old man who was dumped on a park bench after several hospitals refused to admit him. The film tells the story of Dante Remus Lazarescu, whose allegorically suggestive name hints at the circles of hell he is about to endure. He has a terrible headache and has been vomiting, so he calls an ambulance. While he waits for the ambulance and his neighbors assist him, we learn details about his life. Mr. Lazarescu is an alcoholic who lives alone with his three cats. He is sixty-two years old, a former engineer who is now retired. His wife died eight years ago and his daughter lives in Canada. His relationship with his sister, who lives far away, is fraught as he owes money to his brother-in-law. Eventually the ambulance arrives, but the last ninety minutes of the two-and-a-half-hour film are devoted to the paramedics trying to find a hospital that will admit Mr. Lazarescu because a major highway accident is creating chaos in hospital emergency rooms. Eventually, the increasingly incoherent and nonresponsive Mr. Lazarescu is diagnosed with a blood clot in his brain caused by falling in the tub while waiting for the ambulance. The CT scan also indicates he has inoperable liver cancer. As one doctor ironically observes, Mr. Lazarescu needs brain surgery so he can go home and die from cancer. The film ends with a nurse washing and shaving him in preparation for surgery.

Like *Cigarettes and Coffee*, *The Death of Mr. Lazarescu* is a film about navigating the social codes of an economy with a growing precariat class. Unlike Mr. Tomescu in the latter, Mr. Lazarescu lacks the familial support system to administer bribes successfully. The best he can offer is that his sister, arriving the next day, can compensate Mioara, the female paramedic. We see only one direct attempt at bribing, a minor character's attempt to bribe a doctor in the background of a scene, but this is nevertheless an important subtext to the film that audiences familiar with the communist-era health-care system would recognize. This practice of bribing doctors has continued in the post-communist era in Romania and is so widespread that it has been reported on in the international press. There are several reasons why. While Romania, as Ban argues, embraced neoliberalism in the early twenty-first century, its health-care system has remained largely public, though privatization has accelerated since Romania joined the EU, with the number of private hospitals doubling from 2011 to 2017.[55] Thus, Romanian health care combines the worst aspects of the communist system with the social relations produced by neoliberalism. This makes it the appropriate institutional setting for Puiu to dramatize his ideas about history and cinematic realism and to develop his aesthetic, which counters capitalist realism. A 2009 *New York Times* article describes the widespread practice of bribing doctors and its peculiar social codes. According to the article, "Some doctors say that the bribery culture is so endemic that when they refuse bribes, some patients become distraught and mistakenly conclude it is a sign that their illnesses are incurable. Doctors and patients say the bribery follows a set of unwritten rules. The cost of bribes depends on the treatment, ranging from $127 for a straightforward appendix-removal operation to up to more than $6,370 for brain surgery. The suggested bribery prices are passed on by word of mouth, and are publicized on blogs and Web sites."[56] While Romania has made efforts to change this culture of bribery, systemic problems remain. For example, doctors are poorly paid in comparison to the majority of EU nations, which has also contributed to a mass exodus of doctors from the country. European Commission data indicate that "Romania lost half its doctors between 2009 and 2015."[57] However, the phenomenon of patients who "become distraught and mistakenly conclude it is a sign that their illnesses are incurable" when their bribes are refused also suggests the more intractable problem of internalized ideology. Professional ethics register as the traumatic opposite: an honest doctor who refuses bribes creates anxiety over death because it is impossible to imagine honestly functioning social institutions. The irony, as Puiu's *Cigarettes and Coffee* explores, is that this internalized ideology of communist corruption is strengthened rather than dissolved under the transition to neoliberalism. As the father in that short says, "Nothing has changed. It's like the old times, with coffee and cigarettes." Yet the social codes have changed and have increased in complexity. This theme is evident in several Romanian New Wave films. For example, in Cristian Mungiu's 2016 film *Graduation,* Romeo is a doctor who expedites a liver transplant for an official in exchange for him fixing the results of his daughter's scholarship exams. Assaulted on her way to school, Eliza, his daughter, misses an exam and thus needs a very high score on the final one in order to be accepted to Cambridge University. The film explores the convoluted personal and social aftershocks of this quid pro quo. By the end, Romeo's principled self-image is systematically destroyed. Similarly, in the 2013 film *Child's Pose,* Cornelia is a wealthy, domineering mother who bullies and bribes officials in an attempt to save her son, who killed a poor child in a car accident.

While Puiu critiques Romania's transition into neoliberalism and its health-care system in *The Death of Mr. Lazarescu,* he also develops his transcendental style as a counterpoint. Here the material absence emphasized in the film is Mr. Lazarescu himself, who increasingly disappears from Puiu's frames. For example, we are first introduced to Mr. Lazarescu as he feeds his cats and experiences stomach pains. Oleg Mutu's cinematography centers him in the frame, following his actions with a handheld camera.

Mr. Lazarescu dominates the frame when he calls for an ambulance, tends to his varicose veins, and argues with his sister and brother-in-law on the telephone. Indeed, for its first fifteen minutes *The Death of Mr. Lazarescu* employs an aggressive docudrama style as we are introduced to Mr. Lazarescu's apartment and learn his backstory. Interestingly, the camera does not immediately follow Mr. Lazarescu outside his apartment when he knocks on the door of the married couple, Sandu and Mihaela, across the hall to ask for a painkiller. For more than a minute, the camera lingers in his apartment, observing him from a distance as he waits in the hallway for the return of his neighbors, who assume he is drunk again and are called away by burning food. We watch as people pass him on the stairs and the motion lights turn off. As the camera dwells in the darkness of his apartment, the long take calls attention to itself as a shot, emphasizing the three static frames that envelop Mr. Lazarescu: his doorframe in the foreground, the dimly lit hallway, and the neighbor's open door in the background. Though Puiu eventually cuts to position the camera in the hallway, the long take achieves a subtle alienation effect that anticipates Mr. Lazarescu's fate.

Once his neighbors and Mioara, the paramedic, enter his apartment, Mr. Lazarescu begins to recede from the film. The cinematography focuses on other people. In one comedic composition, his neighbors bring him a pill and tend to him while he lies down on the couch. Seated in front of him on the couch, Sandu quibbles with Mioara about his burnt finger. Moreover, the camera does not follow Mr. Lazarescu when he rushes to the bathroom to be sick. Instead, it lingers on Sandu, who is talking with an upstairs neighbor who arrives to return a drill. Mr. Lazarescu is offscreen for nearly two minutes before Mioara and Sandu find him dazed in the tub, where he presumably fell and hit his head, causing his hematoma. Once Mioara places him in the ambulance, Mr. Lazarescu's condition slowly deteriorates and the narrative shifts focus to her attempts to find a hospital to treat him. For example, in the sequence at the first hospital, the cinematography privileges her interactions with the cruel doctor who berates Mr. Lazarescu for his drinking and mocks him for the size of his liver before ordering him transferred to another hospital for a CT scan. Similarly, there is an extended long take outside Mr. Lazarescu's ambulance, where Mioara and other paramedics discuss the traffic accident that is overwhelming area emergency rooms.

Once they arrive at the second hospital, the camera highlights the chaos of the emergency room, where multiple traffic accident victims have been sent. Visually, this is the most complex sequence in the film. The tone is much different from that of the early scenes where the camera primarily follows Mr. Lazarescu's actions and maps the spatial continuity of his apartment. In this hospital sequence, the camera disorients spectators with the amount of information it presents. In her analysis of this key moment, Dominique Nasta writes, "Stylistically, the sequence from the second hospital is one of the film's most dazzling and challenging ones. Puiu refuses classical editing with frequent cuts; he asked the cinematographer to move not before but after an action. During an unusually long shot, Mutu's camera constantly wanders from inside the consulting room to the waiting room and to different annexes, tracking all the characters, as if their actions were far more important than Lazarescu's ever-growing pains."[58] The camera disorientates spectators by tentatively panning in different directions. It is uncertain where it should fix its gaze. For example, in one chaotic moment, we watch as Mioara helps Mr. Lazarescu dress after a female physician assistant examines him. The camera pans right to follow another physician assistant leaving a private room and pans back to Mioara and Mr. Lazarescu. Then it pans to the female physician assistant, who is on the telephone. It lingers on her before she sits down to speak with a couple we see waiting in the emergency room. The camera pans back to Mr. Lazarescu, who is told to lie down again and wait for the neurologist to arrive. It returns to the physician assistant as the neurologist enters, and we follow the latter into the room to examine Mr. Lazarescu. Despite the visual chaos of the sequence, Mr. Lazarescu is treated with more respect and dignity than he was at the first hospital or will be at the third hospital, where he is transferred for surgery after a CT scan of his head and liver.

By the third hospital, the dazed Mr. Lazarescu is slurring his speech. Mioara tries to explain what has happened but is treated rudely by the physician assistant. The surgeon who arrives is more interested in finding a charger for his cell phone and asks Mioara which family member has accompanied Mr. Lazarescu, which is a coded question indicating his willingness to accept a bribe. He also demands he sign a waiver despite the fact that he is in no condition to do so. Unable to sign, Mr. Lazarescu is released to the next hospital by the surgeon. This forces Mioara to take him to a fourth hospital, where he is finally admitted for surgery. The film concludes with a series of long takes in the pre-op room. We watch as Mr. Lazarescu is shaved and cleaned by nurses. It is here that Puiu references *The Retirement Home,* as the nurse's gesture when she wipes him with a sheet recalls the nurse's gesture at the end of the documentary. Though the film's title foretells his death, we never learn whether the immediate cause is the surgery or his liver cancer. The final image is of Mr. Lazarescu lying in bed as he waits to be taken to surgery. This may feel like an anticlimactic conclusion, but it is a necessary ending for Puiu's transcendental style. Mr. Lazarescu's death is not as important as his physical and mental disappearance from the camera's frame as the narrative transpires. To return to Filimon's characterization of Puiu's work, the ending also confronts the audience with "the sacred dimension of the profane world." As with the first third of the film, Mr. Lazarescu is once again the center of the frame. The final shot consists of a static frame that runs for two minutes. The audience is forced to gaze voyeuristically on his body and reflect on the bureaucratic nightmare that they have witnessed for two and half hours. And yet the care and respect finally shown by the nurses to Mr. Lazarescu after his trip to four hospitals recall Schrader's taxonomy of transcendental style, in particular the disparity between the harshness of everyday reality and the expression of passionate commitment. After shaving Mr. Lazarescu, one of the nurses teases him and says he looks handsome now. She also returns to make sure he is comfortable by adjusting his covers. Her compassion transcends the fixed nature of the camera's frame, which is why the film concludes, since there is nothing else it can represent.

Aurora is the second of Puiu's intended six-part series of Bucharest stories. It is more austere than *The Death of Mr. Lazarescu*, where Puiu disrupts his fixed frames with chaotic handheld camera sequences. In comparison, *Aurora* is minimalist and thematically opaque. Its three-hour running time consists almost entirely of fixed frames of its protagonist, Viorel, played by Puiu himself, as he wanders around Bucharest, paces around his unfinished apartment, and murders four people over a period of a few days. On first viewing, the plot is nearly impossible to discern, as Puiu withholds most background information until the final sequence, where he clarifies some details. We learn that Viorel is a divorced engineering consultant. He has two daughters. It is implied in the beginning of the film that either he has left his job or he has been fired. He appears to have a sexual relationship with Gina, a divorced woman who provides him with pills, perhaps a sedative since he has not been sleeping. When his mother-in-law, Pusa, and her partner, Doru, visit his apartment with food from a memorial service, we also learn that his father died several years ago. Eventually, Viorel purchases a rifle and continues to stalk his wife, Amalia, from a distance. Perhaps suspecting a past affair, he kills his wife's notary and a woman he was with. He also kills his ex-in-laws. Later he harasses women at a high-end clothing store while looking for someone. He removes one of his daughters from school—the other one is away on a field trip—and takes her to Pusa's apartment. However, he leaves her with the neighbor because he does not have a key. In the end he arrives at the police station to confess to the murders.

To understand *Aurora*, it is important to analyze its thematic intersections with *The Death of Mr. Lazarescu*. The two films, in fact, share some characters. For example, Gina, the divorced woman who provides Viorel with sedatives, is one of the doctors in the earlier film. Pusa's neighbor is Mioara, the paramedic who heroically tries to find a hospital that will admit Mr. Lazarescu. More importantly, Viorel and Mr. Lazarescu share the same profession. They are both engineers, a once dignified profession in Eastern bloc communist societies that championed industry but that has lost its status in the neoliberal era. In other words, Viorel, like Mr. Tomescu in *Cigarettes and Coffee* and Mr. Lazarescu, is another outmoded man who is disappearing from society under neoliberalism. He lacks, however, the neighborly and familial support that those characters have. He has already physically disintegrated by the beginning of the film, so his murders are presented as a fait accompli. And yet, the film provides some clues regarding his past. In her careful reading of the camera's attention to seemingly mundane plot details, Filimon argues that *Aurora* is "anchored in a specific postcommunist reality" of widening social and economic inequality.[59] Filimon, for example, explains how details in Viorel's childhood apartment, perhaps decodable only to Romanian spectators, imply that his dead father was a member of the privileged class and likely part of the Securitate, the Romanian secret police. In comparison, Viorel is now divorced and lives in an unfinished apartment. However, his ex-in-laws live in a large house in the suburbs, which suggests a cultural and economic clash between the old communist order and the new neoliberal society. Similarly, the notary whom he also murders is characterized as running a successful business with several locations. This anxiety over class explains why Viorel exaggerates social slights from people he encounters throughout the film, such as the women in the high-end clothing store. As Filimon convincingly argues, Viorel is motivated by his desire to reassert his patriarchal authority.

While *Aurora* lends itself to such sociological explanations for Viorel's behavior, the relentless alienation effect produced by the visual style ultimately disrupts any identification with him. The camera rarely follows Viorel's actions. Instead, the cinematography allows him to walk in and out of frame during several shots. For example, we are first introduced to Viorel in a distant shot of him at work as he smokes in a courtyard. The camera is angled against the wall, which obscures our field of vision when he drifts to the right of the frame. In the next shot we watch again from a distance inside the factory as he walks upstairs with another man. The cumulative effect of this visual strategy over three hours is that Viorel remains psychologically opaque even when confessing his crimes to the police at the end. When they ask him about his motivations for murder, he provides a rambling answer in which he claims that the justice department cannot comprehend the complexity of his relationship with his ex-wife.

Though the film is too lengthy to analyze formally in detail, a close reading of a few key scenes highlights how the camera's dispassionate gaze obscures Viorel as a character and invites spectators to reflect on the absence of his personhood. For example, in the scene where we are introduced to his relationship with Gina, the first shot begins with a close-up of him in a darkened room smoking by a window. Viorel turns around as we hear her daughter yell. The camera is placed behind Viorel's shoulder while he stares into the hallway as Gina and her daughter walk past. Given our previous, distant introduction to Viorel at work, we first assume he is now at home and perhaps does not want to bother his family with his smoking. However, the length of the shot emphasizes Viorel's isolation. This isolation is further highlighted by a composition in which the camera gazes from the kitchen as Viorel stands in the doorway of Gina's room and momentarily watches her dress before walking off-frame. It remains in its fixed position while Gina talks to Viorel. Later, when the two are in the kitchen, Gina tries talking to him about her daughter's response to "Little Red Riding Hood" at school. The camera is positioned behind Gina as the blank and impassive Viorel listens, dissociated from the conversation.

During the scenes set in Viorel's unfinished apartment, Puiu employs a visual design that he will further develop in *Sieranevada* where the camera creates a maze of doorframes and clashing foregrounds and backgrounds. This is particularly noticeable in the scene in which Pusa and Doru visit him after a memorial for his father, which is staged as one stunning five-minute sequence shot. Indeed, this is one of the key shots in the film for understanding its transcendental style. It begins with Viorel in the extreme foreground in a room as he dresses. He walks offscreen down the hallway as we hear Pusa open the door. The camera remains in its fixed position as she and Viorel enter the frame and meet in the hallway. She then walks into the kitchen in the background while Viorel exits again and Doru enters. Viorel continues to dress, entering and exiting the frame, while Doru tries to make small talk about the renovations. Eventually they leave. In an interview with *Film Quarterly,* Puiu explains why he employed the distancing technique of a fixed camera position:

> There's that statement from [Rudolph] Arnheim in his *Film as Art* that a filmmaker is obliged to choose things from reality and if you choose one thing you don't choose something else. If you point the camera in this direction, you are going to lose what's happening behind the camera. This is the condition of the filmmaker. So I decided for every scene to have one shot from a very precise position—not in order to expose everything to camera, but to cover the space logically. If someone has to go from the armchair in the living room to the toilet, then maybe you can still get something from the sound of the flush. Cinema allows you to do this, to vary elements in order to build up the cinematographic sentence. I don't know if I've succeeded in this but the statement I want to make is that life is more important than cinema. I think that life is more important than cinema.[60]

Puiu's answer echoes his refusal of Bazinian realism as a description of his work. Even more so than *The Death of Mr. Lazarescu, Aurora* clarifies his skepticism about realism in cinema and its ability to represent history. As he explains, the camera can only select one aspect of reality at a time. Similarly, the camera can map "space logically," but it cannot "expose everything." Thus, the formal design of *Aurora* invites spectators to transcend the restrictions of the camera's framing of reality that Puiu selects. In narrative terms, in order to understand Viorel's absent personhood, it is necessary to reflect on the mundane details onscreen as well as the life offscreen, which is circumscribed by the fixed camera frame and sound design. According to Puiu, "Life is more important than cinema," a statement that recalls Tarr's claim that he follows "the logic of life" in his work. Such an affirmation may feel counterintuitive given the bleakness of *Aurora*. If Mr. Lazarescu disappears across the course of his narrative, only to be shown respect and care in the end by the nurses who prepare him for surgery, then Viorel is already lost at the beginning of *Aurora*.

This makes it difficult for spectators to accept the disparity between the harsh reality the film depicts and the transcendence it invites. In that regard, *Aurora* resembles Robert Bresson's *L'Argent* (1983), where Yvon, an oil-truck driver, descends into murder and mayhem because he unwittingly passes along counterfeit money. Like Yvon, Viorel will only find grace once he confesses and is imprisoned. While this may be a fatalistic ending, Puiu will provide a more hopeful vision of the same themes in his next Bucharest story.

In *Sieranevada,* Puiu further develops the fixed-camera cinematography of *Aurora*. Of the three Bucharest stories to date, it is the most ambitious in its visualization of the daily familial and social ramifications of post-communist malaise and disillusionment with narratives of history. Though the film is less opaque than *Aurora,* discerning the exact nature of the relationships between the many characters still requires careful attention. Backstories are purposely withheld. However, the film primarily focuses on Lary, a former doctor who we learn now sells medical supplies for a private company. Interestingly, the credits reveal that Lary was one of the doctors in *The Death of Mr. Lazarescu,* the surgeon who refuses to operate because Mr. Lazarescu cannot sign his waiver form. Lary and his wife, Laura, attend the Romanian Orthodox fortieth-day after death commemoration for his deceased father, Emil, in his childhood apartment. Beyond this premise, the plot of *Sieranevada* is minimalistic. The majority of the three-hour film is set in this apartment after Lary and Laura arrive for the ceremony, with notable exceptions. Dramatically, the film is structured as a series of revelations, political arguments between family members, and dryly comedic mishaps. These include the following incidents: the priest presiding over the ceremony is late, which prevents everyone from eating; Lary's cousin Cami inappropriately arrives with a drunken friend who passes out; characters engage in conversations about conspiracy theories and the legacies of Romanian communism; and we learn, at an inopportune moment, that Uncle Tony has been having an affair. Even more humorous is the storyline of the thin Sebi, one of Lary's cousins, who is supposed to wear one of Emil's suits as a ritual of forgiveness during the ceremony, but nobody has bothered to tailor the large suit for him.

While the minimalistic plot of *Sieranevada* unfolds as a comedy, Puiu's fixed camera style conveys a more melancholy vision of a fractured society whose characters struggle to reconcile with the past absent a guiding belief system in history. The long-take style, more demanding than the style of either *The Death of Mr. Lazarescu* or *Aurora,* forces spectators to intensely experience this malaise. Though *Sieranevada* is set primarily in an apartment, it begins with a distant shot of Lary parking his company car as Laura exits with one of their daughters, whom they are leaving, presumably, with Laura's mother. Their other daughter is away on a trip. Lary's car blocks the street and a delivery truck starts honking. The shot continues, with the camera panning slightly on its axis, as Lary circles the block while Laura, carrying several bags, argues with her daughter. Eventually, Lary returns and parks again. At six minutes, this opening shot appears to lack a clear narrative purpose on first viewing. We are distanced from Lary and Laura as characters, and waiting for a car to circle the block feels like an absurdist parody of slow cinema that privileges dead time. On a second viewing, however, it becomes clear that the opening shot conveys an image of Romanian society that is fracturing under the stress of neoliberalism. In particular, the careful framing subtly conveys social and economic inequality. For example, in the foreground, the text visible on Lary's car is the website address for Medist Solutions, the private health-care firm for which he now works. This is contrasted with the background, where we see graffiti sprawled across the building, suggesting a different social and economic status. As the subsequent sequence clarifies, Lary and Laura are upper-middle class and are more economically successful than their parents. In a stark formal contrast to the durational aesthetic of the opening shot, Puiu employs jump-cuts while the camera gazes from the back seat as Laura yells at Lary, who has purchased the wrong dress for his daughter's Disney-themed school play. Laura is upset because now their daughter will be dressed like the "stupid peasant" girl whom she hates. Once they settle their argument, they discuss taking a vacation to Thailand.

These themes of class entitlement and social fragmentation are reinforced later when, during the ceremony, Laura goes to the grocery store because she is tired of waiting for the priest to arrive. Returning to the neighborhood, she stops at another store for cigarettes and has to telephone Lary for help because their car is blocked by that of another driver, in whose spot she has temporarily parked. When Lary arrives, he sees Laura arguing with an older woman-whom she insults about dwindling state pensions, implying that she is lower class. The confrontation escalates when another man intervenes and the other driver returns. Lary is shoved while Laura exacerbates tensions by yelling insults. While the situation is eventually defused, the scene highlights the lack of social cohesion produced by a system in which the privatization of the common good rewards a new professional class. Yet, despite their economic privilege, Lary and Laura are not happy. Before they return to the ceremony, there is a stunning ten-minute shot of them parked elsewhere. The static camera gazes from the back seat as Lary tearfully explains to Laura that he knew his father was a serial cheater. Moreover, he wonders why his father could not detect it when his brother would lie to him since he himself was so dishonest. When asked whether he ever told his mother, Lary explains that he is certain she was aware of his father's infidelity, just as Laura is aware when he is lying. Laura understands that Lary has just indirectly confessed to his own infidelity. She replies that she needs a few days to think about what he said and that they need to return to the ceremony.

Though these car scenes help establish the theme of social inequality, the majority of *Sieranevada* is set in an apartment, where Puiu's transcendental style visualizes an alternative to post-communist malaise. It is here that the fixed-camera aesthetic forces spectators to dwell on the possibility of reconciling with the past when faith in historical progress has disappeared. For example, the first shot when Lary enters the apartment runs for nearly four minutes as the camera remains in the hallway, panning in a circle as people walk past. As in *Aurora*, this formalist visual composition creates a convoluted maze of doorframes and rooms. Indeed, it is difficult for spectators to spatialize the apartment. In an interview for the website Mubi, Puiu explains why he rigorously adhered to a fixed camera position throughout the film. On the one hand, he says the fixed camera perspective is meant to invoke the spirit of the father since in the Orthodox tradition the soul wanders the earth for forty days after death. More importantly, when asked specifically about the absence of point-of-view shots in the film, Puiu explains,

> The point was to encapsulate a statement connected to the idea of point-of-view in the style of the film. We are condemned in life to have just one position regarding an event that is unfolding in front of our eyes. Even if you change your position you have the same point-of-view because it is not the physical position but your position is in your brain. The filters that allow you to decode the significance of an event that is unfolding in front of your eyes are in your brain.[61]

In other words, the cinematography in *Sieranevada* is dialectical. In order to represent the characters as locked in their individual points of view, the camera itself must be restricted to the singular perspective, which invokes the presence of the father's spirit. This problem of film form, however, also bespeaks the difficulty of reconciling with history, which *Sieranevada* dramatizes. Consider, for example, the various conversations and arguments the characters have. Lary discusses with his cousins conspiracy theories about the Romanian revolution, 9/11, and the *Charlie Hebdo* shooting. While only Sabi is a devoted conspiracy theorist, other characters express their weariness with official history. Similarly, when Lary's aunt Evelina, a staunch party loyalist, and his sister, Sandra, a devout religious royalist, have a heated argument about communism, both are exposed as hypocrites. Criticizing the communists for their lack of humanism, Sandra will nevertheless use an anti-Semitic slur against Marx and Lenin. On the other hand, despite her antireligious sentiment and expressed desire to close churches, Aunt Evelina will respectfully participate in the ritual prayer when the priest arrives. Both characters vehemently assert their stories about history even when their behavior suggests they have lost some faith in them. Yet *Sieranevada* concludes more optimistically than either *The Death of Mr. Lazarescu* or *Aurora*. Lary's tearful, indirect confession of infidelity to his wife evidences a hope for inner transformation that allows him to embrace the sacred ritual of memorializing the past. Confronting his father's flaws allows him to confess to his own infidelity. In the humorous final shot, everyone finally sits down to eat while Sabi enters with his poorly tailored suit to enact the ritual forgiveness for the departed Emil. Suddenly, the women are called away when Cami's drunken friend awakes and starts crying and vomiting in the bathroom. Lary laughs joyfully. By embracing the absurdity of the situation, he realizes that the symbolism of the fortieth-day after death ceremony is as much about memorializing the past as it is about creating a sacred ritual for the present. Puiu appropriately concludes with this scene. As he explains in the Mubi interview, the camera cannot shift its point of view to represent this new reality. It is left for spectators themselves to decode this "unfinished cinema."

Both Tarr and Puiu develop unique long-take styles that critique capitalist realism. They immerse spectators in a radically materialist vision of the present. To return to the quote from Rancière, this present is framed as "the time after all stories, the time when one takes direct interest in the sensible stuff in which these stories cleaved shortcuts between projected and accomplished ends,"[62] Both directors recognize that the narratives of historical progress advanced by communism and neoliberalism dematerialize the present and must be countered with an "unfinished cinema," inspired by Tarkovsky, where spectators dwell on cinematic time as an inner subjective experience.

But this is where Tarr and Puiu diverge. For Tarr, there can be no reconciliation with the past because there is only the disappearing present. In his late films, the specter of the apocalypse haunts the malaise of the end of history. There is no transcendence; there is only immanence. Yet this is precisely why his vision is humanist in its demand that spectators feel compassion for his miserable and hopeless characters. On the other hand, Puiu returns to the mystical perspective of Tarkovsky. Perhaps because of their shared Eastern Orthodoxy, both embrace a radical cinematic materialism as a means for achieving spiritual and political transformation. Thus, at the conclusion of *Sieranevada,* Puiu can suggest historical reconciliation with Romania's past for his characters who have gathered in ritual mourning. The lesson is that in order to escape post-communist malaise and imagine a new Europe, a political modernist aesthetic must both mourn the past and reconcile with it. This twin problem of mourning and reconciliation is the overarching concern of the late films of Theo Angelopoulos, the most grandiose of political modernists in Balkan cinema. His last films, as the next chapter argues, offer a prescient vision of mapping a new Europe while using cinema as a means of reconciling with the past.

4 • THEO ANGELOPOULOS, GREECE, AND THE ENDS OF EUROPE

I. A NEW COLLECTIVE DREAM

Late Style and Political Commitment

During a forty-year career that spanned thirteen features and several short films, Theo Angelopoulos developed an ambitious political modernist style. With his complex long takes, he sought to dramatize twentieth-century Greece and understand the dialectical relationship between myth and history. In his later films, he explored the regional identity of the Balkans, told melancholy stories about borders and migration, and examined whether cinema can help us reconcile with the past and imagine a new future. He died in a traffic accident while filming *The Other Sea* in January 2012. The synopsis published on his website indicates that the unfinished film would have been a sprawling and ambitious work about Greece and the social and political unrest produced by the debt crisis and austerity. There would have been additional subplots about human trafficking and a theatrical troupe attempting to perform Bertolt Brecht's *Threepenny Opera.*

Angelopoulos's career consists of two distinct periods, which are subdivided by critics, and Angelopoulos himself, into thematically linked trilogies.[1] The first encompasses his seventies films, which focus on the traumatic nature of Greek history in the twentieth century, especially its civil war and military dictatorship in the late sixties. During this period, he gained an international reputation for his three Brechtian epics, *The Traveling Players* (1975),

The Hunters (1977), and *Alexander the Great* (1980), which represent contemporary Greek history as a clash between fascism and communism. In these films, Angelopoulos employs a radical long-take tableau style that avoids close-ups and continuity editing. The effect estranges spectators and emphasizes group identities over individual character identification. *The Traveling Players* is the best known of the trilogy. Set during the years 1939 to 1952 and containing only eighty shots during its four hours, it follows a theatrical troupe that travels through Greece as it attempts to perform a play about peasants. The nonlinear narrative constantly displaces spectators in history. A cut may retreat ten years into the past, or a camera pan within a sequence shot may also mark a shift in time. This aesthetic strategy is further developed in *The Hunters*, a film about a group of bourgeois hunters who discover the corpse of a communist partisan from the Greek Civil War. Angelopoulos's Brechtian tendencies culminate in *Alexander the Great*, a bleak and allegorical three-and-a-half-hour film about a bandit who tries to establish an egalitarian community and turns into a Stalinist dictator.

While Angelopoulos's place in the canon of global art cinema is assured, the majority of his work remains difficult to see and is unavailable on streaming services or has not been released on home video in the United States. Perhaps this is why scholarly criticism of Angelopoulos is limited in comparison to that of other international directors who were influential during the seventies. To date, Andrew Horton's *Films of Theo Angelopoulos: A Cinema of Contemplation* is the only English-language monograph to provide a general overview of his career. However, Angelos Koutsourakis and Mark Steven's 2015 collection, *The Cinema of Theo Angelopoulos*, represents a significant advancement in Angelopoulos scholarship. Divided into sections on "authorship, "politics," "poetics," and "time," the essays in the comprehensive collection interpret his films for their formal, thematic, and political contributions to the modernism of global art cinema. The critical consensus in the collection is that Angelopoulos's seventies films are more politically radical than the films from his second period, which include *Voyage to Cythera* (1984) through *The Dust of Time* (2008). For example, in his essay "Angelopoulos and Collective Narrative," Fredric Jameson argues that Angelopoulos's seventies films are uniquely revolutionary in how they develop a collective narrative that formalizes the ideological conflicts that characterize twentieth-century Greek history. As much as he admires the later films, according to him, they drift into existential and metaphysical themes about borders and exile. For example, of *Ulysses' Gaze* (1995) he writes that it is "more humanist than historical" and is primarily concerned with "metaphysical messages about life and death."[2] This is a fair assessment since Angelopoulos himself mentioned in interviews his disillusionment with ideology and history. Thus, it is not surprising that Jameson should consider Angelopoulos's first period to be characterized by the more radical cinema. These films closely adhere to classical definitions of counter-cinema. In particular, they express a clear political commitment and, similar to Miklós Jancsó's sixties and early seventies films, radically redefine the codes of narrative cinema according to Marxist perspectives about history.

While Angelopoulos's second period may be less avowedly Marxist, Jameson's phrase "more humanist than historical" invites the question, Does disillusionment with ideology necessarily constitute a retreat from political commitment? As chapter 3 argues, cynicism about communist narratives of historical progress permeates the films of Cristi Puiu and Béla Tarr. Nevertheless, both directors work through the post-communist malaise they represent by offering different antidotes to capitalist realism, be it the pessimistic humanism of Tarr or the transcendental style of Puiu. What is unique about Angelopoulos's later films is that they already exhibit a similar malaise by the early eighties. This is because Greece's post-communist era began much earlier than 1989. The defeat of the communist insurgency in the Greek Civil War, 1946 to 1949, by the British- and American-backed right-wing government army meant that Greece became the only Balkan nation that was not part of the second world. Decades of political and social unrest gave rise to the anti-communist Greek military dictatorship from 1967 to 1974, during which Angelopoulos began directing features. By the eighties, as the first wave of neoliberalism was embraced in the West and debt crises began to unravel communism in Eastern Europe, it became clear that there were no longer viable political alternatives to capitalism. To that extent, the Brechtian aesthetic of Angelopoulos's seventies films and its chronicling of history became outmoded in the era of neoliberalism. Recall Brecht's own criticism of György Lukács's theory of realism discussed in chapter 1. For Brecht, Lukács became formalistic and "remote from reality" because he failed to grasp the evolution of capitalism. To be clear, my point is not that Jameson or other Marxist analysts of Angelopoulos have failed to grasp the evolution of capitalism. Even a cursory reading of Jameson's essay would invalidate that notion. Rather, this chapter argues that branding Angelopoulos's later films as "humanist" ignores their emergent politics and risks the formalism that Brecht himself warns against by promoting nostalgia for past aesthetic forms.

In his essay "Tracks in the Eurozone: Late Style Meets Late Capitalism," Mark Steven challenges the notion that Angelopoulos's late films represent a retreat from political commitment. As suggested by his title, Steven interprets his late period through the lens of Edward Said's concept of "late style," whereby an artist develops an unresolvable and contradictory style. Thus, Steven acknowledges that Angelopoulos's late films, especially *The Dust of Time*, often lack the formal complexity of his earlier work. Yet he argues that this is because "the challenge faced by Angelopoulos is to present capitalism's post-war defeat of the left at the same time as delineating a prehistory for the future left's unpredictable resurgence."[3] In other words, whereas Angelopoulos's Brechtian films chronicle history with formal precision, the latter films have the more difficult task of representing "how the collective atomises" while searching for new politics in the post-utopian landscape, where socialist alternatives to capitalism have been exhausted.[4] This chapter develops Steven's argument about Angelopoulos's late style. The first part analyzes *The Suspended Step of the Stork* (1991) and *Eternity and a Day* (1998) in order to argue that their images of borders and exile both express post-communist malaise and articulate new forms of belonging. The second part develops this analysis of borders and exile in relation to the self-reflexivity of *Ulysses' Gaze* and *The Dust of Time*, two films about directors that envision cinema as an apparatus that can help us reconcile with the past in order to imagine a new future politics.

Exiled from History

In *Voyage to Cythera*, Angelopoulos introduces the themes of borders and exile that will define the second half of his career. It is also the first of his three films about a director who uncovers the past and tells a personal story. *Voyage to Cythera* defies straightforward summation since Angelopoulos purposely blurs the boundaries between fantasy and reality. The plot follows the alienated Alexander, a director who is in production on his new film. His father, Spyros, has returned from Russia after thirty-two years in exile—a topical storyline in 1984 since exiled communist rebels from the civil war were granted amnesty in Greece in the early eighties and began returning. However, there are implications that this may be the story of Alexander's film. In other words, Alexander's film may be about a director trying to tell the story of his father's return. Unlike other mise en abyme narratives, such as *Mulholland Drive* and *8½*, *Voyage to Cythera* never reveals the presence of a film crew in order to distinguish footage from reality. The confusion is established in the opening scenes. In the first shot, Alexander, a young boy, wakes up to the sound of soldiers outside and his mother calling his name. Next we see him running through the streets. He sneaks up on a German soldier and knocks something out of his hand. Running away, he finds a corner and hides. Suddenly, from offscreen we hear a voice instructing him what to say. The film cuts to a shot of Alexander, the director, waking up as his wife calls for their son Spyros, who resembles the young Alexander from the previous scene. The diegetic relationship between these two scenes is unclear. The editing suggests that Alexander is awakening from a dream that blended his past and anxiety about the present. On the other hand, this could be a scene from the film he is directing. This dream logic continues once Alexander leaves his apartment for the film studio. While on set, he stops at the casting call for "his father." Dozens of men in trench coats take turns approaching the casting directors to speak their line, "It's me." Alexander leaves and walks past a crew and men lined up outside waiting to audition. When he enters the dining hall, he becomes transfixed by an old man who is selling lavender. He follows him for several minutes to a port. Inexplicably, the old man disappears. Alexander hears Voula, his sister, calling his name as he sees a large ship arriving in the distance. Suddenly the narrative focus shifts as Alexander and Voula awaits the arrival of their father. As Spyros disembarks the large ship, the camera zooms into a close-up as he shouts, "It's me," to his children. It is apparent that the same actor, Manos Katrakis, portrays both the man selling lavender and Spyros.

Despite what this description suggests, *Voyage to Cythera* has little in common with contemporary "mind-game" films such as *Inception* or with classical art cinema surrealism. The purpose of its blurring of fantasy and reality is not to turn spectators into narrative detectives or to liberate the unconscious mind. Rather, the narrative obscurity of *Voyage to Cythera* expresses the disillusionment over the end of socialist alternatives to the market. Consider what happens to Spyros. After an awkward reunion at home, Alexander and Voula drive their father and mother, Katerina, to a small, dilapidated village in northern Greece. This is their childhood home. In a memorable sequence shot, Spyros and an old friend walk through the village cemetery and Spyros calls out the names of old friends as he reads their tombstones.

However, his memorialization is futile because the village will be denied the opportunity to reconcile with its past, its ideological struggles as well as its rural identity. Private capital has arrived in the form of a company that wishes to purchase homes in the village and develop a resort. Everyone but Spyros agrees to sell, which negates the deal. This creates tensions in the village and further alienates Spyros from his children. Only Katerina stays by his side. They try to elude the police, who wish to deport him for the commotion he caused since he is a refugee without any official nationality. He is arrested at a train station. However, his deportation is delayed when the police miscommunicate with a Russian ship. Cruelly, the police are ordered to keep him in international waters. They place him on a raft. Katerina demands to join him. The film ends with the bleak image of the two of them huddled on the raft. It is daybreak. Katerina says she is "ready." Spyros unhooks the rope and we watch as they drift into the sea.

As the first part in his *Trilogy of Silence, Voyage to Cythera* establishes a melancholy tone. However, the ending is open to two contradictory readings. On first viewing, it offers no hope for an emergent politics that can reconcile with the past and counter the privatization of the present. The final image implies that Spyros and Katerina drift into oblivion. This interpretation aligns with the next film, *The Beekeeper,* which retreats further into apolitical despair. In it, Marcello Mastroianni portrays a depressed and alienated beekeeper. He remains trapped in his memories and eventually commits suicide. And yet the ending of *Voyage to Cythera* also lends itself toward a more optimistic, allegorical reading. When asked about the title in an interview, Angelopoulos explained, "Cythera is the island glorified by poets, the island of love, the island of Aphrodite. The title has to reflect the full spirit of the film."[5] In other words, Spyros and Katerina are determined to depart for elsewhere, a utopian place that the film cannot articulate so it must remain offscreen. This ambiguity between the end of a journey—the exit from history of Spyros and his communist ideals—and a new beginning recalls Jean-Antoine Watteau's famous painting *The Embarkation for Cythera,* which, despite its title, implies that the French aristocrats are in fact departing Cythera.[6]

The final film in the trilogy, *Landscape in the Mist,* further explores this idea of the circular journey. In it, a brother and sister, named once again Alexander and Voula, leave home in search of their father, who lives in Germany, according to their mother. The children believe that Germany borders Greece. However, the film implies that the mother is lying and does not know the identity of their father. After a harrowing journey, they eventually reach a border near a river and sneak onto a small rowboat. From offscreen we hear a border guard yell, "Halt," and then the sounds of gunfire. The film concludes with the poetic image of the children walking through fog. The fog recedes and they approach a solitary tree on a landscape and embrace it. Though this ending appears to confirm Jameson's argument that in his second period Angelopoulos is more concerned with "metaphysical messages about life and death," there is concrete political symbolism to the imaginary Greek-German border, decodable by Greeks who lived under the military dictatorship that began in 1967. In *And the Weak Suffer What They Must?*, former Greek finance minister Yanis Varoufakis begins his analysis of the euro crisis with a personal story about how he would huddle with his parents under a red blanket so they could listen to a West German international radio station without their informant neighbor hearing them. He writes, "I was gripped by a sense of excitement at the strangeness of our predicament: to find out what was happening in our very own Athens, we had to travel, through the airwaves, and veiled by a red blanket, to a place called Germany."[7] During the dictatorship, West Germany symbolized the utopian hopes for a democratic, unified Europe. However, this meaning was inverted during the financial crisis. In Varoufakis's subsequent memoir, *Adults in the Room*,[8] about his failed negotiations to end Greek austerity, the Greek-German border now symbolizes the undemocratic nature of the bond market and the boundary between Europe's core—its financial institutions and neoliberal technocrats—and its debtor nations. This historical gap between the dictatorship and the financial crisis highlights an important aspect of Angelopoulos's later films: what registers as metaphysical, such as the ending of *Landscape in the Mist*, bespeaks an emergent political modernism in response to the omnipresence of capitalism and the market's destruction of the utopian dreams of the past. This emergence is further explored in *The Suspended Step of the Stork* and *Eternity and Day*, where crossing borders becomes an allegory of hope for the possibility of a new politics.

The Great Migration Elsewhere

Released in 1991, the first film of *The Border Trilogy*, *The Suspended Step of the Stork*, has become prescient. Its images of a militarized border, stranded refugee populations, and migrants floating dead in the Mediterranean Sea invoke the Europe of 2015 and its refugee crisis. The film tells the story of

Alexander, a television journalist reporting on the refugee population in an unnamed border town. Once he arrives, he believes he has found a missing Greek politician living among the refugees. The opening shot of *The Suspended Step of the Stork* resonates with the iconic image that will define the refugee crisis twenty-four years later: the death of Alan Kurdi, the three-year-old Syrian boy who drowned when his family tried to reach the Greek island of Kos, a few miles from the coast of Turkey. In the shot we see boats in the port of Piraeus with helicopters circling in the air. The camera subtly guides us to the bodies floating in the water as Alexander states in his voice-over that this incident haunted him as he traveled to the border town. He explains that the bodies are Asian refugees who were denied political asylum and drowned after jumping overboard. Later in the film there is another prognostication when Alexander and his crew are filming the refugees living in abandoned train carriages on the edge of town. In a stunning two-minute shot, the camera pans across a line of train cabs. We see families standing in the doorways. From offscreen we hear a man shouting that he was forced to leave because of chemical weapons. This bleak shot resembles images from the Idomeni refugee camp that Greek authorities shut down in 2016, which, according to the *Guardian*, was "Europe's largest informal refugee camp," with encampments set up along railway lines.[9] Though the actual refugee crisis was not prolonged—the number of asylum seekers arriving by sea in Italy, Spain, and Greece declined significantly in 2016—the political aftershocks will reverberate for decades.[10]

The events of 2015 were not Western Europe's first major refugee crisis to capture headlines since the nineties. In 1991, the collapse of its communist regime sparked a panicked exodus of Albanians. In August of that year, more than ten thousand Albanians boarded a cargo ship for Italy, an event that is dramatized in Gianni Amelio's 1994 film *Lamerica*.[11] This exodus would signal future trends. Since the end of communism, there has been mass migration from Eastern Europe to the West. According to the *Economist*, "From 1992 to 2015, so many people left Eastern Europe that its population shrank by 18m, or about 6%, according to UN figures," a trend that is reversing given the labor shortages in Eastern Europe.[12] The numbers are even more staggering when one considers specific national contexts such as the Polish population in the United Kingdom. From 2004 to 2016 the number of Polish-born residents grew from 94,000 to 911,000.[13] Similarly, in 2017 there were more than one million Romanians living in Italy, "making them the largest group of foreign nationals in the country," as well as a convenient target for xenophobic politicians.[14]

Given these immense demographic shifts, immigration has become a common theme in contemporary European art cinema. There have been numerous great films about refugees, racism, and the legacies of Western European colonialism since the nineties, but it is beyond the scope of this chapter to survey them.[15] Rather, my aim is to distinguish Angelopoulos's long-take style from the dominant realism of slow cinema. The latter is exemplified by Pedro Costa's astonishing trilogy about Cape Verde immigrants living in Lisbon: *Bones* (1997), *In Vanda's Room* (2000), and *Colossal Youth* (2006). Beginning with the second film, Costa shot with digital video and available lighting on location and improvised with nonprofessional actors. This documentary-like mode of production is justified by Costa in an interview with *Four by Three* magazine when he explains, "Realism is film and film is reality—the reality of film. It is ingrained in the medium that film can only show reality."[16] The severity of Costa's definition of cinematic realism is evident in the trilogy. The long takes and fixed camera positions create a claustrophobic realism that entraps spectators within the lives and spaces of its dispossessed and disadvantaged characters. In contrast, Angelopoulos's long takes frequently abandon realism. This has led to some critical disagreement about whether his theatrical style should be considered slow cinema. For example, Ira Jaffe avoids analyzing his work in *Slow Movies: Countering the Cinema of Action*, explaining that "his rendering of human subjectivity, of his characters' recollections and imaginative wanderings, entails frequent departures from chronological time and external reality—twin mainstays of slow movies."[17] In addition to the Proustian quality that Jaffe mentions, Angelopoulos's long takes are highly mannered in their depiction of human behavior and in their self-conscious pictorialism.

The latter is evident throughout *The Suspended Step of the Stork*. After the opening image of the dead migrants in the port of Piraeus, there is a lengthy tracking shot that begins with the camera following a military jeep from a distance. The jeep stops and Alexander exits with a colonel. The camera continues to track, reframing them as they walk past a line of privates near the river at the border. They state their names, but some of them also speak poetic phrases such as, "Here time doesn't go by," which the Colonel and Alexander do not acknowledge. Describing these peculiar intrusions of the inner thoughts of the soldiers, Andrew Horton argues that, "at that exact intersection of the realistic image and the improbable line, Angelopoulos's metarealism begins."[18] By "metarealism," Horton means that these disruptions are not intended as classical surrealism, where reality is fused with dream images; rather, Angelopoulos stretches the boundaries of reality toward the poetic. While this is an astute observation about the film's style, these meta moments of mannered human behavior do have an additional rhetorical function. They establish a discourse about the possibility for new forms of human communication across borders. Indeed, the idea of communicating across borders is introduced in the subsequent shot, where the Colonel walks Alexander past the border gate and onto the bridge. He stops at the colored line and asks Alexander, "Do you know what borders are?" The camera follows as the Colonel walks up to the line and explains to Alexander, "This blue line is where Greece ends." The Albanian soldier from the next checkpoint walks toward them with his rifle. In reference to the film's title, the Colonel raises his foot over the line and says, "If I take one more step I'm elsewhere. Or I die." His exaggerated performance highlights the ontological arbitrariness of militarized borders that curtail the hybridity and intersubjectivity of human experience. It invites spectators to ask, How can a blue line signify the end of Greece and the beginning of Albania? What does it mean to be elsewhere?

These abstract questions are not meant to depoliticize borders or reduce the plight of refugees into a universal condition of exile. Rather, the repeated references to migrating "elsewhere" articulate the liminality of Greek identity produced by changing European borders. As Reece Jones explains in *Violent Borders: Refugees and the Right to Move*, the belief that globalization in the nineties would erode political borders in Europe was misguided. He writes, "The reality is that EU borders were not removed in the 1990s, but simply moved to different locations. As internal border restrictions were loosened in the Schengen Area, more focus was placed on the external boundaries of the European Union at the Mediterranean and on its eastern edges."[19] This is why *The Suspended Step of the Stork* could predict the migrant crisis of 2015. It understood that the end of communism in Europe meant that Greece, and the entire Balkan region, would revert to its Enlightenment identity as the boundary between civilized Western Europe and the barbaric other, a boundary reinforced by Western stereotypes of Greeks as "lazy" in order to justify morally the need for austerity.[20] Thus, *The Suspended Step of the Stork* imagines Greece as the dialectical threshold to elsewhere. For the multiethnic refugees trapped in the unnamed border town, it is the threshold between past and present and between terror and freedom. For Greeks, it means they are trapped between Greece and elsewhere.

This concept of "elsewhere" is integral to the plot of the unnamed missing politician, portrayed by Marcello Mastroianni, whom Alexander believes he has found while reviewing footage he and his crewed filmed of the refugees. Throughout the film, we only learn a few key details about the missing politician. He is the author of a 1980 book *Despair at the End of the Century*, which ends with the question that we hear Alexander read to his girlfriend: "What are the key words we could use to make a new collective dream come true?" Later, in an old news report Alexander watches, we discover that Mastroianni's character was a member of Parliament in the unity government that formed after the end of the dictatorship. He was considered a figure of hope. In footage we see him about to give a speech in Parliament, which he cuts short with a poetic line and walks out. Angelopoulos never confirms whether the refugee character that Alexander encounters is also the missing politician. Did he abandon electoral politics and flee in search of a new "collective dream"? Or is Mastroianni playing two different roles? The ambiguity is reinforced when Alexander confronts the missing politician's ex-wife, portrayed by Jeanne Moreau, who explains that her husband's personality changed after his first disappearance. She is convinced that he died after his second disappearance. When she arrives at the border town to see Mastroianni's character, she tells Alexander that he is not her husband.

This uncertainty regarding the identity of Mastroianni's character is important for this theme of pursuing a new collective dream. During Alexander's first encounter with the character in a train boxcar, he listens to him tell a young boy a parable about such a dream:

> When the earth begins to burn because it will have come too close to the sun, the people of our planet will have to go. It will be the beginning of "The Great Migration" as it will come to be known in history. So, people will leave their homes, wherever these might be, by any available means they can get their hands on, and they will all go to the Sahara Desert. There, a child has left a kite, flying very high in the sky. And all the people, young and old, will hold on to the string, and the whole of mankind will rise into space in search of another planet. Some will be holding a small plant in their hand, other a rosebush, or a handful of grain, or a newborn animal. And one of them, all the poems ever written by man. It will be a very long journey.[21]

The parable is both apocalyptic and hopeful. In it, the world ends but history begins anew elsewhere in an event that will be known as "the Great Migration." Compared with the Brechtian aesthetics of Angelopoulos's seventies films, which demystify history and politics, this self-conscious mythologizing seems like a regression into ideological obscurity. Yet such mythologizing allows *The Suspended Step of the Stork* to imagine a new political modernism and the "prehistory for the future left's unpredictable resurgence," to quote Mark Steven. In other words, in the film, myth and history are not opposed. In that regard, it invokes Max Horkheimer and Theodor Adorno's central thesis in *Dialectic of Enlightenment* that "myth is already enlightenment; and enlightenment reverts to mythology."[22] Adorno and Horkheimer argue that both myth and the Enlightenment's belief in instrumental rationality are modes of representing reality. In mythology the natural world is ordered by deities and exists outside the control of humans, whose fate is decided. As they explain, "In Homer, Zeus represents the sky and the weather, Apollo controls the sun."[23] Instrumental rationality promises to demythologize the world but reverts to a mythic order when it evolves into a totalizing capitalist system that dominates nature and reduces humans to subjects. As in classical myths, humans no longer control their fate; the market does. Such is the case with the neoliberal expansion of Europe. This is encapsulated by the story Varoufakis tells of meeting to negotiate the end of Greek austerity measures with German finance minister Wolfgang Schäuble, who reportedly declared, "Elections cannot be allowed to change an economic programme of a member state!"[24] Against this mythic order of the financial market celebrated as the end of history in 1991, *The Suspended Step of the Stork* presents a hopeful countermyth that imagines new forms of belonging that emerge from the existential malaise of border life.

This hope for new forms of belonging is visualized during the border wedding ceremony that Alexander's television crew films, where the daughter of Mastroianni's character, on the Greek side of the river, marries the groom on the Albanian side. Since the film never confirms the identity of Mastroianni's character, it is uncertain whether she is his actual daughter. Her unnamed character is first introduced in the scene in the hotel bar. Alexander enters as she stares at him from a distance. The scene develops slowly, but they eventually look at each other. She follows Alexander to his room. The film cuts to a melancholy close-up of her sitting forlornly while Alexander reaches out with his hand to console her. As he walks her back to the bar, he asks her who the other man is whose name she called out. Later in the film, Alexander sees her walking with some friends and follows her to her boxcar home, where the refugees live. She is seated with her younger brother and sister, whom she orders to bed. She explains that their mother died when they crossed the border and that her father is working late. Mastroianni's character enters and recognizes Alexander from their previous encounter. He offers him a drink, explaining that he had been working the entire day trying to repair the telephone lines. Telling Alexander, "Our home is your home," he then digresses into a brief poetic monologue in which he states, "We've crossed the border but we're still here. How many borders must we cross before we get home?" A stunned Alexander declines the invitation to stay for dinner and leaves. Later in the film, in a restaurant, Alexander meets the Colonel again, as well as a member of his crew who explains they will be filming a wedding by the river. As the daughter of Mastroianni's character walks past in the distance, the Colonel mentions that she is the bride. Alexander is visibly distraught. When he returns to his hotel room, we notice that she has followed him. The two go inside together one last time. The film then cuts to the wedding ceremony.

The fourteen-minute, eight-shot border wedding sequence is the formal centerpiece of *The Suspended Step of the Stork* and the culmination of its countermyth about border life. As such, it merits close consideration. It begins with a three-minute tracking shot of people walking through barren trees. In the distance we see trucks and cars parked. The camera continues to track past a group of refugees and Mastroianni's character standing next to his daughter in her wedding dress. Everyone is standing behind a small hill. The camera tracks up the hill and focuses on a military truck in the distance, on the other side of the river, driving past. Later in the sequence it becomes clear that the refugee community has timed the ceremony around the military patrols. The camera stops as the truck drives off-frame. In the distance we see the groom's party emerge from behind a hill. They run toward the river while we see the bride's party emerge from the foreground. The two parties wave at each other. Angelopoulos cuts and zooms in on the groom approaching the river with a white flower. The next image is of a priest riding his bicycle toward the bride's party in Greece. He begins the ceremony by blessing the bride and the groom, who is on the other side of the river. The length of the shot emphasizes the absurdity of the border that divides the couple. The absence of the groom is highlighted by the crowning ritual common in

Eastern Orthodox wedding ceremonies. The two crowns are joined by a white ribbon, which the priest places over the heads of the couple. Here, however, Mastroianni's character must hold the crown in the air as his daughter walks in a circle while their wedding party throws rice at them. This is followed by two brief shots where the groom raises his flower and walks in a circle, indicating that he is joined by the crown. He then walks to the river and throws the flower into the water. Then the bride walks toward the river and throws the crowns and ribbon into the water. In the next image, we watch as the bride kisses her father and is swarmed by her wedding party. As Mastroianni's character walks away, we hear a gunshot in the distance, signaling that the military patrol is about to return. Both wedding parties disperse over the hills. The camera lingers on the military truck that drives across frame. As it leaves, the bride and groom enter the frame again. They stop near the river and raise their hands toward each other. The sequence concludes with images of Alexander and his crew, who are filming the ceremony. He watches as the bride runs crying from the river toward her father. They depart with their wedding party, the members of which are shown clapping to the sound of accordion music.

Alexander has one more encounter with Mastroianni's character and his daughter back in town. He finds the two of them dancing together in the street. She explains to Alexander that she grew up with her husband and she has faith that one day he will cross the river to take her away. Mastroianni gives one last poetic monologue about how the roaring river beckons him to take another journey elsewhere. This is the last we see of him. Later, in the penultimate scene, Alexander once again returns to the border, where he passes another group of soldiers. One of them mentions that it is New Year's Eve. Just as the Colonel did at the beginning of the film, Alexander walks past the border gate toward the line that marks the end of Greece and the beginning of Albania. He repeats the Colonel's gesture and raises his foot above the line. In the final scene, he approaches the river again and meets the Colonel, who explains that several eyewitnesses have reported contradictory sightings of Mastroianni's character departing in different directions. In the distance Alexander sees Mastroianni's daughter, who runs away. He again encounters the young boy who, earlier in the film, we saw listening to the story about the Great Migration. He tells Alexander that he saw Mastroianni's character walk on water while carrying his suitcase and disappear once he crossed the border. The film concludes with an image of Alexander walking down the road as the camera tracks backward to reveal men in yellow suits climbing up the telephone poles to install new cable. The camera creates a painterly tableau with the yellow color blending into the overcast sky while Alexander walks toward the river.

The Suspended Step of the Stork expresses muted optimism in its belief that new historical forms of belonging can emerge. The mythic trajectory of Mastroianni's character is central to this. He begins as a unifying postdictatorship politician who abandons governance to live as a refugee and transforms into a Christlike figure who disappears from the narrative. His character expresses the hope that the post-communist end of history celebrated in the early nineties can give rise to a new collective dream that is not the marketplace. However, as the horrific Yugoslav wars erupt, the subject of *Ulysses' Gaze*, which is analyzed in section II, this countermyth for a new politics becomes more elusive. History returns with a vengeance. In *The Suspended Step of the Stork*, the border functions as the dialectical threshold to elsewhere and for a new, emergent politics. In subsequent films, this dialectic shifts into the past. As such, borders become sites for working through the past in order to imagine a new political future. These films acknowledge, to quote Adorno, that "the past will have been worked through only when the causes of what happened then have been eliminated."[25] This is why, in *Eternity and a Day*, the last film in the border trilogy, the boundaries between the past and present will collapse in order to map a new future.

A Stranger Everywhere

Eternity and a Day tells the story of a dying poet named Alexander. The narrative follows his final day before he is supposed to enter the hospital. Since his wife died, he lives fixated on the past and his unfinished projects. On the way to visit his daughter, who is unaware of his illness, he saves a young Albanian boy from the police, who are chasing him and other migrant boys because they have been washing windshields at intersections. They part ways but circumstance will bring them together again. He brings his daughter some letters from Anna, his wife, and tries to leave his dog with her, claiming that he will be traveling. She informs him that she and her boyfriend have sold the family home by the sea. This visibly upsets Alexander, who has fond memories of the place. He leaves and goes to a pharmacy. He again encounters the young Albanian boy, who is grabbed by human traffickers who engage in illegal adoptions. Alexander follows the traffickers and purchases the boy's freedom. The rest of the film explores the friendship that develops between the two, who spend the day together before the boy sneaks aboard a ship departing from the port.

What distinguishes *Eternity and a Day* from other European art films about alienated bourgeois artists is that Alexander's fixation with the past is framed as an unfinished political project that is linked to the fate of the Albanian boy. This allows the film to synthesize two visions of belonging, Alexander's romantic nationalism and the young migrant boy's rootlessness and emergent cosmopolitanism. This tension between the two is introduced in the scene where Alexander visits his daughter and we learn that he abandoned writing his own poems once his wife died. Instead, he has been trying to complete Dionysios Solomos's unfinished nineteenth-century poem about the Greek War of Independence, "The Free Besieged," which was inspired by the Third Siege of Missolonghi in 1825, where the defeated Greek forces resisted the Ottoman invasion for over a year. The importance of the Greek War of Independence in the Western European romantic imagination should be emphasized. Famously, Lord Byron joined the cause and died from a fever during the Second Siege of Missolonghi in 1824. Though the Greeks were defeated in these battles, Western powers would intervene in the war and an independent Greek state was established in 1830.

The political implications of Alexander's desire to complete Solomos's poem must also be understood in relation to his memory of the day September 20, 1966, which he spent with his wife and friends to celebrate the birth of their daughter at their seaside home. We are introduced to Alexander's recollections of this day when his daughter reads a letter from Anna as he mentally drifts back to the day. Throughout the film he becomes increasingly lost in the memory, whose date is politically symbolic in addition to being personally important. It is a late summer day before the Greek military junta in the spring of 1967. When the houseguests arrive, we hear a conversation between two men. One of them mentions that this will be "the last carefree summer" because there is talk that the military will intervene in the next election. The other man dismisses this suggestion. Though this is the only allusion, the military coup haunts the remainder of the film. When juxtaposed to his desire to complete Solomos's poem, the meaning of this memory is apparent. In both cases, Alexander romanticizes moments of political defeat. He suffers from what Enzo Traverso defines as "left-wing melancholia." In *Left-Wing Melancholy: Marxism, History, and Memory*, he argues that the decline of communism in the eighties accelerated a crisis in Marxism whereby historical consciousness could no longer "project [us] into the future" in order to imagine utopia and is instead reduced to the "remembrance of the vanquished." Traverso explains, "When communism fell apart, the utopia that for almost two centuries had supported it as a Promethean impetus or consolatory justification was no longer available; it had become an exhausted spiritual resource. The 'structure of feelings' of the left disappeared and the melancholy born from defeat could not find anything to transcend it; it remained alone in front of a vacuum. The coming neoliberal wave—as individualistic as it cynical—fulfilled it."[26] Angelopoulos already explores this melancholy of historical defeat and spiritual exile in *Voyage to Cythera* with the character of Spyros. The difference is that Spyros's fate is left unresolved as he drifts out to sea, whereas Alexander's illness means he has no future. However, the contradiction that Angelopoulos synthesizes is Alexander's desire to complete "The Free Besieged." While a retreat into nostalgia and romantic nationalism, it gives voice to the young boy's cosmopolitan future as he escapes his nightmarish past. Indeed, the boy's past is abstractly visualized in the haunting six-minute shot where Alexander drives him to the Albanian border so he can return home. The shot begins with Alexander's car driving on a dirt road in an overcast, snow-filled landscape. They stop and exit the car. For several minutes the boy tells the harrowing story of escaping from the armed gangs in his village and how another boy named Selim led him and others to safety through a trail. As he finishes his story, the camera tracks up the hillside as it slowly reveals a border fence shrouded in fog. In the distance, past the fence, we see a watchtower and several humans standing still with their arms raised. The fog and the whiteness of the snow completely flatten the depth of field. Beyond the Greek-Albanian border lies nowhere, an unrepresentable space. This is a stark contrast to the river border in *The Suspended Step of the Stork*, where the extended depth of field conveys the ability of the arbitrarily divided people to triumph over the landscape and stage a wedding. As the camera comes to a stop in this shot, Alexander and the boy walk up the path toward the entrance. An ominous-looking military guard walks toward them. Frightened, the boy says that he lied and has no one to care for him. Alexander grabs the boy and they flee back to the car.

In the eight-minute sequence that follows, Alexander tells the boy a fictional account of how the poet Solomos returned from Italy to Greece during the War of Independence to compose his "Hymn to Liberty," whose first two stanzas would become the national anthem of Greece. The first long take begins with Alexander and the boy walking to a food truck to order a sandwich. The camera follows them as they walk along the river. Alexander begins his story,

> Once there was a poet in the last century. A great poet. He was Greek but he grew up and lived in Italy. One day he heard that the Greeks who were living as slaves under the Ottomans had taken up arms to fight them. Then memories of his forgotten homeland stirred inside him, his childhood on the island, the face of his mother still living there. He could not rest. He would wander around, talking to himself. Every night he would dream of his mother. A bride, dressed in white, she was summoning him.[27]

Alexander's version of Solomos differs from the actual historical figure in important ways. In truth, Solomos was born and raised on the Greek island of Zakynthos. He spent several years in Italy studying literature and law. He returned to Zakynthos before the War of Independence, unlike in Alexander's story, where the siren call of nationalism beckoned him home. Alexander continues his story. The camera tracks along the water ahead of him and the boy. We now see Solomos standing by the river and hear his inner monologue about departing for Greece. He tells himself that, as a poet, he must "sing for the revolution, mourn for the dead, invoke the lost face of liberty." He enters a stagecoach and rides away. The surrealism of the shot, which collapses late twentieth-century Greece and early nineteenth-century Italy, invites spectators to consider the similarities between the two poets. Like Solomos, Alexander sees himself as invoking "the lost face of liberty." However, in the remainder of the film, the parallels with the Albanian boy become more important. The boy, after all, is the one who must speak in an unfamiliar language and discover the words that give meaning to his exile and departure for elsewhere. The film now cuts to a boat rowing to shore. Alexander mentions that Solomos, whose early poetry was written in Italian, returned to his home island to sing for the revolution but did not know the Greek language. The camera zooms out to reveal people working by the shoreline. It continues until we see Solomos sitting in ruins speaking all the new words he has learned. Alexander explains that he would buy words from local peasants. The camera follows him as he speaks more new words and encounters a peasant woman whom he pays. Alexander and the boy enter the frame and walk through the ruins past Solomos. Alexander explains that that is how "Hymn to Liberty" was written but that Solomos would lack the words to complete "The Free Besieged."

The friendship that develops between the two centers on the game they play in which the boy sells words to Alexander. In the extended middle sequence, set along a boardwalk near a port, a tired Alexander sits down on a bench. Attempting to raise his spirits, the boy offers to find him a new word. He wanders and returns with *xenitis,* which Alexander defines as "an outsider, a stranger, an emigrant." The boy adds, "a stranger everywhere." When asked whether he just heard the word, the boy confesses he learned it from the women who lived in his village. Their definitions highlight their different experiences of homeland. For Alexander, homeland is the return to the mental space before historical defeat and exile. Thus, as soon as the boy searches for another word, Alexander drifts back into his memory of his perfect day in 1966. However, his extended reverie is disrupted by the young boy's version of homeland. Another refugee boy has drowned in the port. Concerned about the young boy, who disappears, Alexander finds him crying in a nearby abandoned building. He explains to Alexander that the boy who drowned is Selim, who led him and others to safety while crossing the border. Alexander helps his friend steal some of Selim's clothes from the morgue so the refugee children can memorialize him. In the same abandoned building, he watches as they burn Selim's clothes and mourn his loss. One of the boys wonders who will guide them across the sea when they depart at night. In his analysis of the film, Lasse Thomassen argues that Angelopoulos hints at an emergent cosmopolitan identity through the children. He writes, "The community of refugee children in *Eternity and Day* is a community of those who are strangers everywhere, xenitis. They are neither simply Greek nor simply Albanian (or some other determinable national identity). They cannot be recognized according to national distinctions. They are the neither/nor of the either/or—the neither Geek nor Albanian, neither European nor non-European."[28] In other words, because the children are "strangers everywhere," they have no fixed national identity. Consequently, they lack a concept of home to which they can return, unlike Alexander, who can mentally return to his perfect day and dwell in the past. Their homeland exists only on the horizon of the future. As Thomassen explains, "This is a community without stable or clear limits, a community that is not like an inside to an outside. It is a community without a fixed centre; for instance, it is scattered across the city, only gathering momentarily."[29] This vision of community should not be confused with Michael Hardt and Antonio Negri's notion of "the multitude," criticized in chapter 2, which they define as "composed of innumerable internal differences that can never be reduced to a unity or a single identity."[30] The community of children in *Eternity and a Day* forms a unified nonidentity rather than a multiplicity of internal differences that have converged. This allows the film to reveal an emergent Kantian cosmopolitan belonging that transcends political and economic borders. Kant articulates the famous third article about hospitality in his essay "To Eternal Peace." According to Kant, "It is the right to visit [*Besuchscrecht*] which belongs to all men—the right belonging to all men to offer their society on account of the common possession of the surface of the earth. Since it is a globe, they cannot disperse infinitely, but must tolerate each other. No man has a greater fundamental right to occupy a particular spot than any other."[31]

In other words, to be a xenitis, "a stranger everywhere" like the refugee children, negates the current world order of economic and political borders. This negation expresses the hope that we might someday think through "the common possession of the surface of the earth." However, *Eternity and a Day* can only defer this hope into the future. Before the young boy departs by sea, he and Alexander briefly ride a bus. In this surreal sequence, they watch as a student couple breaks up, a political protester with a red flag falls asleep, and a musical trio performs. They also encounter the poet Solomos, who recites a poem that he leaves unfinished. As he gets off the bus, a distraught Alexander asks him, "How long does tomorrow last?" a question he will ask again in the film's final scene. After the bus ride, however, Alexander drives the boy to a port so he can sneak aboard a ship with other boys as they depart for elsewhere. The boy "sells" him another word, *argadini*, which they translate as "very late" and "deep into the night." While it is very late for Alexander, who is dying, the journey is only beginning for the young boy.

In the end, Alexander resists checking into the hospital and visits the empty beach house his daughter sold. The film leaves open the question of whether he has reconciled with his past. He once again replays the memory of his perfect day with his wife and friends. As he walks the beach with Anna, he reminds her that he once asked her, "How long does tomorrow last?" Her answer is the film's title, "An eternity and a day." With this, Alexander's memory of this perfect day dissolves and he walks toward the sea, shouting the words he purchased from the young boy. This implies that Alexander has finally exhausted his project of completing the Solomos poem, which the boy will undertake on his journey. The conclusion reminds us that we must continually work through the past if we are to envision an emergent cosmopolitan identity for the boy. In the final image, Alexander regresses further into his memory of the past. As he stands silently in front of the sea, on the soundtrack we hear his mother calling his name. This echoes the sequence from the beginning of the film where Alexander dreams of swimming in the sea as a child while his mother calls his name from a distance. As *Ulysses' Gaze* and *The Dust of Time* indicate, Angelopoulos imagines cinema itself as an apparatus that can help us further reconcile with the past and discover images that reveal a new future politics.

II. CINEMA AS PAST AND FUTURE

A Lost Gaze

In *Ulysses' Gaze* and *The Dust of Time*, Angelopoulos returns to the metacinematic themes first introduced in *Voyage to Cythera*. Both tell stories about unnamed directors credited only as A. The former stars Harvey Keitel as a Greek American director who travels throughout the Balkans and the war-torn former Yugoslavia to find undeveloped reels from the Manaki brothers, whose 1905 short *The Weavers*, about their grandmother, is considered the first film shot in the Balkans. The A in *The Dust of Time* is portrayed by Willem Dafoe. He is not searching for footage. He is completing a film about his mother, Eleni. Both films meditate on cinema's ability to work through the past. In *Ulysses' Gaze*, the era filmed by the Manaki brothers, encompassing the Balkan Wars, is juxtaposed to the war in Bosnia during the nineties. In *The Dust of Time*, the aftermath of the death of Stalin blends with the end of communism and the end of the twentieth century.

With its three-hour length, *Ulysses' Gaze* recalls the epic ambitions of Angelopoulos's seventies films. However, its narrative structure of the cyclical journey situates it within his second period. Released in between *The Suspended Step of the Stork* and *Eternity and a Day*, *Ulysses' Gaze* is the second film of the border trilogy. Unlike those films, however, it is more concerned with the porous cultural and political boundaries between past and present than it is with the existential realities of migration and exile. This idea is introduced in the opening sequence, where we see footage from *The Weavers* with voice-over from A, who explains that it is the first film from Greece and the Balkans. But he immediately wonders whether this is true. Is it the first cinematic gaze? Angelopoulos dissolves from *The Weavers* to a black-and-white image of the sea. The camera zooms out to reveal a man standing next to Yanaki Manaki, who is hunched over a camera as he tries to film a passing blue ship. The man explains that the year is 1954 and he is an apprentice for Yanaki. Color now infuses the image as Yanaki collapses into the arms of his apprentice. The camera follows him as he walks across the screen toward A, who has been listening the entire time. He explains to A that Yanaki mentioned the existence of three undeveloped reels from the turn of the century. The camera now follows A as he watches the passing ship and we hear his inner monologue about searching for the reels. Yanaki and his camera are no longer visible. In his analysis of this sequence, John Orr describes the aesthetic as a "startling innovation in the time-image." He explains, "Within the sequence shot Angelopoulos has shifted time around in unexpected ways. The film buff appears to be an anachronism, intruding into the time-space of an earlier history, but as the camera moves back, it retrospectively turns Manakis [Manaki] into a figure of history, who has intruded into the time-space of the present, that of Keitel, his distant successor."[32] Nonlinear narrative structures can be found in Angelopoulos's early films. In *The Traveling Players,* for example, a cut or a camera pan within a shot might displace us back in time. The difference here is that this sequence shot is simultaneously set in the past and the present. The temporal structure is a Möbius strip where the present intrudes into the past and the past is archived in the present. This surreal temporality, which Orr describes as "hallucinatory time-travel,"[33] defines A's journey throughout the Balkans to Sarajevo to find the undeveloped reels. In one of the most obscure sequences in the film, A crosses the border to Bulgaria in the present and is transported to 1915, where he enacts an incident in which Yanaki was sentenced to death for treason. At the last minute, his sentence is commuted to exile for the duration of the First World War. While this digression into the past represents an unguided excursion into A's fantasy where he identifies with his knowledge of Yanaki's story, it also highlights how the aftershocks of empires in the region complicate our understanding of identity and national origins. Thus, when A's fantasy transference into Yanaki's identity dissolves, he is shown crossing the Bulgarian border again. Asked by the guard his destination, he responds, "Philippopolis," which is the ancient Greek name for Plovdiv, one of the oldest cities in Europe, which has been conquered numerous times throughout its history. The guard corrects him and repeats, "Plovdiv."

For A, the journey to find the undeveloped reels is both personal and political. Though the two realms blend together throughout the film, *Ulysses' Gaze* is more critical of the personal aspect of A's journey than it is of the political meaning of finding the undeveloped reels. As Smaro Kamboureli argues, the film "radically questions origins." He explains, "*Ulysses' Gaze* suggests that home and nation are not always aligned: that they are, in fact, at odds with each other. Showing that the Balkans have long been a region where people of different ethnic backgrounds moved and settled in the midst of other ethnic groups, *Ulysses' Gaze* exposes the 'insanity' of trying to establish new national borders against the fluidity of diasporic movements."[34] This misalignment between home and nation is evident in how the film complicates A's backstory. Following his encounter with Yanaki's apprentice, A returns to Florina, his hometown in Greece, after several decades for a screening of his film. However, the screening is disrupted by religious protests and has been moved outside. In a self-reflexive twist, the soundtrack from his film is an English-language version of *The Suspended Step of the Stork*. We hear the scene where Alexander encounters the missing politician, who ruminates on how many borders he must cross before he reaches home. A tells his guides how much he would like to stay in town for personal reasons but he must depart again. The religious protesters interrupt the screening outside and confront the spectators. Since *Ulysses' Gaze* is also a loose retelling of *The Odyssey*, A sees for the first time the Penelope figure—here she is an old lover—who will reappear throughout the film as different women associated with the homeland to which A cannot return. He encounters Penelope again in the town of Monastiri, otherwise known as Bitola, in the Republic of North Macedonia, where the Manaki brothers moved from Greece. This time Penelope is a guide in the Manaki brothers' museum. Later A encounters her on a train traveling to Skopje and Bucharest. He explains his reasons for wanting to find the undeveloped reels and accepting the documentary project, describing it as "a way out" from another film he was trying to make. More importantly, he describes the reels as "the first glance, a lost glance, a lost innocence" and states that finding them might help him recover his "own first glance, lost long ago."

Ulysses' Gaze, though, implies that A's lost gaze and lost innocence can never be localized within national borders and cannot be recovered. When he arrives in Bucharest, we learn that A's family is from the port city of Constanţa, which historically had a large Greek population. After the Second World War, Romanian communists oppressed the bourgeois Greek communities, many members of which returned to Greece, an event that is dramatized in this sequence. It begins when A steps off the train and sees his mother. Her clothes indicate that we have drifted back into the forties. The two board a train for Constanţa. They arrive and walk the streets among Russian soldiers and a communist parade. A's return to his Constanţa home is depicted with a stunning ten-minute sequence shot that unfolds across successive New Year's Eves between 1945 and 1950. It begins with the adult A interacting with his family. He watches as his father returns from prison camp. Members of the People's Confiscation Committee arrive to abduct a family member. More members arrive in 1950 to loot their home. We learn that the father has secured a permit for the family to leave Romania and migrate to Greece, presumably to Florina, where A began his journey. The father explains that eighty families will be leaving the city. He expresses regret and mentions that his family has lived in Constanţa for centuries. The dream logic of the shot concludes with everyone posing for a family portrait with A, now a young child, who joins the photo. He has regressed psychologically before he departs for Greece. A can never return home because home is only a mental image, a surreal memory that intrudes into the present. Like the missing politician in *The Suspended Step of the Stork*, A must keep crossing borders and departing for elsewhere. The reality of national origins in the Balkans is, as Kamboureli argues, "diasporic movements" rather than localizable identity.

Ulysses' Gaze is more ambiguous about the political implications of A's quest to find the three reels. Whereas his personal journey to return home must be perpetually deferred, A does find and develop the reels. However, *Ulysses' Gaze* never reveals their contents to the audience. When asked in an interview about his choice to withhold what A sees, Angelopoulos explained that he did initially shoot something but decided against showing anything because "it was concrete" and he instead wanted to emphasize that A "reached his goal" by developing the film.[35] This invites the question of what A imagines he will see on the reels and how we should understand his political goal. On the train to Bucharest, he explains to Penelope, "The Manaki brothers went around photographing and filming people. They were trying to record a new era, a new century. Over 60 years they photographed faces, events, in the turmoil of the Balkans. They weren't concerned with politics, or racial questions, with who were their friends. They were interested in people." He adds, "All the ambiguities, the contrasts, the conflicts in this area of the world are reflected in their work."[36] In other words, the reels might contain a fleeting vision from the past of the underlying social unity in the Balkans. For A, cinema is a utopian medium that can transcend political and cultural divisions in order to chronicle the historical aftershocks of modernity, "a new era, a new century." Yet, as *Ulysses' Gaze* repeatedly emphasizes, these aftershocks also reveal the fragility of cinema's utopian potential. If cinema is, as is often claimed, a universal language, then the wars of the twentieth century and the turmoil that the Manaki brothers chronicled fragment this language and disperse it into the archive. This idea is introduced in the scene where A visits the home of the Manaki brothers' museum and encounters Penelope. He stares at the front door while Angelopoulos cuts to documentary footage of Miltiades Manaki walking down the street.[37] Miltiades explains that he and his brother arrived in Monastiri because times were difficult in Ioannina, Greece. His monologue is interspersed with archival footage from the Balkan Wars and the First World War. He explains that "all the great armies of Europe have trudged through this street," which would change names depending on the army. Angelopoulos cuts to a shot of A inside the museum, where noise from a projector indicates that the documentary footage has been playing. A is looking at one of the brothers' original cameras, which are now encased in glass, a blunt representation of how the utopian hope of cinema is museumized. When he leaves the museum, he visits the ruins of the Manaki brothers' movie theater. As he stands in front of the remains of the theater, we once again hear the soundtrack from the documentary. Miltiades explains, "We opened with a French film, *Rin-Tin-Tin,* but the reel was in horrible shape, it kept falling apart. We kept it together with pins. The musicians we'd hired kept loosing track. Business gradually picked up. But we were up to our neck in debt up until 1939, just before WWII when our cinema burnt down. The film we were showing, a Chaplin comedy, caught fire and that was the end of our cinema."[38] This image of a movie theater in ruins, which will be repeated when A arrives in Sarajevo, articulates the ephemerality of cinema. The film print, the delivery medium for the majority of the twentieth century, decays with each screening and falls apart. However, there is a deeper anxiety about the impermanence of cinema reflected in the refusal of *Ulysses' Gaze* to show the footage that A finds. This anxiety concerns cinematic time itself. Any image of unity the footage might contain can only be fixed as the past. It cannot invent a new future. Cinema is, as Mary Ann Doane argues, an archive of time susceptible to temporal decay.[39] In her brilliant work *The Emergence of Cinematic Time: Modernity, Contingency, the Archive,* she argues that cinematic time emerged in the late nineteenth century when our philosophical, scientific, and economic concepts of time were radically transformed. As such, it was imagined to be an apparatus with unparalleled ability to represent time.

Doane begins her book with an analysis of James Brander Matthews's iconic 1895 nightmarish short story, "The Kinetoscope of Time," where an unnamed narrator finds himself in a mysterious place with four kinetoscopes. He looks through the first two, where he watches fictional scenes from myth and literature. The narrator is approached by a mysterious man who says he witnessed all of the events and explains that fact is often inferior to fiction. He offers the narrator a deal. The remaining two kinetoscopes can show images from his past or future, provided the narrator gives him a year of his life in return. The narrator refuses and returns to town, where he discovers an engraving of the mysterious man that indicates he was from a previous century. Commenting on the story, Doane argues,

> Its rhetoric echoes that which accompanied the reception of early cinema, with its hyperbolic recourse to figures of life, death, immortality, and infinity. The cinema would be capable of recording permanently a fleeting moment, the duration of an ephemeral smile or glance. It would preserve the lifelike movements of loved ones after their death and constitute itself as a grand archive of time. As André Bazin would later point out, photographic technology "embalms time, rescuing it simply from its proper corruption." But because time's corruption is "proper" to it, its fixed representation also poses a threat, produces aesthetic and epistemological anxiety "The Kinetoscope of Time" registers this threat as the complicity of the machine with the demonic; hence the protagonist's refusal to look.[40]

A's monologue to Penelope about the Manaki brothers indicates that he, too, imagines cinema as an apparatus capable of archiving time and the ephemeral moments of humanity. Unlike the Matthews story, *Ulysses' Gaze* does not present the threat of accessing this archive of time as a demonic bargain. Rather, as the film's discourse about unlocalizable origins suggests, the threat of fixing time is inherently political. In other words, if *Ulysses' Gaze* were to reveal the content of the footage that A develops, then it would express the very nostalgia for fixed origins that the film criticizes as dangerous to the Balkans. The political meaning, then, of A's journey, accessing the Manaki brothers' archive of time, is that we should mourn the past rather than uncritically re-create it politically.

The film's demand for mourning over nostalgia is visualized through A's means of travel to Serbia from Romania. After the ten-minute sequence shot that depicts A's surreal return to his home in Constanţa, he awakes at night in a hotel room with Penelope. In the morning she takes him to the port, where a ship awaits. This ship carries unique cargo, a giant dismantled statue of Lenin that we presume has been sold to a museum. For more than a minute, we watch as a crane loads it onboard. Eventually it departs down the Danube. For several minutes, the film cuts between a long shot of the statute traveling down the river—Lenin's finger pointing to the sky and A barely visible next to it—and a shot of groups of people who have gathered by the river, clearly in awe of the image. In his analysis of this stunning sequence, Traverso describes it as a "funeral of Lenin, a broken and fallen statue leaving the stage of history," which "depicts the remembrance of communism as a work of mourning."[41] According to Traverso, this work of mourning is the central theme of the film. He writes,

> The end of communism as the end of a utopia and an act of remembrance as a ceremony of mourning both solemn and tragic, found its most poignant expression in Theo Angelopoulos's *Ulysses' Gaze* (1995), a movie devoted to the war in the former Yugoslavia. The erasing of the past, the rescue of its legacy, and the preservation of its memory are the film's connecting thread. The journey of its hero in the middle of a country devastated by war, looking for a lost fragment of film—the first Greek movie, whose last copy is conserved at Sarajevo's film archive, in a besieged city—is the metaphor of a collapsed world whose fall has swept away its hopes and utopias.[42]

Traverso correctly observes that *Ulysses' Gaze* mourns the end of communism as the end of utopia rather than as its specific failure as a historical political project. This is the symbolism of riding the dismantled Lenin statue into the former Yugoslavia. As chapter 2 argues, the ideological aim of Josip Broz Tito's Yugoslavia was to build "brotherhood and unity" between various ethnicities, but this project of unity quickly unraveled in the eighties when Yugoslavia experienced a severe economic downturn. Thus, the end of Yugoslavia signifies the collapse of the utopian dream of social unity in the Balkans. To that extent, *Ulysses' Gaze* risks depoliticizing communism. Rather than mourning the defeat of the politics of class struggle, it mourns the loss of a metaphysical unity in the past. This would confirm Fredric Jameson's criticism of Angelopoulos's second period of films that they are ultimately "more humanist than historical." A similar interpretation of the symbolism of the Lenin statue in the film can be found in Vrasidas Karalis's *History of Greek Cinema*, where he writes, "There are so many aspects to this film: it is a journey—the archetypal odyssey—to the origins of Balkan cinema, to the original gaze of unity and authenticity so savagely lost after the collapse of the last 'internationalist' project—the grand utopia of brotherhood and unity. The broken gigantic statue of Lenin, offered to the real god of Europe, the bloodline of all its civilizations, the river Danube, is a funeral of all ideologies that go back to the beginning of cinema, coinciding with the beginning of social questioning and unrest."[43] Though Karalis argues that the sequence with Lenin's statue critiques the transition to free-market capitalism, "the real god of Europe," he concludes that it memorializes "all ideologies that go back to the beginning of cinema." Since the birth of cinema coincides with the ideological struggles of the twentieth century, the sequence is a funeral for the end of history. However, the melancholy of the sequence obscures its nascent optimism. Though it is a funeral for the lost utopia for communism, the sequence also calls for a new cinematic modernism to imagine a new historical unity for the region. This is why Angelopoulos cuts from the sequence of A riding the ship to a nighttime shot of him seated on the statue where he reads from the diary of Miltiades Manaki, who describes his first encounter with cinema:

> In the early months of 1905 in Bucharest, Romania we were told that in England and France you could buy a machine for making moving pictures. We could hardly believe it. It took our breath away. But we had to believe it because we saw one of these moving pictures with our own eyes. The people in these pictures looked like puppets. They moved jerkily like puppets. But that didn't matter. We were completely fascinated. My brother Yanakis was so excited. He

> couldn't rest until he got ahold of this magic machine and take it back to Monastiri. He saw it in his dreams. He raved about it.[44]

The description of the camera as a "magic machine" invokes Doane's argument that the emergence of cinematic time would establish an archive for "lifelike movements" and "fleeting moments." The archive, however, is imperfect, its temporal gaps registering as the jerky movements of the people Miltiades saw on screen. Yet it is these dreamlike imperfections of the cinematic images that give the archive its psychological power. It invades our dreams because it is an imperfect replica of life. Moreover, this subconscious power is also inherently political, allowing for ideological reproduction. It is important to emphasize that A reads Miltiades's diary on a statue of Lenin, who acknowledged the ideological power of cinema. He is frequently quoted as telling Anatoly Lunacharsky, the first commissariat for education after the revolution, that cinema is the most important art for designing the new communist future. In his "Directives on the Film Business," Lenin, for example, explains that "special attention should be given to organising film showings in the villages and in the East, where they are novelties and where our propaganda, therefore, will be all the more effective."[45] Thus, while the sequence depoliticizes communism into mourning for a lost utopia, it also demands a new political modernism in cinema. Yet, as the end of *Ulysses' Gaze* indicates, we must finish mourning for a lost utopia before we can, as Mark Steven argues, imagine "a prehistory for the future left's unpredictable resurgence."

Once in Belgrade, A meets with a journalist friend who takes him to a man who used to be in charge of the archives. He lives in a dilapidated retirement home. He explains to A that he once possessed the reels from the Manaki brothers but was not able to develop them so he gave them to another archivist in Sarajevo. In a humorous scene in a bar that emphasizes the film's critique of searching for national origins, A and his friend overhear an argument between two men about whether Serbs or Albanians arrived first in the Balkans. A's friend explains, "They're arguing over who came first to the Balkans, the Serbs or the Albanians, only to come to the conclusion that it's all Hegel's fault for influencing Marx." Afterward A and his friend walk the streets toasting various artists, then A decides he must depart for Sarajevo by river. His journey is depicted as a surreal digression into the past, into the First World War, where he encounters Penelope again, this time as a Bulgarian housewife whose husband died in the war. A returns from this temporal digression and arrives in Sarajevo in the morning. The dream logic continues. In a series of shots, we see A running down streets past destroyed buildings and a UN truck. The sound of shelling can be heard. Absurdly, A asks people running for cover, "Is this Sarajevo?"

Eventually he finds the archivist Ivo Levy at an underground food market. Ivo and A run through the streets to his film archive, which is the basement of a destroyed film theater, an image that deliberately echoes A's visit to the ruins of the Manaki brothers' theater near their museum in the Republic of North Macedonia. War has once again fragmented the utopian potential of cinema. Ivo has relocated all his equipment and film prints to the basement. Showing A around, he mentions some of the film prints he has, including *Birth of a Nation*, *Metropolis*, and *Persona*. An exhausted A collapses and goes to sleep. He awakes at the arrival of Ivo's daughter, who lives on the other side of the city. This is his last encounter with Penelope. Together A and Ivo are able to develop the footage from the Manaki brothers, which they process and leave to dry. As Ivo explains, it is a foggy day, which means the city can return to normal since snipers lack visibility. He mentions that a youth orchestra of Serbs, Croats, and Muslims gathers to play music across the city. Ivo and A walk the foggy streets of Sarajevo as people watch the orchestra perform. They also watch a performance of *Romeo and Juliet* and walk past a graveyard where we see a burial ceremony. These are the images of unity and peace that A imagines might be contained on the reels of film. For the first time in *Ulysses' Gaze*, we are given a glimpse of a possible future, one where the divisions of the present have been overcome. However, these utopian images quickly slip into the past. Though A and Ivo reunite with Ivo's extended family, the fog becomes more dense. They become lost and wander too far from the city, then encounter Serbian paramilitaries who murder everyone except for A, who stands impotently in the distance. We hear their bodies thrown into the river. As the troops leave, he rushes toward their bodies and cries.

In the final scene, A has returned to Ivo's theater. We hear the sound of the film projector and the light flickering onscreen. It is clear that A has just watched the developed reels. Angelopoulos cuts to a close-up of A, who has been crying. He recites a soliloquy as Odysseus speaking to Penelope about his return in which he promises to tell her about "the whole human adventure" and "the story that never ends." Angelopoulos cuts to the credits as we continue to hear the projector flickering. Like *Voyage to Cythera*, *The*

Suspended Step of the Stork, and *Eternity and a Day, Ulysses' Gaze* ends with a character departing again for elsewhere. The difference here is that A has completed his journey. Though he believed that his journey would be a homecoming, the political meaning of developing the reels of the Manaki brothers has been to mourn the lost utopia and the lost unity in the Balkans. Having completed its mourning, *Ulysses' Gaze* reconciles with the past and suggests another journey to discover a new cinema with images of unity, a theme Angelopoulos revisits in his final film, *The Dust of Time.*

The Dust of Time: "Nothing Ever Ends"

The Dust of Time is the second part of a loose trilogy about twentieth-century Greek history. It follows *The Weeping Meadow* (2004), which is about a Greek community whose members return to Greece in 1919 after the Russian Revolution. It focuses on Eleni, a young girl who is adopted by a family. She falls in love with her adopted stepbrother, Alexi, and gives birth to twin sons who are sent to private school. Eleni and Alexi run away when she is forced to marry her stepfather, Spyros. The film follows their lives for several decades through the Metaxas dictatorship, the Second World War, and the Greek Civil War. Eleni's story ends in tragedy as Alexi travels to America in hopes that the family can emigrate. He enlists in the war and dies on the battlefield in the Pacific Ocean Theater. Her sons die fighting on opposing sides of the civil war. *The Weeping Meadow* begins brilliantly with a Brechtian long take of the Greek community members walking in the estuary of a river toward the camera. A self-reflexive narrator explains that this is "scene one" and redundantly describes the arrival of the community while Spyros himself narrates their exile from Russia to someone offscreen. The heightened artifice provocatively suggests the impossibility of periodization and narrating history. However, the remainder of the film does not explore this idea. Though it contains his signature pictorial beauty, *The Weeping Meadow* is also, by Angelopoulos's standards, a linear historical epic with few digressions into theatricality and fantasy. It summarizes his more radical films that cover the same historical period, such as *Days of '36* and *The Traveling Players.*

The Dust of Time is more innovative in its political modernism than *The Weeping Meadow*. Like *Ulysses' Gaze,* it tells the story of a director credited only as A, portrayed this time by Willem Dafoe. Though it is not a sequel to *Ulysses' Gaze,* it functions as a postscript, reworking its themes about cinema and reconciliation with the past. Its narrative is as spatially and temporally digressive, but *The Dust of Time* downplays the self-conscious mythologizing of *Ulysses' Gaze* and is not structured as an epic journey. Moreover, Angelopoulos deemphasizes his signature sequence-shot style. He even parallel edits at times to express the film's interplay between dream, memory, and representation, which hints at unfulfilled stylistic evolution since he died filming the intended third part of the trilogy, *The Other Sea*. The relative lack of long takes turns *The Dust of Time* into one of Angelopoulos's most narratively obscure films and necessitates multiple viewings in order to understand its plot. The use of long takes in *Ulysses' Gaze* and *Eternity and Day* establishes a visual continuity for the blurring between history, fantasy, and memory. In comparison, *The Dust of Time* lacks this continuity and fragments the relationship between past and present. However, it is also this fragmentation that allows the film to suggest an emergent future rather than retreating into the archives to reestablish the defeated utopian projects of the past, such as the incomplete Solomos poem Alexander tries to finish in *Eternity and a Day* or the undeveloped reels of the Manaki brothers that A searches for in *Ulysses' Gaze*. In other words, its speculations about cinema's ability to imagine a new political modernism as an antidote to the malaise of capitalist realism in postcommunist Europe make it the most optimistic of Angelopoulos's late films.

The A in *The Dust of Time* is directing a film about his mother, Eleni. She is not the same character from *The Weeping Meadow*. This Eleni was exiled to the Soviet Union after the Second World War and the Greek Civil War. She eventually migrates to North America. During her exile, she becomes involved in a love triangle with Jacob, a German Jew, and Spyros, a Greek communist, who also arrives in the Soviet Union. Spyros is A's father. The present-day setting of *The Dust of Time* is 1999 in Rome and Berlin. The plot is structured around A's struggles with his film and his failed marriage. His daughter, also named Eleni, runs away. Eventually, Eleni and Spyros arrive in present-day Berlin in 1999 to visit and celebrate New Year's Eve. The two reunited and married in the seventies. Jacob also arrives in Berlin.

The film begins with a slow zoom of A driving onto the lot of an Italian film studio. On the soundtrack, we hear his voice-over, "Nothing ended. Nothing ever ends. I return to where I let a story slip into the past, losing its clarity under the dust of time and then unexpectedly at some moment it returns like a dream. Nothing ever ends."[46] His thoughts are a guide for the narrative structure of *The Dust of Time*, whose story, indeed, loses its clarity as Angelopoulos cuts between present-day Europe and Eleni's past in

Siberia, the United States, and Canada. Similar to *Voyage to Cythera, The Dust of Time* blurs the boundaries between events from Eleni's life, the film A is directing, and his imagination of events derived from reading his mother's letters. In particular, the opening sequence jarringly keeps slipping into the past. As A exits his car, Angelopoulos cuts to a shot of Spyros on a train to Moscow as he illegally acquires travel permits and papers. The opening sequence continues to cut between Spyros on the train and A walking down the hall of the studio while talking to his assistant about the film's producers, who are concerned about a break in the shooting schedule. On first viewing, the editing reads as crosscutting intended to establish narrative simultaneity between the characters and events. However, the characters' clothing clarifies that these are different historical periods. The sequence becomes more abstract as it continues, invoking the "dust of time" of the title. A sound bridge links Spyros memorizing his papers and A walking through the studio toward the footage of his current film being printed. It is here that *The Dust of Time* becomes self-reflexive and visualizes the theme of how the cinematic apparatus can help us reconcile with the past. The title credits appear onscreen while A looks carefully at the print. The camera zooms closer to A as we begin to hear Russian voices and the sound of a parade. It is unclear whether this is A's imagination or whether it is the soundtrack to his footage. The sound becomes louder as the camera rests on A's face. Angelopoulos then cuts to black-and-white footage of Stalin, who is waving to a cheering crowd. Further dislocating the audience, Angelopoulos moves the camera away from the screen to reveal a crowd watching the footage, placing us again in the past, in the Russian city of Temirtau. Spyros has arrived and he, Eleni, and Jacob are in an audience of communist exiles from the Greek Civil War watching the footage. A young Greek communist runs into the screening with news that something has happened in town. As we shall learn, Stalin has died.

The self-reflexive nature of the sequence establishes the cinematic formalism by which *The Dust of Time* aims to reconcile the past and present and ultimately suggest a hopeful vision for the future with its final image of Spyros and A's daughter in front of the Brandenburg Gate. But before it can convey this hope, the film must define its past and present. As Mark Steven argues, the opening sequence establishes that the past "is monumentally socialist, whereas the present, with its talk of producers, financiers and budgetary constraints, is decisively bound to the market. It is as though the film itself, *The Dust of Time,* wants to allegorise its own historical location, stretched between these two moments and the political forces that define them."[47] In other words, like *Ulysses' Gaze, The Dust of Time* is concerned with representing the transition from socialism to free-market capitalism. It does so, however, without depoliticizing communism into an abstract lost utopia. Consider the fundamental difference between the visual metaphors the films employ to represent the death of communism. *Ulysses' Gaze* memorializes Lenin and the death of utopian ideology in the scene where A travels the Danube. In contrast, in *The Dust of Time,* the death of Stalin represents the end of communism and precipitates the imprisonment, exile, and wanderings of Eleni, Spyros, and Jacob. Stalin's death is also the structuring absence at the heart of the film's temporal digressions. Absent his vision of historical progress, the film recedes into blurring diegetic realities.

As the opening sequence continues, Spyros and Eleni travel into town when they hear that something has happened. On the streetcar, another man mentions that the whole town is in an uproar. Next we see people walking to the town square and gathering in front of a statue of Stalin. In one of the film's few Brechtian long takes, the camera cranes upward to reveal hundreds of people listening to a loudspeaker that is announcing the death of Stalin. The shot continues to linger as the crowd disperses, emphasizing, as Steven argues, "how the collective atomises, decoupling down to the singular individual."[48] This dispersal of collective politics is not mourned beyond this scene. Rather, Angelopoulos cuts from the image of the last person leaving the town square back to the present, where A and his assistant visit the orchestra scoring his film. This visit is interrupted by a phone call from his daughter, who we learn has run away. A rushes home, where he finds a lost letter from his mother. As he reads the letter, the film cuts back to the empty town square. It is night. The streetcar is stranded in the middle of the road. Two people approach it and discover Spyros and Eleni inside having sex, and the couple is arrested. The diegetic reality of the scene is indeterminate. The editing suggests A is imagining it as a scene for his film. If so, his is a regressively melodramatic imagination given the historical events depicted in the narrative. As Steven argues, the film shifts "from an epic of monumental historiography to the differently affective realm of sexual and familial relations" in order to disperse history into a "post-utopian" narrative.[49] The death of Stalin in the film signifies the shift from collective politics to the personal melodrama of A's life. He was conceived the night his parents were arrested.

Three years later, Eleni places him on a train to Moscow to live with Jacob's sister. Later in life, he is alienated from his personal relationships. Like his counterpart in *Ulysses' Gaze*, his current film project is an attempt to reconstruct history.

The second sequence in *The Dust of Time* about Stalin visualizes the forgetting and fragmenting of history. It is 1956 in Siberia. Eleni and Jacob visit a cultural center. We hear a voice-over from a letter she wrote, which was presumably read by A for his film project. She references the Twentieth Congress of the Communist Party of the Soviet Union, which is where Nikita Khrushchev denounced the personality cult of Stalin. In a stunning shot, Eleni and Jacob walk up the stairs to the center. Busts and statues of Stalin are visible everywhere. While this is the film's only explicit reference to the period of de-Stalinization, the entire narrative structure of *The Dust of Time* formalizes the political problem of what comes after Stalin. Recall from the introduction that Evgeny Dobrenko argues that the cult of personality surrounding Stalin "left without an answer the question of what there would be 'after communism'" and introduced a new temporality in which the future was "concluded" and "the present itself underwent complete de-realisation."[50] In other words, the contradiction of Stalinism was such that the present was shifted into the past as a prehistory for the communist utopia to come, which also shifted the present into a future that has been concluded. This temporal delirium is emphasized by how the film transitions into present-day Europe from 1956. Angelopoulos cuts to a shot of A walking through the Italian sound stage and then dissolves to a shot of him walking through his daughter's room in Berlin. As A is in his daughter's room, he receives a phone call and learns that his parents' plane has been diverted to a different airport because of a terrorist attack. These surreal leaps in space and time structure the remainder of the film. In one sequence, multiple characters' points of view combine into a memory of the past. In it, an adult A drives his father, in the past, to a bar in Ontario where Eleni works. This immediately cuts to a scene, in present-day Berlin, where Jacob, Eleni, and Spyros enter a bar. As Spyros walks through the bar, he remembers his reconciliation with Eleni.

The present-day setting of *The Dust of Time* is repeatedly visualized as an era after the end of history. Consider how Angelopoulos represents the arrival of Spyros and Eleni at the airport. Because of the terrorist attack, they are in line waiting for a digital body scan. This is in stark contrast with the "monumentally socialist" past, when Spyros and Eleni were Greek communist exiles in the Soviet Union. Here the atomization of the present extends beyond the marketplace. In a close-up, we watch as the elderly Spyros stands in front of the scanner, his nude body projected on a screen for a guard to view. Once a committed socialist, he is reduced to a digital image of bare life. In addition to this image of a body digitized and severed from any collective politics, *The Dust of Time* references Francis Fukuyama's thesis about the end of history in a letter from A to his mother that we hear him read. He states,

> Berlin. 10 November 1989. Mother, here yesterday we lived a historic moment. The Berlin Wall no longer exists. In the streets both yesterday and today thousands of Germans visiting and celebrating, singing, dreaming. Some hasten to predict that the end of the Cold War also meant the end of history. I know like father you'll have reservations about all of this, but it's time we saw a new era. We finished shooting. Both the crew and actors have either left or are leaving. I'm staying. Her name is Helga. When she secretly crossed from East to West Berlin one terrifying night seventeen years ago she was only fifteen. And an unexpected meeting. In the crowd I caught sight of Jacob and Aunt Rachel and her husband Dan. They were on their way to Leipzig to find their old family home. Mother, last night I dreamt that we walked together among the ruins of the wall but when I turned to look at you it wasn't you. A little girl. A little Eleni held out her hand to me.[51]

The optimism that A feels as a result of the reunification of Berlin—meeting his ex-wife, dreaming of a daughter, and seeing Jacob—fades by 1999. In the present, Jacob is still in love with Eleni and will commit suicide. We also learn that Eleni is terminally ill. The reconciliation between the two Elenis, grandmother and granddaughter, the latter of whom is found by the German police, is temporary. The older Eleni lies down in her granddaughter's bed. Nevertheless, *The Dust of Time* maintains its hopeful demand that "it's time we a saw a new era." However, for the film it is the post-communist era that emerged after the fall of the Berlin Wall, the era of the atomized marketplace and the digital security state, that now needs to fade. In the final sequence, A arrives with a doctor for his mother. We can hear the New Year's Eve celebration outside. The camera zooms in on Spyros and cuts one last time to the past. Eleni is running happily down the street in Siberia. In the distance we can see Spyros chasing her. We return to the present with A and the doctor in the adjoining room. A is crying. The sequence becomes theatrical.

A looks up as he hears an unnaturally strong wind blow open the shutters in Eleni's room. As he enters the room, the curtains drift and we see his daughter at her grandmother's bedside. The camera zooms in on Spyros, who begs for Eleni to wake up. The camera rests on a close-up of his outstretched hand, which his granddaughter takes, then the two walk out on the balcony. Further confounding our sense of the reality of this image, A narrates, "Outside it was snowing. The snow was falling silently on the city that was still sleeping, on the deserted streets, the waters of the canals, on all the dead and the living, on time past and on time passing. On the universe."[52] His words appropriate language from the iconic ending of James Joyce's short story "The Dead." But there is a crucial distinction: whereas the snow falling in Joyce suggests a melancholy ending to Gabriel's story, in Angelopoulos's iconography, snow, like the mist and fog that repeat throughout his films, represents the possibility of historical emergence, a "new era." Such is the case with the snow and fog at the end of *Ulysses' Gaze,* which afford a fleeting moment of peace in Sarajevo.

The same is true for the dreamlike final image of the film. As Spyros and the young Eleni walk out onto the balcony, Angelopoulos cuts to a shot of them in front of the Brandenburg Gate. They hold hands as they run in slow motion, smiling in the snow, toward the camera. The image conveys the historical symbolism of the Brandenburg Gate since Prussian king Frederick William II first ordered its construction in the late eighteenth century. Having been the site of many key moments from the era of Napoleon to that of the Nazis, it came to symbolize the ideological division of the Cold War. Once the Berlin Wall was erected, the gate became inaccessible. Thus, the image of the elderly Spyros, once a Greek communist, running with his granddaughter in front of the gate synthesizes the past with the present in order to suggest hope that the post-communist malaise about the end of history will give way to a new era. Compared with the endings of *The Suspended Step of the Stork* and *Ulysses' Gaze,* which imply uncertain futures for their characters, *The Dust of Time*'s ending gives cinematic form to the future. Notably, Angelopoulos decided against showing the footage that A develops in *Ulysses' Gaze,* fearing that the utopian image the Manaki brothers filmed would be too concrete. Here, however, Angelopoulos ends with a self-reflexive image of cinematic time itself and its ability to imagine a new temporality for history. Time is spatialized in the shot. The snow falls. Spyros and Eleni run in slow motion to the camera, which zooms in on them. In his analysis of Alain Resnais, Gilles Deleuze writes in *Cinema 2: The Time-Image,*

> This is what happens when the image becomes the time-image. The world has become memory, brain, superimposition of ages or lobes, but the brain itself has become consciousness, continuation of ages, creation or growth of ever new lobes, re-creation of matter as with styrene. The screen itself is the cerebral membrane where immediate and direct confrontations take place between the past and the future, the inside and the outside, at a distance impossible to determine, independent of any fixed point. . . . The image no longer has space and movement as its primary characteristics but topology and time.[53]

This passage appropriately describes the final time image of *The Dust of Time*, which is about "topology and time." The topology is the shape of European history itself, trying to fulfill the EU motto "United in diversity." The hope represented by Spyros and the young Eleni running together with hands joined does not transcend the history that transpired around the gate. Yet it is a moving invitation for a new cinematic modernism that can engage in discourse about, as Deleuze writes, the confrontations "between the past and the future." Angelopoulos's final film of the trilogy, *The Other Sea,* would have directly confronted the aftershocks of the euro crisis. Rather than mourn its incompletion because of his accidental death, we can look to the final time-image of *The Dust of Time* as an invitation to advance European history past its post-communist malaise.

CONCLUSION

ONCE UPON A TIME THERE WAS A EUROPE

One of the arguments of this book is that the aftershocks of the European debt crisis have created parallels between the collapse of Yugoslavia and the disintegration of the EU. As chapter 2 discusses, the immediate causes of Yugoslavia's disintegration can be traced to the economic crises of the seventies. Unable to sustain its levels of foreign debt, Yugoslavia was forced by the International Monetary Fund to implement austerity and market reforms to service its debt during the eighties. In this unstable political environment, nationalistic politicians like Slobodan Milošević gained in popularity. Yugoslavia's decline also revealed the wealth inequality between its various republics, which the communist federal government could not alleviate. Consequently, the wealthiest republics, Slovenia and Croatia, were the first to secede.

Though Yugoslavia's economic collapse was substantially more severe than the downturn faced by the EU in the aftermath of the 2008 debt crisis, a similar degree of wealth inequality has been exposed. Data from 2017 regarding the gross domestic product per capita and actual individual consumption by household shows the gap between southern and northern Europe. At the bottom of both categories are the candidate and applicant states of Serbia, the Republic of North Macedonia, Bosnia, and Albania.[1] Of the twenty-eight member states, Croatia and Bulgaria rank last. Such wealth inequality contributes to the rise of right-wing Euroskeptic parties throughout the continent. The Alternative for Germany party, the Freedom Party of Austria, and the Northern League in Italy have all made substantial electoral gains by channeling legitimate economic discontent into anti-immigrant xenophobia. Concerned by this rise in right-wing populism, the European Commission invoked Article 7 of the Lisbon Treaty against Poland in December 2017, while the European Parliament did so against Hungary in September 2018 for violating basic European values. Article 7 explains that four-fifths of the European Commission or the Parliament can censure a member state for breaching the European values articulated in Article 2, which explains, "The Union is founded on the values of respect for human dignity, freedom, democracy, equality, the rule of law and respect for human rights, including the rights of persons belonging to minorities. These values are common to the Member States in a society in which pluralism, non-discrimination, tolerance, justice, solidarity and equality between women and men prevail."[2] While the egalitarian and democratic goals of the article are praiseworthy, in practice the EU, which began as a free-trade agreement, has always privileged markets over democracy. In *Adults in the Room: My Battle with the European and American Deep Establishment*, Yanis Varoufakis explains, "The EU began as a cartel of big business limiting competition between central European heavy industries and securing export markets for them in peripheral countries such as Italy and, later, Greece."[3] In the past Greece could address its structural deficits by devaluing its currency, but this became impossible once it adopted the euro. Thus, the financial crisis of 2008 exacerbated Greece's debt and left it without any monetary policy flexibility.

In his memoir, Varoufakis details his failed attempt, as Greek minister of finance in 2015, to renegotiate the terms of the Greek bailouts. The lengthy memoir repeatedly indicates how the International Monetary Fund and financial institutions of Europe subverted democracy in order to promote bank bailouts and impose austerity measures on Greece, a process summarized by Wolfgang Schäuble, the German finance minister, who is quoted as saying that elections cannot be allowed to change economic policy. Varoufakis's memoir highlights why the dispute over Greek financial policy contributed to the rise of right-wing populism. At the beginning of the book, he writes,

> The story it tells is not only symbolic of what Europe, Britain and the United States are becoming. It also provides insight into how and why our polity has fractured. . . .
>
> Shortly after the ruthless suppression of our rebellion, the opposition lost its momentum in Spain; no doubt many voters feared they would suffer a fate similar to ours. Having observed the leaders of the European Union and its allies

> callously disregard democracy in Greece and scare off the Spanish, many supporters of the Labour Party in Britain went on to vote to leave the European Union in June 2016. Brexit boosted Donald Trump. Donald Trump's triumph blew fresh wind into the sails of xenophobic nationalists throughout Europe and the world.[4]

Varoufakis draws a clear connection between the Greek bailouts, Brexit, and the rise of "xenophobic nationalists" throughout Europe. Since the publication of his memoir, the formal end of the Greek bailout program was announced for 2018, though it will still take years for the debt crisis to be fully resolved and for the economy to recover.[5] As Varoufakis explains, the bailout program exposed the undemocratic core of the EU and has intensified Euroskepticism by right-wing nationalists who are exploiting discontent with the EU.

The long-term repercussions of the Brexit vote are also likely to intensify this dynamic. At the time of this writing, there is still no agreement for the United Kingdom's orderly exit from the EU, which was initially scheduled to conclude in March 2019, two years after the government invoked Article 50 of the Treaty on European Union, which describes the withdrawal of a member state. Though the withdrawal date has been extended, there is little indication that the United Kingdom can avoid a "hard exit" in which they have not negotiated a customs union or access to the EU common market. The lack of a customs union, in particular, threatens to renew hostilities in Northern Ireland because it would no longer have an open border with the Republic of Ireland. The disastrous negotiations in the UK Parliament resulted in the resignation of Tory prime minister Theresa May in May 2019.

The political deadlock of Brexit can be explained by the ending of Emir Kusturica's 1995 film *Underground,* which ambitiously traces the history of Yugoslavia from the Second World War to its dissolution. Though the film has been criticized for representing the Balkans as culturally backward, its final image predicts a possible future for Europe. *Underground* begins when the partisan Marko hides people from the Nazis in a Belgrade cellar. He convinces the group, which includes his brother Ivan and best friend, Blacky, that the Second World War never ended. They manufacture weapons for Marko, who leads a double life as a close confidant of Josip Broz Tito and as an arms trafficker. Eventually Blacky emerges above ground in the sixties. *Underground* then leaps ahead thirty years to the Yugoslav wars in 1992. Blacky is leading a militia as he searches for his son, who was also in the underground cellar. Marko is now a war profiteer, trying to broker an arms deal. Blacky's militia kills Marko and his wife, Natalia. Blacky himself commits suicide by jumping in a well. In a fantastical ending, the characters are reconciled for a wedding at the banks of a river. As they dance joyfully, Ivan turns to the camera and says that one day they will tell their children fairy tales that begin, "Once upon a time there was a country." In the final image, the land literally ruptures and drifts out to the water as characters dance obliviously. In her astute reading of the film's surreal conclusion, Rosalind Galt writes, "The film is thus predicated on an impossible time, as well as an impossible space. There is no time at which Yugoslavia, or any of its various states, existed as a coherent and boundaried space. Not only is there no Yugoslavia now, but there never was an uncontested Yugoslav identity. Thus, to be nostalgic for a point of 'once upon a time there was a country' is to set up a nostalgia for an impossibility."[6] Galt's insightful analysis of the ending also applies to the political deadlock facing Europe since the debt crisis. Europe is torn between two competing visions of impossible space and impossible time, both of which erode the potential for a more authentic democratic union. On the one hand, the neoliberal EU promotes the impossibility of the end of history and the promise of free-market capitalism to spread the values described in Article 2 of the Treaty of Lisbon. However, as the Greek bailout program proves, when markets and democracy decouple during economic downturns, the interests of markets take precedent. In contrast to the neoliberalism of the EU, the right-wing nationalists claim to support a European unity, which has never existed, against the encroachment of Islam. Viktor Orbán, for example, defines his goal as follows: "We are working on building an old-school Christian democracy, rooted in European traditions."[7] Such nationalistic rhetoric about defending Western tradition against a decline in values has its corollary in the self-image of the former Yugoslav republics and how they defined themselves in relation to the Balkans and Europe. As Slavoj Žižek observes, "For the Serbs, [the Balkans] begins down there in Kosovo or Bosnia, and they defend the Christian civilization against this Europe's Other; for the Croats, they begin in orthodox, despotic, Byzantine Serbia, against which Croatia defends the values of democratic Western civilization; for Slovenes, it begins with Croatia, and we are the last outpost of the peaceful *Mitteleuropa*; for many Italians and Austrians, they begin in Slovenia, the Western outpost of Slavic hordes." Žižek extends this chain of the geographic imaginary all the way to Britain. Though his text was published in 2000, the inclusion of Britain resonates differently after Brexit. Žižek writes that, for "British opponents of the European Union for whom—implicitly, at least—the whole of continental Europe functions today as a new version of the Balkan Turkish Empire, with Brussels as the new Istanbul, a voracious despotic center which threatens British freedom and sovereignty . . ." The result of the Brexit vote is the culmination of what Žižek argues is the "identification of continental Europe itself with the Balkans, its barbarian Other."[8] In other words, European identity has always defined itself as the boundary between civilization and barbarism, even internally. This is why it is impossible to spread democratic values via the free market to unify the continent. The Greek debt crisis and the subsequent austerity measures proved that there is no cultural solidarity between Europe's core and periphery nations, especially during an economic downturn.

THE UTOPIAN HOPE OF CINEMATIC TIME

Throughout this book, I have sought to update the discourses of political modernism and counter-cinema and argue that the geopolitics of Eastern Europe and the Balkans allow us to rethink possibilities for both. It is essential to articulate new representational strategies that can imagine alternatives to the political malaise of contemporary Europe. As chapter 3 argues, these strategies can be found in the films of Béla Tarr and Cristi Puiu, whose long-take styles immerse spectators in the materiality of cinematic time in order to critique communist and capitalist narratives of historical progress. Similarly, the last films of Theo Angelopoulos examine the potential of cinematic time to help us reconcile with the past and map the reemergence of the political Left defeated by the collapse of international communism.

Angelopoulos's films in particular address a larger historical question related to rethinking political modernism and art cinema and revisiting the debate regarding modernism versus realism. His work asks us to consider the role of utopian hope in imagining alternatives to the malaise of the post-communist order. This issue also frames Ernst Bloch's defense of modernist aesthetics against György Lukács's realism. In other words, Bloch's larger critical project is to rethink the utopian possibilities of Marxism. In his afterword to the collection *Aesthetics and Politics,* Fredric Jameson writes, "Bloch's Utopian principle aims at jarring socialist thought loose from its narrow self-definition in terms which essentially prolong the categories of capitalism itself," adding that his "priorities suggest the need to think the 'transition to socialism' in terms of radical difference, of a more absolute break with that particular past."[9] This principle of moving socialism away from the "categories of capitalism itself" that Jameson describes has new relevancy in the context of post-communist Eastern Europe and the Balkans, where the failures of the regions' communist past and the capitalist present both contribute to the sense of political malaise. As chapter 3 explains, neoliberal market reforms during the nineties and the early years of the new century were justified as pragmatic reforms that would dismantle the last vestiges of communist state power. However, when neoliberalism itself failed with the financial crash, the political identity of Eastern Europe and the Balkans experienced further derealization. To reiterate Boris Groys's argument, the end of communism already meant the unmooring of identity from a modern universal history that would unite all people. The debt crisis, in turn, accelerated economic instability and privileged undemocratic austerity politics. Consequently, for most people in the regions, neither a return to the communist past nor a future of capitalist prosperity seems possible, which is why the political parties of the extreme Right have been able to gain electoral power by presenting themselves as an alternative to the EU.[10] To untangle this political deadlock, we must reaffirm Bloch's utopian principle of hope, even if we do not accept the entirety of his uniquely messianic Marxism. Consider the 1964 interview between Bloch and Theodor Adorno where the two discuss the meaning of utopia. Adorno articulates the notion that utopia resides "essentially in the determined negation, the determined negation of that which is." As such, he warns "not to conceive of certain utopias in detail" lest we lose the ability to know "what the false thing is." At the same time, Adorno acknowledges that the disappearance of the utopian element from socialism transforms it into an ideology of domination. Though often in agreement with Adorno, Bloch nevertheless describes his understanding of utopia as "a process of being" for which Marxism functions as a precondition. As he states, "Only when all the guests have sat down at the table can the Messiah, can Christ come."[11] Bloch's critical innovation, according to Enzo Traverso, is that "rather than a 'cold utopia' depicting socialism as a future inscribed into the laws of history," Marxism is a form of "anthropological optimism" and humanism that would fulfill the egalitarian project of the Enlightenment. As Traverso explains, Bloch understood utopia in messianic terms as "the realm of 'not yet'" toward which we hope.[12]

Most of the films analyzed in this book are not invested in direct representations of utopia. Despite lacking in concrete utopias, the principle of hope expressed by this book resides in the materiality of cinematic time and its ability to critique the present while also conveying the "not yet" of the allusive emergent possibilities for a new world. As I argue in chapter 3, this formalization of the materiality of cinematic time in the long take is the great aesthetic innovation of Andrei Tarkovsky. Throughout *Sculpting in Time,* Tarkovsky synthesizes discourses of modernism and realism, arguing for film images that allow for both subjective spectator responses and concrete representations of the totality of life. Tarr translates this synthesis into a discourse on the post-communist condition. Despite the pessimism of their surface themes, his work nevertheless conveys a haptic humanism regarding the lived reality of his characters. Tarr intensifies Tarkovsky's style by further elevating the sequence shot into an expression of the materiality of time. Similarly, the films of Puiu convey the message, as he describes, that "life is more important than cinema,"[13] echoing the desire of Tarkovsky and Tarr to extend the meaning of the film image beyond the frame.

The late films of Angelopoulos articulate a political hope that is deeply intertwined with a self-reflexive discourse about the nature of cinematic time. Thus, in *Ulysses' Gaze,* the mourning for the end of communism is mapped against a search for lost film footage. Though the film is ambivalent about the search for ethnic and national origins, it is committed to the idea that cinema emerges from the impulse to create an archive of time that can help us reconcile with the past and glimpse an emergent future. In Angelopoulos's late films, the sequence shot and the time image express a utopian Marxist historiography, one where the future is not concluded by the laws of scientific communism or neoliberalism, which reduces all future life to market transactions. This is why many of his films end with images of the "not yet," with characters departing for elsewhere, a new space that extends "beyond the edges of the screen" toward an unrepresentable future.[14] Even his flawed final film, *The Dust of Time,* with its sprawling personal and collective histories, articulates this "not yet," which is ultimately the reemergence of a Left that has lost its utopia.

This resurgence is necessary if Europe is to avoid the fate predicted by Jan Švankmajer in his self-described "work of agitprop," *The Death of Stalinism in Bohemia,* from 1990, which is analyzed in chapter 2. Recall that Švankmajer's dizzying stop-motion animation history of communism in Czechoslovakia, from Klement Gottwald to the Velvet Revolution, ends with the startling image of the bust of Stalin rescued from the trash, from the dustbin of history into which Leon Trotsky condemned the Mensheviks, and is painted with the colors of the then-Czechoslovakian flag. Echoing the opening of the film, where the bust of Stalin gives birth to Gottwald, this freshly painted, reanimated Stalin is placed on the operating table and is cut open for a cesarean delivery of a new totalitarian nationalistic leader. Here, again, we should consider the parallels between the dissolution of Yugoslavia and the rise in xenophobia and right-wing politics in the EU since the debt crisis. In his prescient short film, Švankmajer imagines a future Europe whose mass movements are nationalistic, a haunting prospect that echoes the political and social instabilities of the thirties. To counter this regression into the worst horrors of European history, new cinematic political modernisms can imagine emergent historiographies, such as the ones expressed throughout this book. A new principle of hope is needed to establish the resurgence of a Left that has overcome its melancholy regarding the end of communism and has reconciled with the legacies of Stalinism. It must counter both Europe's growing nationalism and its zombie neoliberalism, which privileges markets over democracy. In order to imagine this Left, cinema can still be the most important art.

ACKNOWLEDGMENTS

The writing of this book would not have been possible without the generous support of Columbia College Chicago and my department, Cinema and Television Arts. I began researching and writing this project while on sabbatical in 2015. Since then, I have benefited from professional development funds that allowed me to present versions of these chapters at conferences, especially at the annual Society for Cinema and Media Studies conference. I have also been privileged to teach courses on some of the filmmakers analyzed in this book. In 2018, I was especially happy to teach an entire course on Béla Tarr and slow cinema attended by amazing and dedicated students. I would like to thank chairs Bruce Sheridan and Eric Scholl for giving me the freedom to teach such courses.

Though I began working on this book in 2015, the origins of the project are much earlier. No doubt my interest in nationalism, social disintegration, and European integration stems from watching, with horror and confusion, news reports about the unraveling of the former Yugoslavia in the early nineties. I visited family in the former country a few times in the eighties, so I was particularly struck by how quickly it collapsed politically and socially. I wanted to understand why. One of the arguments of this book is that the rise of right-wing populism in Europe since the financial crisis of 2008 has unfortunate parallels with the disintegration of Yugoslavia.

Many of the ideas and methods in this book were first formed while finishing my PhD at the University of Wisconsin–Milwaukee. As a modern studies student, I was able to develop and synthesize my various interests in Marxism, nationalism, political philosophy, film theory, and art cinema. I was honored to study with Marcus Bullock, Peter Paik, and Patrice Petro, who generously commented on early versions of a few of these chapters. I would also like to thank Gilberto Blasini, Andrew Martin, and Tasha Oren for their support while I was at the University of Wisconsin-Milwaukee. I am grateful when I can catch up with everyone at conferences.

The discussion of Dušan Makavejev in chapters 1 and 2 is revised from my essay "The Impermanent Revolution Rotor: Dušan Makavejev's Final Manifesto," in *Dušan Makavejev: Eros, Ideology, Montage*, edited by Vadim

Erent and Bonita Rhoads (Prague: Litteraria Pragensia Books, 2018). Similarly, the analysis of *Pretty Village, Pretty Flame* in chapter 2 is condensed and revised from my essay "Did Somebody Say 'Communism' in the Classroom?," in *Blackwell Companion to East European Cinemas*, edited by Anikó Imre (London: Blackwell, 2012).

Several colleagues asked about my progress, offered their encouragement, listened to my frustrations, or answered my questions about their own books, particularly Kevin Cooper; Ron Falzone; Karla Fuller; Susan Kerns; Suzanne Leonard, who generously read portions of this book; Adam Ochonicky; and Joe Steiff. I am also grateful for the patience and support of my editors Leslie Mitchner and Nicole Solano. Lastly, I would like to thank my friends for keeping me sane during the writing of this book, especially Dave Clark, for all the concerts; Dave Laskowski, for whose music addiction I may be responsible; Steve Matuszak and Todd Chase for always taking me to all the record stores in Minneapolis; Eric Russell and Jennifer King Russell for the many years of friendship; and the world's greatest trivia team, the B Sharps, who forgive my terribleness at questions about the Oscars despite being a film professor. Most of all, I would like to thank my mother, Milka Samardzija; my father, Milan Samardzija; and my sister, Tanja Vasicovschi, for all of their love and support.

NOTES

INTRODUCTION

1. "Hungary to Stop Financing Gender Studies Courses: PM Aide," Reuters, August 14, 2018, https://www.reuters.com/article/us-hungary-government-education/hungary-to-stop-financing-gender-studies-courses-pm-aide-idUSKBN1KZ1Mo.
2. "Hungary 'Slave Law' Protesters Target State Broadcaster," BBC News, December 18, 2018, https://www.bbc.com/news/world-europe-46600035.
3. Nigel Farage, "Nigel Farage: Why You Should Vote for Brexit This Thursday," *Independent,* June 20, 2016, https://www.independent.co.uk/voices/eu-referendum-brexit-nigel-farage-on-why-you-should-vote-to-leave-a7091021.html.
4. Angelina Giuffrida and Jennifer Rakin, "Furore over European Parliament President's Mussolini Comments," *Guardian,* March 14, 2019, https://www.theguardian.com/world/2019/mar/14/furore-over-european-parliament-president-antonio-tajani-mussolini-comments.
5. Nico Baumbach, *Cinema/Politics/Philosophy* (New York: Columbia University Press, 2019), loc. 206 of 6199, Kindle.
6. D. N. Rodowick, *The Crisis of Political Modernism: Criticism and Ideology in Contemporary Film Theory* (Berkeley: University of California Press, 1994), 12.
7. Rodowick, xiv, xv.
8. Baumbach, *Cinema/Politics/Philosophy,* loc. 227.
9. Baumbach, loc. 227.
10. Rodowick, *Crisis of Political Modernism,* xxiv–xxv.
11. Rosalind Galt and Karl Schoonover, "Introduction: The Impurity of Art Cinema," in *Global Art Cinema: New Theories and Histories,* ed. Rosalind Galt and Karl Schoonover (London: Oxford University Press, 2010), loc. 328 of 10444, Kindle.
12. Galt and Schoonover, loc. 412.
13. David Bordwell, *The Poetics of Cinema* (New York: Routledge, 2008), 151–170.
14. Galt and Schoonover, "Introduction," loc. 377.
15. Galt and Schoonover, loc. 377.
16. Galt and Schoonover, loc. 497.
17. Christina Gerhardt and Sara Saljoughi, "Introduction: Looking Back: Global Cinema and the Legacy of New Waves around 1968," in *1968 and Global Cinema,* ed. Christina Gerhardt and Sara Saljoughi (Detroit: Wayne State University Press, 2018), loc. 144 of 9302, Kindle.
18. Dina Iordanova, *Cinema of the Other Europe: The Industry and Artistry of East Central European Film* (London: Wallflower, 2003), 13.

19. Boris Groys, "Beyond Diversity: Cultural Studies and Its Post-Communist Other," in *Art Power* (Cambridge, MA: MIT Press, 2008), loc. 1922 of 2368, Kindle.
20. Evgeny Dobrenko, *Stalinist Cinema and the Production of History: Museum of the Revolution*, trans. Sarah Young (New Haven, CT: Yale University Press, 2008), 6.
21. Jeffrey Herf, *Reactionary Modernism: Technology, Culture, and Politics in Weimar and the Third Reich* (London: Cambridge University Press, 1984).
22. Dobrenko, *Stalinist Cinema*, 6.
23. Lev Manovich, *The Language of New Media* (Cambridge, MA: MIT Press, 2002), 203.
24. Groys, "Beyond Diversity," loc. 1922.
25. For example, first published in 1985, and then in a revised second edition in 2005, Peter Hames's *The Czechoslovak New Wave* is one of the best English-language monographs.
26. The latter is evident in Mira Liehm and Antonin J. Liehm's groundbreaking *The Most Important Art: Eastern European Film after 1945* (Berkeley: University of California Press, 1977).
27. Larry Wolff, *Inventing Eastern Europe: The Map of Civilization on the Mind of the Enlightenment* (Stanford, CA: Stanford University Press, 1994).
28. The parallels are not exact, as Todorova, in particular, acknowledges that "Balkanism" differs from "Orientalism" because "the Balkans have a concrete historical existence" politically and geographically." Maria Todorova, *Imagining the Balkans* (New York: Oxford University Press, 1997), 12.
29. Nataša Kovačević, *Narrating Post/Communism: Colonial Discourse and Europe's Borderline Civilization* (London: Routledge, 2008), 16.
30. Kovačević, 16–17.
31. Ewa Mazierska, Lars Kristensen, and Eva Näripea, "Introduction: Postcolonial Theory and the Postcommunist World," in *Postcolonial Approaches to Eastern European Cinema: Portraying Neighbours On-Screen*, ed. Ewa Mazierska, Lars Kristensen, and Eva Näripea (London: I. B. Tauris, 2014), 16.
32. Mazierska, Kristensen, and Näripea, 17.
33. Mazierska, Kristensen, and Näripea, 21.
34. Groys, "Beyond Diversity," loc. 1915.
35. See, for example, Étienne Balibar, *Politics and the Other Scene*, trans. Christine Jones, James Swenson, and Chris Turner (New York: Verso, 2002), 146–176. In the essay "Ambiguous Universality," he distinguishes between three forms of universality. "Real universality" is the global interdependence of legal and political systems. "Fictive universality" is akin to the representational norms produced by institutions and cultures. In related terms, "symbolic universality" can be explained as the idealistic, aspirational form of universality that guides critiques of institutions and norms and demands for liberty and equality.
36. Romanian photographer Bogdan Gîrbovan has a fascinating project called *10/1* where he took ten pictures of identical-looking units in a ten-story apartment complex. See http://girbovan.ro/10pe1-2008.
37. Mark Fisher, *Capitalist Realism: Is There No Alternative?* (London: Zero Books, 2009).

38. "Russian Critic Accidentally Reviews 'Creatively' Dubbed, Bootleg 'Iron Lady,'" NPR, March 22, 2012, https://www.npr.org/2012/03/22/149151840/russian-critic-accidentally-reviews-creatively-dubbed-bootleg-iron-lady.
39. "Thatcher and Her Tussles with Europe," BBC News, April 8, 2013, https://www.bbc.com/news/uk-politics-11598879.
40. Francis Fukuyama, "At the 'End of History' Still Stands Democracy," *Wall Street Journal*, June 6, 2014, https://www.wsj.com/articles/at-the-end-of-history-still-stands-democracy-1402080661.
41. Francis Fukuyama, "The History at the End of History," *Guardian*, April 3, 2007, https://www.guardian.co.uk/commentisfree/2007/apr/03/thehistoryattheendofhist.
42. Francis Fukuyama, *Identity: The Demand for Dignity and the Politics of Resentment* (New York: Farrar, Straus and Giroux, 2018), 166, 167.
43. Walter Laqueur, *After the Fall: The End of the European Dream and the Decline of a Continent* (New York: St. Martin's, 2012), loc. 188 of 4931, Kindle.
44. Terry Eagleton, "A Shelter in the Tempest of History," *Red Pepper*, February 1, 2002, https://www.redpepper.org.uk/A-shelter-in-the-tempest-of.

CHAPTER 1 EASTERN EUROPEAN NEW WAVES AND POLITICAL MODERNISM

1. Peter Wollen, "Godard and Counter Cinema: *Vent d'Est*," in *Readings and Writings: Semiotic Counter-Strategies* (London: Verso, 1982), 79.
2. Jonathan Rosenbaum, "*WR*, Sex, and the Art of Radical Juxtaposition," Criterion Collection, June 18, 2007, https://www.criterion.com/current/posts/643-wr-sex-and-the-art-of-radical-juxtaposition.
3. Rosenbaum.
4. Roger Ebert, review of *Closely Watched Trains*, RogerEbert.com, May 29, 1968, http://www.rogerebert.com/reviews/closely-watched-trains-1968.
5. D. N. Rodowick, *The Crisis of Political Modernism: Criticism and Ideology in Contemporary Film Theory* (Berkeley: University of California Press, 1994), 12.
6. György Lukács, "Realism in the Balance," trans. Rodney Livingston, in *Aesthetics and Politics: The Key Texts of the Classic Debate within German Marxism* (New York: Verso, 1977), 32.
7. Lukács, 33.
8. Lukács, 40.
9. Ernst Bloch, "Discussing Expressionism," trans. Rodney Livingston, in *Aesthetics and Politics*, 22.
10. Bertolt Brecht, "Against Georg Lukács," trans. Stuart Hood, in *Aesthetics and Politics*, 68.
11. Wollen, "Godard and Counter Cinema," 91.
12. Karl Radek, "Contemporary World Literature and the Tasks of Proletarian Art," speech delivered at the Soviet Writers' Congress, August 1934, Marxists Internet Archive, https://www.marxists.org/archive/radek/1934/sovietwritercongress.htm.

13. Andrei Zhdanov, "Soviet Literature—The Richest in Ideas, the Most Advanced Literature," speech delivered at the Soviet Writers' Congress, August 1934, Marxists Internet Archive, https://www.marxists.org/subject/art/lit_crit/sovietwritercongress/zdhanov.htm.

14. Ksenya Gurshtein and Joanna Raczynska, "Artists, Amateurs, Alternative Spaces: Experimental Cinema in Eastern Europe, 1960–1990," National Gallery of Art, accessed September 4, 2019, https://www.nga.gov/content/ngaweb/features/experimental-cinema-in-eastern-europe.html.

15. Dina Iordanova, *Cinema of the Other Europe: The Industry and Artistry of East Central European Film* (London: Wallflower, 2003), 19.

16. John Cunningham, *Hungarian Cinema: From Coffee House to Multiplex* (London: Wallflower, 2004), 96.

17. "Purge in Croatia Follows Rioting," *New York Times*, December 16, 1971, https://www.nytimes.com/1971/12/16/archives/purge-in-croatia-follows-rioting-a-secessionist-movement-in.html.

18. In 1973, the *New York Times* even reported on the controversy caused by *WR*. See Raymond N. Anderson, "Yugoslavia Acts to Indict a Key Film Maker for Derision," *New York Times*, February 2, 1973, https://www.nytimes.com/1973/02/04/archives/yugoslav-acts-to-indict-a-key-film-maker-for-derision.html.

19. The National Gallery of Art entry for *Black Film* provides a brief overview of this period. See Ksenya Gurshtein, "*Black Film*," National Gallery of Art, accessed September 4, 2019, https://www.nga.gov/features/experimental-cinema-in-eastern-europe/documentaries-with-a-human-face/black-film.html.

20. Though I have not heard it credited with doing so, the documentary also likely inspired Abbas Kiarostami's 2008 feature, *Shirin*, which consists of close-ups of women watching a movie in a theater.

21. See Līva Pētersone, "*Ten Minutes Older*," National Gallery of Art, accessed September 4, 2019, http://www.nga.gov/content/ngaweb/features/experimental-cinema-in-eastern-europe/documentaries-with-a-human-face/trace-and-10-minutes-older.html.

22. David Bordwell, "Eisenstein, Socialist Realism, and the Charms of *Mizanstsena*," in *Eisenstein at 100: A Reconsideration*, ed. Al Lavalley and Barry P. Scherr (New Brunswick, NJ: Rutgers University Press, 2001).

23. Bordwell, 25–26.

24. In his classic essay on Godard, Brian Henderson interprets the lateral tracking shots in *Weekend* as formalizing a rejection of bourgeois notions of depth. As he states, "Godard's flat frames collapse this world into two-dimensional actuality; thus reversion to a cinema of one plane is a demystification, an assault on the bourgeois world-view and self-image." Brian Henderson, "Toward a Non-bourgeois Camera Style," *Film Quarterly* 24, no. 2 (Winter 1970–1971): 12.

25. For a detailed history of postwar film clubs in Yugoslavia, see Daniel J. Goulding, *Liberated Cinema: The Yugoslav Experience, 1945–2001* (Bloomington: Indiana University Press, 2002).

26. An earlier version of my analysis of Makavejev's seventies and eighties films can be found in Zoran Samardzija, "The Impermanent Revolution Rotor: Dušan Makavejev's

Final Manifesto," in *Dušan Makavejev: Eros, Ideology, Montage*, ed. Vadim Erent and Bonita Rhoads (Prague: Litteraria Pragensia Books, 2018).

27. Raymond Durgnat, *WR: Mysteries of the Organism*, BFI Modern Classics (London: British Film Institute, 1999), 54.

28. Durgnat, 54.

29. Steven Shaviro, "*Sweet Movie*," *Pinocchio Theory* (blog), September 11, 2007, http://www.shaviro.com/Blog/?p=596.

30. Dušan Makavejev, "*Sweet Movie*: The Gentle Side of 'Destructive Art,'" *Sense of Cinema*, no. 47 (May 2008), http://sensesofcinema.com/2008/feature-articles/sweet-movie-makavejev.

31. Graham Petrie, "I Haven't Changed, the World Has: Miklós Jancsó Interviewed," *Kinoeye* 3, no. 4 (March 2003), http://www.kinoeye.org/03/04/interview04_n01.php.

32. Mira Liehm and Antonin J. Liehm, *The Most Important Art: Soviet and Eastern European Film after 1945* (Berkeley: University of California Press, 1977), 173.

33. Jean-Pierre Oudart, Jean Narboni, and Jean-Louis Comolli, "Readings of Jancsó: Yesterday and Today," in *Cahiers du Cinéma*, vol. 3, *1969–1972: The Politics of Representation*, ed. Nick Browne, trans. Randall Conrad (London: Routledge, 1990), 92.

34. For example, see J. Hoberman, "Red Modernism," *Film Comment*, September/October 2006, http://www.filmcomment.com/article/miklos-jansco. Hoberman writes, "'In Hungary, or at least in Hungarian culture, film nowadays plays the role of the avant-garde,' the venerable Marxist philosopher and critic Georg Lukacs told Yvette Biró, then editor of the Hungarian journal *Filmkultura*, in the course of a celebrated interview held in Lukacs's shabby, book-crammed Budapest apartment during the glorious May of 1968. Lukacs had been particularly impressed by *The Round-Up*. Yet this laconic succession of fluid takes isolating tiny figures in the windswept nothingness of the *puszta* synthesized all that the philosopher repressed." Hoberman implies that it is ironic that Lukács should admire Jancsó's modernism. However, this ignores the extent to which Lukács's ideas about realism and communism evolved over time.

35. Pavle Levi, *Cinema by Other Means* (New York: Oxford University Press, 2012), 97.

36. Levi, 97.

37. Mészáros completed a fourth and final diary film in 2000 called *Little Vilma—The Last Diary*.

38. Catherine Portuges, *The Hungarian Cinema of Márta Mészáros: Screen Memories* (Bloomington: Indiana University Press, 1995), 93.

CHAPTER 2 WHAT HAPPENS AFTER THE END OF HISTORY?

1. "About the Visegrad Group," Visegrad Group, accessed September 9, 2019, http://www.visegradgroup.eu/about.

2. Marton Dunai, "Hungary Builds New High-Tech Border Fence—with Few Migrants in Sight," Reuters, March 2, 2017, https://www.reuters.com/article/us-europe-migrants-hungary-fence-idUSKBN1692MH.

3. Csaba Tóth, "Full Text of Viktor Orbán's Speech at Băile Tuşnad (Tusnádfürdő) of 26 July 2014," *Budapest Beacon*, July 29, 2014, https://budapestbeacon.com/public-policy/full-text-of-viktor-orbans-speech-at-baile-tusnad-tusnadfurdo-of-26-july-2014/10592.
4. György Lázár, "Hungary Is Removing Statue of Philosopher György (Georg) Lukács—He Was Marxist and Jewish," *Hungarian Free Press*, February 16, 2017, https://hungarianfreepress.com/2017/02/16/hungary-is-removing-statue-of-philosopher-gyorgy-georg-lukacs-he-was-marxist-and-jewish.
5. Samuel P. Huntington, *The Clash of Civilization and the Remaking of World Order* (New York: Simon and Schuster, 1996), 288–289.
6. Edward Said, "The Clash of Ignorance," *Nation*, October 22, 2001, https://www.thenation.com/article/clash-ignorance/.
7. Michael Hardt and Antonio Negri, *Empire* (Cambridge, MA: Harvard University Press, 2001), xii–xiii.
8. Hardt and Negri, *Multitude: War and Democracy in the Age of Empire* (New York: Penguin Press, 2004), xiv.
9. Daniel Boffey and Philip Oltermann, "EU Elections: Voters Boost Greens and Far Right to Leave Centrist Groups Diminished," *Guardian*, May 26, 2019, https://www.theguardian.com/politics/2019/may/26/european-elections-centrist-parties-projected-lose-grip-power.
10. Peter Hames, *The Czechoslovak New Wave*, 2nd ed. (London: Wallflower, 2005), 210.
11. Jonathan Jones, "Jan Švankmajer: Puppets and Politics," *Guardian*, December 5, 2011, https://www.theguardian.com/film/2011/dec/05/jan-svankmajer-puppets-politics.
12. An archived version of Švankmajer's essay can be found on the defunct tribute website Jan Švankmajer: Alchemist of the Surreal, which collected his random writings: Jan Švankmajer, "To Renounce the Leading Role," 1990, Jan Švankmajer: Alchemist of the Surreal, https://web.archive.org/web/20060307053301/http://www.illumin.co.uk/svank/script/texts/leadrole.html.
13. Eoin Koepfinger, "'Freedom Is Becoming the Only Theme': An Interview with Jan Švankmajer," Sampsonia Way: An Online Magazine for Literature, Free Speech & Social Justice, June 5, 2012, https://www.sampsoniaway.org/blog/2012/06/05/freedom-is-becoming-the-only-theme-an-interview-with-jan-svankmajer.
14. For an archived version, see Jan Švankmajer, "Coming Attractions," 1997, Jan Švankmajer: Alchemist of the Surreal, http://web.archive.org/web/20060222075734/http://www.illumin.co.uk/svank/script/texts/coming.html.
15. Steven Shaviro, "*Conspirators of Pleasure*," *Pinocchio Theory* (blog), February 11, 2007, http://www.shaviro.com/Blog/?p=555.
16. Švankmajer, "Coming Attractions."
17. Jan Švankmajer, *Touching and Imagining: An Introduction to Tactile Art*, ed. Cathryn Vasselu, trans. Stanley Dalby (London: I. B. Tauris, 2014), loc. 368 of 3454, Kindle.
18. Švankmajer, loc. 383.
19. Anikó Imre, *Identity Games: Globalization and the Transformation of Media Cultures in the New Europe* (Cambridge, MA: MIT Press, 2009), 199, 200.
20. Jan Švankmajer, dir., *Lunacy* (n.p.: Zeitgeist Video, 2007), DVD.

21. The Indiegogo page for *Insects* is still available: "The Last Film by Švankmajer: Insects," Indiegogo, accessed September 9, 2019, https://www.indiegogo.com/projects/the-last-film-by-jan-svankmajer-insects--4#.

22. Michel Field, "Interview with Vera Chytilová," Institut national de l'audiovisuel, video, 4:18, aired February 1, 1994, http://fresques.ina.fr/europe-des-cultures-en/fiche-media/Europe00213/interview-with-vera-chytilova.html.

23. Hames, *Czechoslovak New Wave*, 263.

24. The film is set in the period between the Velvet Revolution and the dissolution of Czechoslovakia.

25. Carmen Gray, "Traps," in booklet for *Traps*, dir. Vera Chytilová (London: Second Run, 2015), DVD.

26. Andrew J. Horton, "Hitchhiking: The Perils and the Romance, Part I, the Perils: Vera Chytilová's *Pasti, pasti, pasticky*," *Central European Review*, January 19, 1999, http://web.archive.org/web/20020629101539/http://www.ce-review.org/kinoeye/kinoeye17old1.html.

27. Kate Connolly, "Bohemian Rhapsodist," *Guardian*, August 10, 2000, https://www.theguardian.com/film/2000/aug/11/culture.features2.

28. Dina Iordanova, *Cinema of the Other Europe: The Industry and Artistry of East Central European Film* (London: Wallflower, 2003), 123.

29. Dennis Lim, "Then as Now, the Terrors of Routine," *New York Times*, January 16, 2009, https://www.nytimes.com/2009/01/18/movies/18lim.html?_r=0.

30. Dora Viceníková, "Naked Allegory," *Kinoeye: New Perspectives on European Film* 2, no. 8 (April 29, 2002), http://www.kinoeye.org/02/08/vicenikova08.php.

31. "Pilot Sues over Bosnian Escape Movie," BBC News, August 20, 2002, http://news.bbc.co.uk/2/hi/entertainment/2205560.stm.

32. Srećko Horvat, "In the Land of Blood and Money: Angelina Jolie and the Balkans," in *What Does Europe Want? The Union and Its Discontents*, by Slavoj Žižek and Srećko Horvat (New York: Columbia University Press, 2015), 68–69.

33. *Je Vous Salue, Sarajevo* is available in *Four Short Films*, dir. Jean-Luc Godard (Munich: ECM Cinema, 2006), DVD.

34. Des O'Rawe, "Voyage(s) to Sarajevo: Godard and the War of Images," in *Post-conflict Performance, Film, and Visual Arts: Cities of Memory*, ed. Des O'Rawe and Mark Phelan (London: Palgrave Macmillan, 2016), 121.

35. Jean-Luc Godard and Youssef Ishaghpour, *Cinema: The Archeology of Film and the Memory of a Century*, trans. John Howe (New York: Berg, 2005), 109.

36. Gavin Smith, "Interview: Jean-Luc Godard," *Film Comment*, March/April 1996, http://www.filmcomment.com/article/jean-luc-godard-interview-nouvelle-vague-histoires-du-cinema-helas-pour-moi.

37. Jean-Luc Godard, dir., *Notre Musique* (New York: Wellspring, 2004), DVD.

38. Lorraine Mortimer, *Terror and Joy: The Films of Dušan Makavejev* (Minneapolis: University of Minnesota Press, 2009), xiii.

39. An earlier version of my analysis of Makavejev's late films can be found in Zoran Samardzija, "The Impermanent Revolution Rotor: Dušan Makavejev's Final Manifesto,"

in *Dušan Makavejev: Eros, Ideology, Montage*, ed. Vadim Erent and Bonita Rhoads (Prague: Litteraria Pragensia Books, 2018).

40. *Manifesto* was released on home video in the United States as *A Night of Love*, dir. Dušan Makavejev (New York: Fox Lorber, 1997), VHS.

41. Dušan Makavejev, dir., *Dream*, in *Danske Piger Viser Alt* (Denmark: Holland House et al., 1996), VHS.

42. *Hole in the Soul* is included as an extra feature on *WR: Mysteries of the Organism*, dir. Dušan Makavejev (Irvington, NY: Criterion Collection, 2007), DVD.

43. *Hole in the Soul.*

44. Steve H. Hanke, "The World's Greatest Unreported Hyperinflation," Cato Institute, accessed September 9, 2019, https://www.cato.org/publications/commentary/worlds-greatest-unreported-hyperinflation.

45. David J. Fox, "'Action' Promotion Is Out of This World," *Los Angeles Times*, March 3, 1993, https://articles.latimes.com/1993-03-03/entertainment/ca-239_1_action-hero.

46. Richard Byrne, "The Last Yugoslav: On Dusan Makavejev," *Nation*, October 28, 2009, https://www.thenation.com/article/last-yugoslav-dusan-makavejev.

47. Jonathan Rosenbaum, "*WR*, Sex, and the Art of Radical Juxtaposition," Criterion Collection, June 18, 2007, https://www.criterion.com/current/posts/643-wr-sex-and-the-art-of-radical-juxtaposition.

48. Ernest Gellner, *Nations and Nationalism* (Ithaca, NY: Cornell University Press, 1983), 71–72.

49. Susan L. Woodward, *Balkan Tragedy: Chaos and Dissolution after the Cold War* (Washington, DC: Brookings Institution, 1995), 18.

50. Woodward, 73.

51. My analysis of the film is a condensed and revised version of Zoran Samardzija, "Did Somebody Say 'Communism' in the Classroom?," in *Blackwell Companion to East European Cinemas*, ed. Anikó Imre (London: Blackwell, 2012).

52. Pavle Levi, *Disintegration in Frames: Aesthetics and Ideology in the Yugoslav and Post-Yugoslav Cinema* (Stanford, CA: Stanford University Press, 2007), 141.

53. Srđan Dragojević, dir., *Pretty Village, Pretty Flame* (n.p.: Pathé, 1998), DVD.

54. Warren Zimmerman, *Origins of a Catastrophe: Yugoslavia and Its Destroyers—America's Last Ambassador Tells What Happened and Why* (New York: Times Books, 1996).

CHAPTER 3 SLOW CINEMA AND THE ESCAPE FROM CAPITALIST REALISM

1. Romania and Bulgaria joined the EU in 2007.

2. Jonathan Romney, "In Search of Lost Time," *Sight and Sound*, February 2010; Nick James, "Being Boring," *Sight and Sound*, July 2010.

3. Dan Kois, "Eating Your Cultural Vegetables," *New York Times Magazine*, May 1, 2011, https://www.nytimes.com/2011/05/01/magazine/mag-01Riff-t.html.

4. Kois.

5. Manohla Dargis and A.O. Scott, "In Defense of Slow and Boring," *New York Times,* June 3, 2011, https://www.nytimes.com/2011/06/05/movies/films-in-defense-of-slow-and-boring.html?_r=1.

6. Manohla Dargis and A.O. Scott, "Sometimes a Vegetable Is Just a Vegetable," *New York Times,* June 17, 2011, https://www.nytimes.com/2011/06/19/movies/critics-discuss-cinema-thats-good-for-you.html?mtrref=www.google.com&gwh=72207695AD6FC2DB1D9425AB04FCD2F9&gwt=pay&assetType=REGIWALLhttps://www.google.com/?gws_rd=ssl.

7. Ira Jaffe, *Slow Movies: Countering the Cinema of Action* (New York: Columbia University Press, 2014), 1, 8.

8. Tiago de Luca and Nuno Barradas Jorge, "Introduction: From Slow Cinema to Slow Cinemas," in *Slow Cinema,* ed. Tiago de Luca and Nuno Barradas Jorge (Edinburgh: Edinburgh University Press, 2016), 10, 16.

9. Steven Shaviro, "Slow Cinema vs Fast Films," *Pinocchio Theory* (blog), May 12, 2010, http://www.shaviro.com/Blog/?p=891.

10. David Bordwell, *Figures Traced in Light: On Cinematic Staging* (Berkeley: University of California Press, 2005), 8.

11. Andrei Tarkovsky, *Sculpting in Time,* trans. Kitty Hunter-Blair (Austin: University of Texas Press, 1987), 118.

12. The term *unfinished cinema* appears in several interviews with Kiarostami, but its clearest expressions can be found in the text he wrote for the Centenary of Cinema celebrations in Paris in 1995 and later included in the press packet for *The Wind Will Carry Us* (1999), where he states, "I believe in a type of cinema that gives greater possibilities and time to its audience. A half-created cinema, an unfinished cinema that attains completion through the creative spirit of the audience, so resulting in hundreds of films. It belongs to the members of that audience and corresponds to their world." For an archived version, see Abbas Kiarostami, "Unfinished Cinema," text written for the Centenary of Cinema, Paris, 1995, http://www.dvdbeaver.com/FILM/articles/an_unfinished_cinema.htm.

13. Rob White, "Cristi Puiu Discusses Aurora," *Film Quarterly,* December 7, 2010, https://filmquarterly.org/2010/12/07/editors-notebook-cristi-puiu-discusses-aurora.

14. Tarkovsky, *Sculpting in Time,* 118.

15. György Lukács, "Realism in the Balance," trans. Rodney Livingston, in *Aesthetics and Politics: The Key Texts of the Classic Debate within German Marxism* (New York: Verso, 1977), 40.

16. Tarkovsky, *Sculpting in Time,* 118–119.

17. Fredric Jameson, *The Geopolitical Aesthetic: Cinema and Space in the World System* (Bloomington: Indiana University Press, 1992), 100.

18. Tarkovsky, *Sculpting in Time,* 218.

19. Slavoj Žižek, *The Fright of Real Tears: Krzysztof Kieślowski between Theory and Post-Theory* (London: British Film Institute, 2001), 104.

20. Jonathan Rosenbaum, "The Importance of Being Sarcastic," review of *Satantango,* Jonathan Rosenbaum's website, October 14, 1994, https://www.jonathanrosenbaum.net/1994/10/the-importance-of-being-sarcastic.

21. Phil Ballard, "In Search of Truth: Béla Tarr Interviewed," *Kinoeye: New Perspectives on European Film* 4, no. 2 (March 2004), https://www.kinoeye.org/04/02/ballard02.php.
22. Slavoj Žižek, "Slavoj Žižek Speaks at Occupy Wall Street: Transcript," Impose, accessed September 10, 2019, http://www.imposemagazine.com/bytes/slavoj-zizek-at-occupy-wall-street-transcript.
23. Mark Fisher, *Capitalist Realism: Is There No Alternative?* (London: Zero Books, 2009), loc. 117 of 1195, Kindle.
24. Fisher, loc. 44.
25. Tarr's comments are included in the booklet for *The Prefab People,* dir. Béla Tarr (Chicago: Facets Video, 2005), DVD.
26. Jaffe, *Slow Movies,* 160.
27. André Bazin, "*Umberto D,*" in *What Is Cinema,* trans. Hugh Gray (Berkeley: University of California Press, 1972), 2:81.
28. Jacques Rancière, *Béla Tarr, the Time After,* trans. Erik Beranek (Minneapolis: Univocal, 2013), 3.
29. *Prefab People.*
30. András Bálint Kovács, "Sátántangó," in *The Cinema of Central Europe,* ed. Peter Hames (London: Wallflower, 2004), 239.
31. John Gray, *Black Mass: Apocalyptic Religion and the Death of Utopia* (New York: Farrar, Straus and Giroux, 2008), loc. 3412 of 4641, Kindle.
32. Terry Eagleton, "Humanity and Other Animals," review of *Straw Dogs,* by John Gray, *Guardian,* February 6, 2002, https://www.theguardian.com/books/2002/sep/07/highereducation.news2.
33. Rancière, *Béla Tarr,* 63.
34. Tarr has since directed two installation pieces, *Muhamed* (2017) and *Missing People* (2019). Intended as a statement on the plight of refugees in Europe, *Muhamed* is a short about a boy playing accordion. A synopsis of *Missing People* can be found on the website of the Vienna Festival, which commissioned the piece. "Béla Tarr: *Missing People,*" Wiener Festwochen, accessed September 10, 2019, https://www.festwochen.at/en/programme/programme/detail/missing-people.
35. László Krasznahorkai, "At the Latest, in Turin," in *The World Goes On,* trans. John Batki (New York: New Directions, 2017), loc. 219 of 3819, Kindle.
36. Krasznahorkai, loc. 219.
37. Krasznahorkai, loc. 219.
38. John Gray, *Straw Dogs: Thoughts on Humans and Other Animals* (New York: Farrar, Straus and Giroux, 2002), 46.
39. Rancière, *Béla Tarr,* 63.
40. Béla Tarr, dir., *The Turin Horse* (New York: Cinema Guild, 2011), Blu-ray.
41. Fisher, *Capitalist Realism,* loc. 44.
42. Jeremy Rifkin, *The European Dream: How Europe's Vision of the Future Is Quietly Eclipsing the American Dream* (New York: Penguin Books, 2004), 7.
43. Monica Filimon, *Cristi Puiu,* Contemporary Film Directors (Champaign: University of Illinois Press, 2017), 147.

44. Filimon, 147–148.

45. Filimon, 7.

46. Dominique Nasta, *Contemporary Romanian Cinema: The History of an Unexpected Miracle* (London: Wallflower, 2013), 155.

47. Paul Schrader, *Transcendental Style in Film: Ozu, Bresson, Dreyer*, new ed. (Oakland: University of California Press, 2018), loc. 462 of 5104, Kindle.

48. Schrader, loc. 301, 306.

49. Schrader, loc. 805, 1487.

50. Cornel Ban, *Ruling Ideas: How Global Neoliberalism Goes Local* (New York: Oxford University Press, 2016), loc. 1544 of 7961, Kindle.

51. Ban, loc. 3462.

52. Filimon, *Cristi Puiu*, 127.

53. Filimon, 129–130.

54. Alina Haliliuc, "*Cigarettes and Coffee* (Cristi Puiu, 2004)," *Senses of Cinema*, September 2017, http://sensesofcinema.com/2017/cteq/cigarettes-and-coffee.

55. "Romania's Private Healthcare Services Market, Up 12% in 2017," Romania Insider, May 22, 2018, https://www.romania-insider.com/private-healthcare-services-market-2017.

56. Dan Bilefsky, "Medical Care in Romania Comes with an Extra Cost," *New York Times*, March 8, 2009, https://www.nytimes.com/2009/03/09/world/europe/09bribery.html.

57. Ginger Hervey, "The EU Exodus: When Doctors and Nurses Follow the Money," Politco EU, September 30, 2017, https://www.politico.eu/article/doctors-nurses-migration-health-care-crisis-workers-follow-the-money-european-commission-data.

58. Nasta, *Contemporary Romanian Cinema*, 155.

59. Filimon, *Cristi Puiu*, 77.

60. Rob White, "Cristi Puiu Discusses *Aurora*," *Film Quarterly*, December 7, 2010, https://filmquarterly.org/2010/12/07/editors-notebook-cristi-puiu-discusses-aurora.

61. Patrick Holzapfel, "The Dead Person Is the Camera: Talking with Cristi Puiu about 'Sieranevada,'" Mubi, November 28, 2016, https://mubi.com/notebook/posts/the-dead-person-is-the-camera-talking-with-cristi-puiu-about-sieranevada.

62. Rancière, *Béla Tarr*, 63.

CHAPTER 4 THEO ANGELOPOULOS, GREECE, AND THE ENDS OF EUROPE

1. There is *The Trilogy of History*, which includes *Days of '36* (1972), *The Traveling Players* (1975), and *The Hunters* (1977), all films about the Greek Civil War and the Metaxas dictatorship. Presumably, *Alexander the Great* (1980) is separate, since it is more allegorical than historical, though some critics group it with the aforementioned films to form a tetralogy. Next there is *The Trilogy of Silence*, which explores existential themes in *Voyage to Cythera* (1984), *The Beekeeper* (1986), and *Landscape in the Mist* (1988). This is

followed by *The Trilogy of Borders*, which includes *The Suspended Step of the Stork* (1991), *Ulysses' Gaze* (1995), and *Eternity and a Day* (1998). The final, unnamed trilogy is intended to encapsulate Greek history from 1919 to the present day. Only *The Weeping Meadow* (2004) and *The Dust of Time* (2008) were completed.

2. Fredric Jameson, "Angelopoulos and Collective Narrative," in *The Cinema of Theo Angelopoulos*, ed. Angelos Koutsourakis and Mark Steven (Edinburgh: Edinburgh University Press, 2015), 100.

3. Mark Steven, "Tracks in the Eurozone: Late Style Meets Late Capitalism," in Koutsourakis and Steven, *Cinema of Theo Angelopoulos*, 147.

4. Steven, 150.

5. Michel Grodent, "A Withered Apple: *Voyage to Cythera*," in *Theo Angelopoulos: Interviews*, ed. Dan Fainaru (Jackson: University of Mississippi Press, 2001), 52.

6. According to Dany Nobus and Nektaria Pouli, Angelopoulos indicated his appreciation for the paining as well as the similarly titled Charles Baudelaire poem. Dany Nobus and Nektaria Pouli, "Syncope and Fractal Liminality: Theo Angelopoulos' *Voyage to Cythera* and the Question of Borders," in Koutsourakis and Steven, *Cinema of Theo Angelopoulos*, 191–205.

7. Yanis Varoufakis, *And the Weak Suffer What They Must? Europe's Crisis and America's Economic Future* (New York: Nation Books, 2016), ix.

8. Yanis Varoufakis, *Adults in the Room: My Battle with the European and American Deep Establishment* (New York: Farrar, Straus and Giroux, 2017), Kindle.

9. Patrick Kingsley and Helena Smith, "Idomeni: Greek Riot Police Move In to Clear Refugee Camp," *Guardian*, May 24, 2016, https://www.theguardian.com/world/2016/may/24/idomeni-greek-riot-police-move-in-before-dawn-to-clear-out-refugee-camp. For photographs of the camp, see Jeanne Carstensen and Jodi Hilton, "Trapped in Greece, These Refugees Wait, Just before Another Frontier," PRI, May 16, 2016, https://www.pri.org/stories/2016-05-16/trapped-greece-these-refugees-await-just-another-frontier.

10. Patrick Kingsley, "Migration to Europe Is Down Sharply: So Is It Still a 'Crisis'?," *New York Times*, June 27, 2018, https://www.nytimes.com/interactive/2018/06/27/world/europe/europe-migrant-crisis-change.html.

11. I analyze *Lamerica* in Zoran Samardzija, "The Great Migration Elsewhere," in *Aftermaths: Exile, Migration, and Diaspora Reconsidered*, ed. Marcus Bullock and Peter Paik (New Brunswick, NJ: Rutgers University Press, 2008). I have appropriated the title for this section since the phrase originates in Angelopoulos's *Suspended Step of the Stork*.

12. "Eastern Europe's Wave of Emigration May Have Crested," *Economist*, August 26, 2017, https://www.economist.com/europe/2017/08/26/eastern-europes-wave-of-emigration-may-have-crested.

13. "Population of the UK by Country of Birth and Nationality: 2016," Office for National Statistics, August 24, 2017, https://www.ons.gov.uk/peoplepopulationandcommunity/populationandmigration/internationalmigration/bulletins/ukpopulationbycountryofbirthandnationality/2016#.

14. Anna Momigliano, "In Italy, Politicians Court Votes by Stoking Racism against Romanians," *Washington Post*, April 23, 2017, https://www.washingtonpost.com/news

/worldviews/wp/2017/04/23/in-italy-politicians-court-votes-by-stoking-racism-against-romanians.

15. For an excellent overview of these films, see Isolina Ballesteros, *Immigration Cinema in the New Europe* (Bristol: Intellect Books, 2015).

16. "On Revenge and Tragedy in Cinema and Life: In Conversation with Pedro Costa," *Four by Three*, accessed September 11, 2019, http://www.fourbythreemagazine.com/issue/death/pedro-costa-interview.

17. Ira Jaffe, *Slow Movies: Countering the Cinema of Action* (New York: Columbia University Press, 2014), 6.

18. Andrew Horton, *The Films of Theo Angelopoulos: A Cinema of Contemplation* (Princeton, NJ: Princeton University Press, 1997), 164.

19. Reece Jones, *Violent Borders: Refugees and the Right to Move* (London: Verso, 2017), loc. 354 of 3839, Kindle.

20. Jasmine Coleman, "Greek Bailout Talks: Are Stereotypes of Lazy Greeks True?," BBC News, March 10, 2015, https://www.bbc.com/news/world-europe-31803814.

21. Theo Angelopoulos, dir., *The Suspended Step of the Stork* (1991), in the box set *The Theo Angelopoulos Collection*, vol. 2 (London: Artificial Eye, 2012), DVD.

22. Max Horkheimer and Theodor Adorno, *Dialectic of Enlightenment*, trans. John Cumming (New York: Continuum, 1999), xvi.

23. Horkheimer and Adorno, 8.

24. Yanis Varoufakis, "Why We Must Save the EU," *Guardian*, April 5, 2016, https://www.theguardian.com/world/2016/apr/05/yanis-varoufakis-why-we-must-save-the-eu.

25. Theodor Adorno, "The Meaning of Working through the Past," in *Can One Live after Auschwitz? A Philosophical Reader*, ed. Rolf Tidemann, trans. Henry W. Pickford (Stanford, CA: Stanford University Press, 2003), 18.

26. Enzo Traverso, *Left-Wing Melancholia: Marxism, History, and Memory* (New York: Columbia University Press, 2016), xiv, 52.

27. Theo Angelopoulos, dir., *Eternity and a Day* (1998), in the box set *The Theo Angelopoulos Collection*, vol. 3 (London: Artificial Eye, 2012), DVD.

28. Lasse Thomassen, "Towards a Cosmopolitics of Heterogeneity: Borders, Communities, and Refugees in Angelopoulos' Balkan Trilogy," in *Cosmopolitics and the Emergence of a Future*, ed. Diane Morgan and Gary Banham (London: Palgrave Macmillan, 2007), 197.

29. Thomassen, 202.

30. Michael Hardt and Antonio Negri, *Empire* (Cambridge, MA: Harvard University Press, 2001), xii–xiii.

31. Immanuel Kant, "To Eternal Peace," in *Basic Writings of Kant*, ed. Allen W. Wood, trans. Carl J. Friedrich (New York: Modern Library, 2001), 449.

32. John Orr, "The Cold War and the Cinema of Wonder," in *The Art and Politics of Film* (Edinburgh: Edinburgh University Press, 2000), 76–77.

33. Orr, 76.

34. Smaro Kamboureli, "Memory under Siege: Archive Fever in Theo Angelopoulos' *Ulysses' Gaze*," in Koutsourakis and Steven, *Cinema of Theo Angelopoulos*, 262, 253.

35. Dan Fainaru, "The Human Experience in One Gaze: *Ulysses' Gaze*," in Fainaru, *Theo Angelopoulos: Interviews*, 98.
36. Theo Angelopoulos, dir., *Ulysses' Gaze* (1995), in *Theo Angelopoulos Collection*, vol. 3.
37. According to Andrew Horton, this is footage from a documentary about the brothers that the Yugoslav government made in 1956. Horton, *Films of Theo Angelopoulos*, 188.
38. *Ulysses' Gaze*.
39. Mary Ann Doane, *The Emergence of Cinematic Time: Modernity, Contingency, the Archive* (Cambridge, MA: Harvard University Press, 2002), 3.
40. Doane, 3.
41. Traverso, *Left-Wing Melancholia*, 79.
42. Traverso, 76–77.
43. Vrasidas Karalis, *A History of Greek Cinema* (New York: Continuum, 2012), 250–251.
44. *Ulysses' Gaze*.
45. V. I. Lenin, "Directives on the Film Business," in *Lenin Collected Works*, vol. 42, trans. Bernard Isaacs (Moscow: Progress, 1971), https://www.marxists.org/archive/lenin/works/1922/jan/17.htm.
46. Theo Angelopoulos, dir., *The Dust of Time* (2008), in *Theo Angelopoulos Collection*, vol. 3.
47. Steven, "Tracks in the Eurozone," 147.
48. Steven, 150.
49. Steven, 150.
50. Evgeny Dobrenko, *Stalinist Cinema and the Production of History: Museum of the Revolution*, trans. Sarah Young (New Haven, CT: Yale University Press, 2008), 6.
51. *Dust of Time*.
52. *Dust of Time*.
53. Gilles Deleuze, *Cinema 2: The Time-Image*, trans. Hugh Tomlinson and Robert Galeta (Minneapolis: University of Minnesota Press, 1989), 125.

CONCLUSION

1. "GDP per Capita, Consumption per Capita and Price Level Indices," Eurostat, June 2019, https://ec.europa.eu/eurostat/statistics-explained/index.php/GDP_per_capita,_consumption_per_capita_and_price_level_indices.
2. The text of the Lisbon Treaty, which took effect in 2009, is available online on the European Commission's website. See "Treaty of Lisbon: Taking Europe into the 21st Century," home page, accessed October 11, 2019, https://ec.europa.eu/archives/lisbon_treaty/full_text/index_en.htm.
3. Yanis Varoufakis, *Adults in the Room: My Battle with the European and American Deep Establishment* (New York: Farrar, Straus and Giroux, 2017), loc. 400 of 11117, Kindle.
4. Varoufakis, loc. 50.
5. According to the *Financial Times*, "Despite strong growth expectations, Greece's economic output in 2023 is forecast to be 17 per cent below 2007 levels, according to International Monetary Fund data. Valentina Romei, "In Charts: Greece's Economy Is

Rebounding—but There Is Far to Go," *Financial Times*, August 17, 2018, https://www.ft.com/content/3067bf9c-8a88-11e8-bf9e-8771d5404543.

6. Rosalind Galt, *The New European Cinema: Redrawing the Map* (New York: Columbia University Press, 2006), 130.

7. Quoted in John Lloyd, "The New Illiberal International," *New Statesman*, July 18, 2018, https://www.newstatesman.com/world/2018/07/new-illiberal-international.

8. Slavoj Žižek, *The Fragile Absolute: Or, Why Is the Christian Legacy Worth Fighting For?* (New York: Verso, 2000), 3–4.

9. Fredric Jameson, "Reflections in Conclusion," in *Aesthetics and Politics: The Key Texts of the Classic Debate within German Marxism* (New York: Verso, 1977), 210.

10. One exception to this dynamic is to become entirely mutable ideologically. As of 2019, the longest-serving leader in Europe is Milo Đukanović of Montenegro, who has held various positions leading the country since 1991. A *New York Times* profile of Đukanović, who faced protests for his corruption, quotes Srdan Kosovic, an editor for an independent media outlet, as saying, "He is very flexible in terms of ideology. . . . He was a communist, a nationalist, a champion of independence, a friend of the West, and is now appealing to a new strain of Montenegro nationalism." Marc Santora, "'Balkan Spring' Turns to Summer, and Hopes for Change Dim," *New York Times*, June 1, 2019, https://www.nytimes.com/2019/06/01/world/europe/balkans-protests-montenegro-serbia-bosnia-albania.html.

11. Ernst Bloch, "Something's Missing: A Discussion between Ernst Bloch and Theodor W. Adorno on the Contradictions of Utopian Longing," in *The Utopian Function in Art and Literature: Selected Essays*, trans. Jack Zipes and Frank Mecklenburg (Cambridge, MA: MIT Press, 1987), 11, 12, 15.

12. Enzo Traverso, *Left-Wing Melancholia: Marxism, History, and Memory* (New York: Columbia University Press, 2016), 70, 119.

13. Rob White, "Cristi Puiu Discusses *Aurora*," *Film Quarterly*, December 7, 2010, https://filmquarterly.org/2010/12/07/editors-notebook-cristi-puiu-discusses-aurora.

14. Tarkovsky, *Sculpting in Time*, 118.

INDEX